Praise for *The Planetary*

"Velchanes takes on each of the aetheric spheres in their ascending Chaldean order, offering penetrating insights from a variety of perspectives. Whereas modern astrology tends to regard the zodiacal signs as personality types and the primary loci of astrological meaning, Soror Velchanes resituates the planets into their rightful roles as distinct concentrations of meaning. She deftly handles the history, theory and practice of planetary magic, giving transformational exercises resulting in a complete integration of planetary consciousness. This amazing resource should be in the personal library of every astrologer, alchemist, and magician."

—**JAIME PAUL LAMB**, author of *The Astrological Goetia*

"Hands down the definitive guide to Planetary Magick! Thoroughly researched, easy to read and follow. This workbook also challenges the practitioner to 'do the work,' as it were. Soror Velchanes presents us with exercises and rituals that provide the magician with tools and techniques to aid them on their life journey while enriching their practice and deepening their expertise."

—**JOSHUA WETZEL**, author of *The Paradigmal Pirate*

"Few, if any, practical workbooks on astrological magick have succeeded the way *The Planetary Magick Workbook* does….While focusing mainly on the classical planets, this workbook is overflowing with astrological theory and techniques, as well as important historical details which help to expand and deepen our understanding of the practices themselves. There is likely no better reference for the modern astrological magick practitioner in a single volume, and I'm happy to say that I have incorporated more than a few of the given exercises into my personal practice with great success."

—**IKE BAKER**, author of *A Formless Fire, Ætheric Magic*, and host of the *ARCANVM* podcast and YouTube channel

"This book will equip you with the tools to create profound, authentic inner initiations. *The Planetary Magic Workbook* uses Peter Carroll's system of chaos monasticisms to guide you through a series of exercises that initiate you into the mysteries of each planet. These small steps, a blend of ancient planetary and chaos magic, foster a profoundly personal and intuitive understanding of planetary mysteries….The book is designed to be usable by both the experienced and beginning magician, ensuring that all readers can

connect with its teachings....It is a beautiful planetary journey that will transform you and give you tools to measure progress in the real world."
—**ANDRIEH VITIMUS**, author of *Hands On Chaos Magic*

"This book offers comprehensive, immersive information for literally everyone. Newcomers to the occult will find practical steps to understanding the classical planets and the roles they play in magic, while seasoned practitioners will discover enlightening methods of integrating planetary energies into their daily lives. In a voice that is firm, experienced, and encouraging, Soror Velchanes combines her extensive knowledge of chaos magic and Western esotericism to guide readers down a truly unique path towards adepthood."
—**THUMPER FORGE**, Chaos Witch and blogger at Five Fold Law

THE

PLANETARY
MAGIC

WORKBOOK

About the Author

Soror Velchanes is a practicing chaos magician and avid paradigm surfer living in Scottsdale, Arizona. A member of the Illuminates of Thanateros since 2003, she occasionally teaches classes on chaos magic, pop culture magic, and more in the Greater Phoenix area. Learn more about her published works at http://www.velchanes.com.

THE
PLANETARY
MAGIC

WORKBOOK

AN EXPERIMENTAL GUIDE TO
UNDERSTANDING AND **WORKING** WITH
THE **CLASSICAL PLANETS**

SOROR VELCHANES

LLEWELLYN
WOODBURY, MINNESOTA

First Edition
First Printing, 2025

Book design by Rordan Brasington
Cover design by Shannon McKuhen
Editing by Laura Kurtz
Interior illustrations by Llewellyn Art Department

Llewellyn Publications is a registered trademark of Llewellyn Worldwide Ltd.

Library of Congress Cataloging-in-Publication Data

Names: Velchanes, Soror author.
Title: The planetary magic workbook : an experimental guide to
   understanding and working with the classical planets / Soror Velchanes.
Description: First edition. | Woodbury, Minnesota : Llewellyn, [2025] |
   Includes bibliographical references. | Summary: "A pragmatic approach
   (incl. coursework) to address the roles and practical applications of
   the planets in a variety of traditions (incl. Western and Eastern
   astrological traditions), illustrating the theory and practice of
   planetary magic that can help a practitioner tap into planetary forces
   for spiritual enrichment, magic, life balance, etc"—Provided by
   publisher.
Identifiers: LCCN 2024058957 | ISBN 9780738779751 (paperback) | ISBN
   9780738779959 (ebook)
Subjects: LCSH: Magic. | Planets--Mythology. | Witchcraft.
Classification: LCC BF1611 .V45 2025 | DDC 133.4/3—dc23/eng/20250106
LC record available at https://lccn.loc.gov/2024058957

Llewellyn Publications
A Division of Llewellyn Worldwide Ltd.
2143 Wooddale Drive
Woodbury, MN 55125-2989
www.llewellyn.com

Printed in the United States of America

Other Books by Soror Velchanes

The Elemental Magic Workbook, 2nd edition (Megalithica Books, 2020)

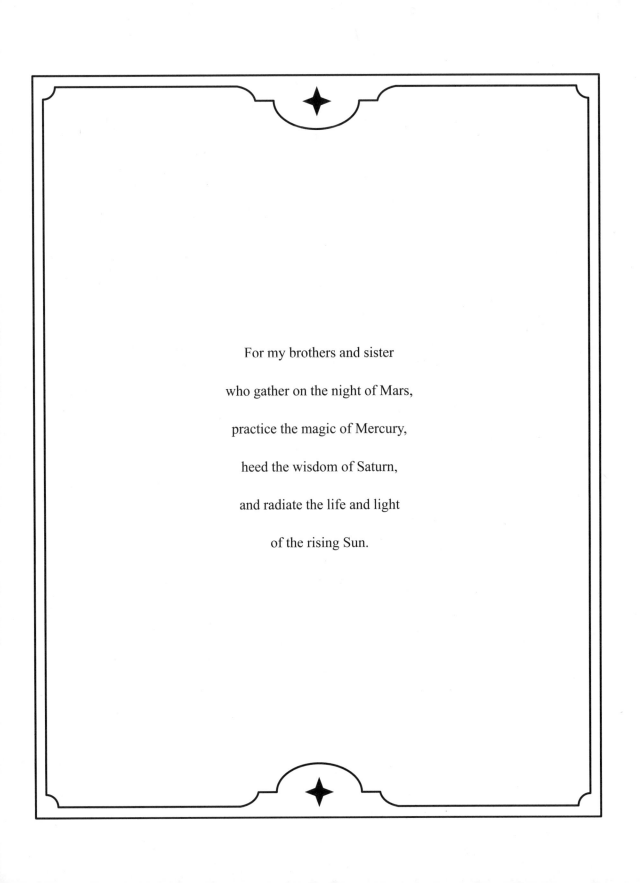

For my brothers and sister

who gather on the night of Mars,

practice the magic of Mercury,

heed the wisdom of Saturn,

and radiate the life and light

of the rising Sun.

Contents

Exercises

Fundamentals

Introduction

Planetary magic is a living, evolving tradition. Since its inception, individuals from diverse backgrounds and preparations have used the planets for spiritual enrichment, life balance, practical magic, and more. Though many paradigms developed additional valuable models, the primary emphasis in this book is placed on understanding and working with the classical planets from Greco-Roman and Hermetic perspectives, with a chaos magic twist. Chaos magic is a modern, results-oriented form of magical practice. In the chaos magic meta-paradigm belief serves as a tool, just like a wand or cup. Here, you will be introduced to both traditional and modern approaches to planetary magic and how they may be effectively blended together.

Who am I? Why should you listen to me? Honestly, who I am doesn't matter. What *does* matter is that I've been practicing magic for a long time—long enough to have encountered many common roadblocks, and long enough to have made *a lot* of mistakes. Keep in mind that you shouldn't blindly listen to me or anyone else. I am not inerrant and I am definitely not infallible. Feel free to modify the rites presented herein to accommodate your personal practice if you deem it necessary. Your magical results will speak for themselves.

The Work

This book has been optimized for self-study. The benefits you will reap will be in direct proportion to your efforts. Chapters should be viewed in sequential order, as latter ones build on previous concepts. A typical chapter is divided into discussion (note-taking) and practice sections. Discussion sections address fundamental planetary magic concepts and principles, thematic attributes specific to each planet, and how each planet affects your life. Take notes as you read.

Discussion content will be reinforced in the practice sections, where you will perform magical work tailored to each planet. This includes an attuning exercise, greeting rite, and guided meditation. You will also find planetary monasticisms, which were inspired by the overarching framework of Peter J. Carroll's "Chaos Monasticism."[1] Planetary monasticisms entail performing magical work tailored toward a specific planet over a span of multiple days. Akin to the Chaos Monasticism, there are three levels of observances: Lesser Observances are intended for someone who regularly has a busy schedule, Extreme Observances are intended for someone who has extended free time, and Greater Observances strike a balance between the two.

You should progress at a rate of no more than one chapter per month. The note-taking for a chapter should take no more than two hours to complete and may be done in one sitting. Magical practice should be commenced for a minimum of thirty minutes each day for the remainder of the month. Previous magical experience is helpful but not required. Here are a few study tips:

- Make sure your environment is conducive to learning. A private, quiet place free of distractions is ideal.
- Develop a routine. Establish a set schedule where you work on a chapter at the same time each day.
- Performing magic in the same locale over a long enough time period will eventually cause an automatic shift in consciousness when you enter, so a consistent location is also helpful.
- Take your time and do not rush. Move on to the next chapter when you have a firm grasp on content in the current chapter.
- Though the planets coexist together in a complex fashion, it is easiest to focus on one planet at a time in the beginning.
- Learning magic is like learning math—proficiency is gained through experience. Practice regularly and often.

---

1. Peter J. Carroll, *Liber Kaos* (Weiser Books, 1992), 187–90.

It is highly recommended that you document your efforts in a magical diary to keep track of information and monitor your progress. Your magical diary may be kept separate from your note-taking book. A magical diary serves as a permanent written record of your work. It is a place to record your rites, results, insights, and more. Your diary does not have to be fancy unless you want it to be. A cheap spiral-bound notebook or bound composition book will suffice. The magical diary will be discussed in detail in chapter 1.

Excerpts from my own magical diary are included throughout this book—hopefully they will give you ideas on how to record your experiences and provide some sense of what you might encounter.

May the Planets Light Your Way

Different aspects of the universe may be influenced through the forces underlying each planet. I don't know what the planets have in store for you—I had no idea what they had in store for me. Now, grab a blank notebook and let the planets light your way!

CHAPTER 1
Getting Started

Congratulations on beginning your planetary journey! Throughout history, individuals from diverse backgrounds and preparations have used the classical planets as means to different ends. In modern times, these ends primarily involve spiritual enrichment, life balance, and practical magic. Working with the planets is a highly personal experience. Your perception, internalization, and interaction with each planet may differ from your peers, even if you share similar personalities or worldviews.

The Planets in the Ancient World

Western astronomy and astrology have origins in Mesopotamia and ancient Egypt. Observation of astronomical phenomena provided a means of calendar-keeping and facilitated prediction of celestial and terrestrial events.[2,3] Many of these events held religious and philosophical significance, as ancient man believed the heavens influenced earthly existence.[4] The earliest discovered astronomical records date back to Mesopotamia, where Babylonians documented their observations on cuneiform tablets. Some of

---

2. Wayne Horowitz, *Mesopotamian Cosmic Geography* (Eisenbrauns, 1998), 162–64.

3. R. A. Parker, "Ancient Egyptian Astronomy," *Philosophical Transactions of the Royal Society of London, Series A* 276, no. 1257 (1974): 53–54.

4. Nicholas Campion, *Astrology and Cosmology in the World's Religions* (New York University Press, 2012), 92–93, 124–25.

the most famous tablets comprise the "Enuma Anu Enlil," which discusses astronomical events and their divinatory implications (omens).

In Babylonian cosmology the universe is composed of three heavenly and three earthly realms, with the fixed stars and *wild sheep* occupying the lower heavens. The fixed stars maintain their relative positions on a rotating jasper ceiling, while the wild sheep (i.e., classical planets—the Sun, Moon, and planets visible to the unaided eye) move through the lower heavens along a narrow band at their own rates. According to "MUL.APIN" and the "Astrolabe" tablets, the arrangement of stars is divine in origin, with particular deities ruling over specific celestial regions.[5]

Greco-Roman Model of the Planets

Babylonian and ancient Egyptian endeavors influenced the natural philosophy of the Greeks. Our word *planet* is derived from *planētēs* (Gk. πλανήτης; wanderer), as the planets wander across the sky in contrast to the fixed stars.[6] Observation of astronomical phenomena became more quantitative, but planets were still viewed as divine and omens still held significance.[7,8] In Aristotelian cosmology the classical planets occupy a heavenly realm composed of aether (αἰθήρ) and are arranged in a complex system of concentric crystalline spheres driven by a prime mover (Figure 1.1).

In this model, the visible sky appears to rotate around a spherical, stationary Earth. The fixed stars maintain their relative positions due to their locale on a single sphere, whereas the *wandering stars* are distributed across multiple spheres rotating at different velocities. The sublunar realm is composed of the four terrestrial elements and is bound by the laws of generation and corruption. Everything above the sublunar realm is filled with aether, the divine quintessence. The information in Figure 1.1 is adapted from Aristotle's *De Caelo* and *Metaphysics*. Planets are arranged by orbital period.

5. John H. Rogers, "Origins of the Ancient Constellations: I. The Mesopotamian Traditions," *Journal of the British Astronomical Association* 108, no. 1 (1998): 18–19.

6. Plato, *Timaeus*, trans. Donald J. Zeyl (Hackett Publishing Company, 2000), 22.

7. Plato, *Epinomis*, trans. W. R. M. Lamb, in *Charmides, Alcibiades I and II, Hipparchus, The Lovers, Theages, Minos, Epinomis* (Harvard University Press, 1927), 458–59.

8. Matthew Dillon, *Omens and Oracles: Divination in Ancient Greece* (Routledge, 2017), 179–88.

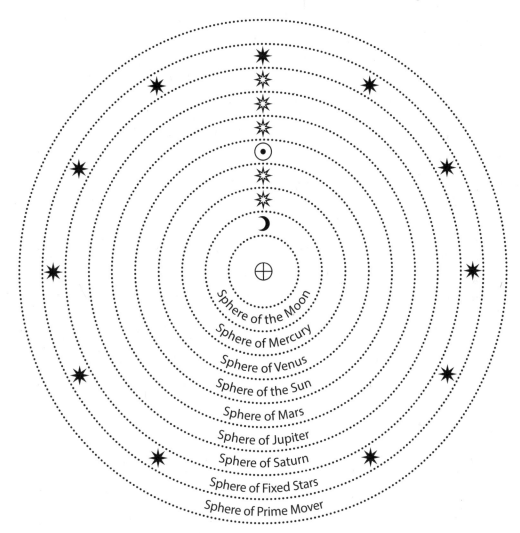

Figure 1.1. Greco-Roman model of the planets

The Western repertoire of astronomical and astrological knowledge was eventually systematized in second-century Egypt, primarily due to the efforts of Claudius Ptolemy. He described the astrological properties of the *wanderers* in terms of Aristotelian physical theory, differentiating them by hot/cold and wet/dry characteristics as determined by their positions relative to the Sun (the source of heat) and Earth (the source of moisture).[9] The hot quality brings together similar things, whereas the cold quality brings together all things, regardless of their similarity.[10] Things that are wet are adaptable in shape, whereas dry things are not.[11] Ptolemy's work compiled all known astronomical and astrological knowledge of the time, and, due to its explanatory and predictive power, remained unchallenged until the Renaissance.

Hermetic Model of the Planets

The origin story of the classical planets appears in "Poimandres" of the *Corpus Hermeticum*.[12] This collection of texts is attributed to the "Thrice Great" Hermes Trismegistus, a combination of the Greek Hermes and Egyptian Thoth. In a vision of the universe's creation, fire manifests from light, followed by air, with the water and earth elements remaining mixed below. Fire and air naturally move upward, whereas water and earth naturally move downward. In a second emanation, seven *governors* (classical planets) ruling fate are created from the upward-moving elements. The *logos* (Gk. λόγος) then rises from the downward moving elements and sends the planets into orbit.

Hermeticist Franz Bardon further explains how planets are organized into zones (Figure 1.2). Each planetary zone has a presence on the physical, astral, and mental planes and is inhabited by various denizens governed by their own laws.[13] Zones are not confined to the planetary spheres—their influence may stretch across the universe. The *All in All* (which many paradigms call *God*) dictates the vibration (and thus characteristics) of each sphere. When we die, we ascend through the zones, shed our vices, and reunite with the Divine.[14]

---

9. Ptolemy, *Tetrabiblos*, trans. F. E. Robbins (Harvard University Press, 1940), 34–37.

10. Aristotle, *On Generation and Corruption*, trans. Harold H. Joachim, in *The Basic Works of Aristotle*, ed. Richard McKeon (Modern Library, 2001), 509–10.

11. Aristotle, *On Generation and Corruption*, 510.

12. Brian P. Copenhaver, *Hermetica: The Greek* Corpus Hermeticum *and the Latin* Asclepius *in a new English translation, with notes and introduction* (Cambridge University Press, 1995), 1–7.

13. Franz Bardon, *The Practice of Magical Evocation* (Merkur Publishing, 2001), 91–94. Originally published in 1956 by Verlag Hermann Bauer.

14. Copenhaver, *Hermetica*, 5–7, 51–52.

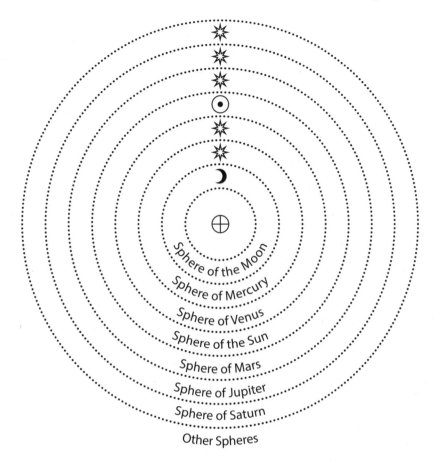

Figure 1.2. Hermetic model of the planets

To make a colored image for your notes, commonly used correspondences are as follows: the Moon, white or silver; Mercury, orange; Venus, green; the Sun, yellow or gold; Mars, red; Jupiter, blue; and Saturn, purple.

Hermetic Qabala

The Qabala (Heb. קבלה) is a cornerstone of the Western esoteric tradition. It is a way of reception (of the nature of the universe) and revelation. Its wisdom can be summarized into one glyph: the Tree of Life (Figure 1.3).

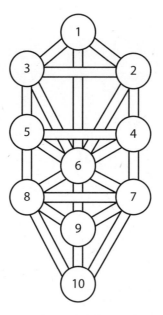

Figure 1.3. The Tree of Life

The Tree of Life is one of the most widespread symbols in Western mysticism. It is a map of the self, all levels of experience, and the universe. It is composed of ten spheres and twenty-two paths. Romanized Hebrew names of each sphere are as follows: 1, *Keter* (Heb. Crown); 2, *Ḥokma* (Wisdom); 3, *Bina* (Understanding); 4, *Ḥesed* (Love or Mercy); 5, *Gebura* (Strength or Might); 6, *Tif'eret* (Beauty); 7, *Neṣaḥ* (Victory); 8, *Hod* (Splendor); 9, *Yesod* (Foundation); and 10, *Malkut* (Kingdom).

Its spheres and paths represent specific archetypal forces. Each classical planet is associated with a sphere and path that we'll explore more deeply in later chapters. A detailed discussion of Qabala is beyond the scope of this book, but a plethora of fantastic literature is available in this day and age if the subject interests you.[15]

The Hexagram

The hexagram (six-pointed star) is significant in many cultures. It is a shape that can be drawn with two equilateral triangles. The earliest discovered hexagrams date back to the ancient world where they served as decorations or spiritual symbols. Medieval

---

15. Soror Velchanes, *The Elemental Magic Workbook: An Experimental Guide to Understanding and Working with the Classical Elements*, 2nd ed. (Megalithica Books, 2020), 224–29.

Hebrews incorporated hexagrams—often inscribed with divine names—into protective amulets.[16,17] Medieval Christians incorporated hexagrams into religious architecture to symbolize the Holy Trinity.[18]

Drawing a hexagram inherently involves working with planetary forces—each point and the center correspond to a classical planet (Figure 1.4). In Renaissance times, Henry Cornelius Agrippa incorporated hexagrams into evocations but did not heavily discuss them in the context of planetary magic.[19,20] In the 1800s, Éliphas Lévi viewed the hexagram as a sign of the union of opposites, the balance of planetary forces, and the macrocosm. He wrote, "The notion of the Infinite and the Absolute is expressed by this sign, which is the grand pantacle—that is to say, the most simple and complete abridgement of the science of all things."[21]

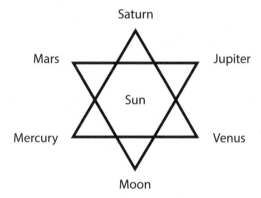

Figure 1.4. The hexagram

16. "Amulets," in *The Jewish Encyclopedia*, ed. Isidore Singer (Funk & Wagnalls, 1906), 1:546–50.

17. "Magen Dawid," in *The Jewish Encyclopedia*, 8:251–52.

18. Judith Neulander, "Conjuring Crypto-Jews in New Mexico," in *Boundaries, Identity and Belonging in Modern Judaism*, eds. Maria Diemling and Larry Ray (Routledge, 2016), 211.

19. Henry Cornelius Agrippa, *Three Books of Occult Philosophy*, ed. Donald Tyson (Llewellyn Publications, 2004). Originally published 1651 by R. W. for George Moule.

20. Henry Cornelius Agrippa, *The Fourth Book of Occult Philosophy*, ed. Donald Tyson (Llewellyn Publications, 2009). Originally published 1665 by J. C. for J. Harrison.

21. Éliphas Lévi, *Transcendental Magic: Its Doctrine and Ritual*, trans. Arthur Edward Waite (Weiser Books, 2001), 45. Originally published in 1854–1856 by Germer Baillière.

Occultist Aleister Crowley modified Lévi's hexagram to symbolize union with the Holy Guardian Angel.[22] In Lévi's arrangement, the upward pointing red triangle symbolizes elemental fire and the downward pointing blue triangle symbolizes elemental water. In Crowley's arrangement, the downward pointing red triangle symbolizes a flame descending upon an altar and the upward pointing blue triangle symbolizes focused aspiration. Crowley also placed a pentagram (five-pointed star) inside a unicursal hexagram to symbolize the union of terrestrial and celestial forces, the microcosm and the macrocosm, man and the Divine. Whereas the pentagram is associated with terrestrial (elemental) forces and symbolizes the microcosm, the hexagram is associated with celestial (planetary) forces and symbolizes the macrocosm. In many Western esoteric practices today, the hexagram continues to symbolize the balance of planetary forces and the heavens as a macrocosm.

---

22. Aleister Crowley, *The Book of Lies* (Samuel Weiser, 1998), 148–49. Originally published in 1913 by Wieland and Co.

Active Work
Your Magical Diary

As mentioned in the introduction, a magical diary serves as a permanent, written record of your work. Do not let anyone view your magical diary—it is a highly personal document for you alone. Also, do not touch someone else's diary or other magical items without their permission—it is considered rude.

Instructions for creating a basic magical diary from a blank spiral-bound notebook or bound composition book are as follows:

- Create a table of contents to record a page number, date, and title for each entry. Leaving a small space to indicate if a rite yielded successful results is helpful but not required.

- Individual entries should begin with the date and title. Additional information (e.g., time, Moon phase, weather …) may also be included if it is important in your tradition or if you feel it is necessary.

- Include a brief description of what you did. Elaborate workings may be referenced or copied in their entirety into the diary. Securely attaching printouts by stapling or taping is another option.

- Record any notes, thoughts, inner feelings, and other details you feel are important afterward. Document them as soon as possible so you don't forget small details.

- Leave a few blank lines to record any results (or lack thereof) you achieve. The manifestation of results varies widely and depends on factors such as the overarching goal and nature of the activity.

- Never write anyone's legal name in your diary. Refer to others by their magical names or initials instead. This will protect people's identities if your diary is accidentally discovered. Better safe than sorry!

An example magical diary entry is shown below. You will be performing this exercise in chapter 2.

October 31, 2021, 11:45pm. *Moon Attunement.* I attuned with the Moon for 10 minutes tonight, alone near the canal. I feel more sensitized to the surrounding environment, especially the water. The Moon's energy was receptive, malleable, and surreptitious.

Keep your diary in a safe, secure place where no one will see it. Update it regularly to keep track of your progress. It is not uncommon for long-term practitioners to have multiple volumes. Sometimes it is fun to look back and see what you were doing years ago! If you already have a magical diary, begin a separate one for your planetary work. Important entries can be referenced or copied into the primary diary.

Meditation

Though many meditation techniques exist, their overarching goal is to focus your energy inward to carefully examine a subject of interest—its underlying forces can be more easily perceived by the subconscious mind. The following procedure can be used to meditate on any topic, including those covered here:

1. Sit down in a comfortable position in a quiet place free of distractions.
2. Close your eyes.
3. Focus your attention on your breath, but make no effort to control the intensity or rhythm of your breathing.

4. If your mind wanders, gently redirect your focus back to your breathing.

5. After a few minutes, transfer your focus from breathing to the subject of interest.

6. If your mind wanders, gently redirect your focus back to the subject of interest.

7. When you are finished, open your eyes and take a moment to become reacquainted with your surroundings. Once you are reoriented you may stand up.

8. Record your results in your magical diary.

When you first start meditating, you may skip steps five and six and just focus on your breath. During this exercise you might also observe peripheral thoughts entering and exiting your mind. Let them go and do not pursue them. Vigilant practice will allow you to consistently redirect your focus back to the subject of interest.

Chapter 1
Homework

After taking notes on the chapter, proceed with the following exercises. Magical practice should be commenced for a minimum of thirty minutes each day for a minimum of one month. You may check off the boxes to keep track of your progress.

☐ Create your magical diary. If you already have a magical diary, begin a separate one for your planetary work.

☐ Practice meditating on any topic for twenty minutes each day for a minimum of one month. You may choose two ten-minute sessions or one twenty-minute session. Record your results in your magical diary.

☐ After meditating, reflect on what you hope to gain from working with the classical planets for another ten minutes each day. Record your thoughts and feelings in your magical diary.

☐ Obtain your natal chart and place it in your magical diary. In astrology, it is believed that the positions of the planets at birth and onward influence the course of an individual's life. To create your natal chart you will need the date, time, and city of your birth. There are many reputable websites where you may obtain a free natal chart online. Choose the *tropical* zodiac and *whole sign* houses. Do not worry about interpreting it for now. We will examine the natal chart, planet by planet, in subsequent chapters.

Chapter 1 Resources

AstroSeek. "Traditional Astrology Chart Calculator." https://horoscopes.astro-seek.com/traditional-astrology.

CHAPTER 2
The Moon Reflects

The Moon provides the foundation necessary to work with the classical planets. Thus, our journey will begin with the Moon. As the Moon reflects the light of the Sun, our unconscious mind reflects our personal self (the "I") and drives us to fulfill our needs. Common Moon symbols are shown in Figure 2.1. They are useful focal points in meditation and magical practice.

(a)　　　　　　　　　　(b)

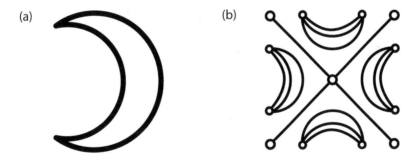

Figure 2.1. The (a) astronomical symbol and (b) planetary seal of the Moon

The Western View of the Moon

In the Greco-Roman model the Moon resides between Earth (at the center) and Mercury.[23] Due to its close proximity to Earth, the Moon is primarily wet and secondarily hot.

---

23. Ptolemy, *Tetrabiblos*, 34–43.

These characteristics dictate its other attributes, such as temperament (i.e., benefic or malefic), sex (masculine or feminine), and sect (diurnal or nocturnal). The benefic (helpful) planets are typically hot or wet, whereas the malefic (harmful) planets are typically cold or dry. The Moon is benefic. In addition, wet planets are typically feminine and nocturnal, whereas dry planets are typically masculine and diurnal. The Moon is feminine and nocturnal.

The classical planets move through the zodiac, which modulates each planetary force. Planetary forces strongly manifest in the sign they rule. The Moon rules Cancer.[24] Planetary forces are also strong when exalted and weak in their fall (the opposite sign). The Moon is exalted in Taurus and its fall is in Scorpio.[25]

In the Hermetic model the classical planets affect the physical, astral, and mental planes on Earth.[26] The Moon affects the liquid on Earth. It is also analogous to our astral body and the astral plane. In a nutshell, the astral plane is the realm of dreams, imagination, and nonmaterial existence underlying physical reality. It is superimposed over the physical plane but consists of higher vibrations. A plethora of literature describing the form and function of the astral plane is present in the modern day and age.[27] Astral life is present in the Moon zone. According to Franz Bardon, denizens of the Moon may be evoked in a white or silver light.[28] These colors of light emulate the Moon zone's vibrations and are thus conducive to manifesting lunar beings.

Gk. *Selēnē* (Σελήνη); Heb. *Levana* (לבנה);
Lat. *Luna*; Ouranian Barbaric *XOAC*

The Lunar Archetype

Planetary archetypes are key concepts in magical thought. The ancients personified these archetypes as deities, but you may think of them as ordering principles within the

---

24. Ptolemy, *Tetrabiblos*, 78–81.

25. Ptolemy, *Tetrabiblos*, 88–89.

26. Bardon, *Magical Evocation*, 292.

27. Dolores Ashcroft-Nowicki and J. H. Brennan, *Magical Use of Thought Forms: A Proven System of Mental & Spiritual Empowerment* (Llewellyn Publications, 2004), 55–61.

28. Bardon, *Magical Evocation*, 128.

human psyche.[29] Deities traditionally associated with the Moon include Khonsu (Egyptian), Artemis and Hecate (Greek), and Diana (Roman).

The Moon is our foundation. It represents our relational matrix, which manifests in our ability to interface with society. It also has ties to our sense of security. The Moon oversees the mother and family life, two important foundations. Exoterically (physically), it is the biological mother who carries and nurtures the developing fetus. Esoterically (metaphysically), it is the Great Mother who oversees the cycles and rhythms of manifestation on Earth. Keywords relevant to the Moon are as follows:

Foundation

Our relational matrix is an important foundation. A solid foundation provides a sense of structure, security, and belonging. An unstable foundation may result in an inability to trust or bond with others. It may also lead to chronic feelings of insecurity and alienation.

Unconscious Mind

The mental processes underlying the unconscious mind influence our perceptions, judgements, and motivations.[30] The lunar force may manifest through dreams or be conveyed via intuition, such as a gut feeling.

Instincts

Instincts are innate behaviors that do not have to be learned. The Moon reigns over our maternal and nurturing instincts. The need to be part of a community is also considered an instinct.

Emotions

Our emotions influence how we relate and respond to others, thus impacting our ability to function in society. This may positively manifest through reaching out to others, being receptive to their needs, and having a sense of community. This may negatively manifest through dependency (as opposed to interdependency) or an inability to empathize.

29. Carl Jung, *Synchronicity: An Acausal Connecting Principle*, trans. R. F. C. Hull (Princeton University Press, 2010), 77. Originally published in 1952 by Princeton University Press.

30. John A. Bargh, "Our Unconscious Mind," *Scientific American* 310, no. 1 (2014): 30–37.

Creation

The Moon reigns over generation and fertility. This is also why the Moon is associated with sex magic. Further, in many cultures the Moon is believed to bear connection to the human menstrual cycle.

Cycles

The Moon exhibits cyclical change as it progresses through its phases. This carries over esoterically, thus in many traditions the Moon reigns over the cycles and rhythms of life on Earth, as well as the rhythms of Earth at large.

Western Moon Magic

The Moon appears to be the same size as the Sun in the sky, so the ancients perceived both luminaries as powerful.[31] In many Western esoteric traditions the Moon is associated with astral, dream, glamoury, cyclical, regenerative, and sex magic. It is also generally associated with spiritual and feminine works.

Moon Phases

The Moon has long held significance in witchcraft, and its phases are of especial interest. The phases represent cyclical change, and each is well suited for a particular type of magic. The phases also reflect different aspects of a triple goddess, as shown in Table 2.1.

Table 2.1. Moon Phase Correspondences in Witchcraft			
Moon Phase	**Magical Activities**	**Triple Goddess Aspect**	**Goddesses**
Waxing	Beginnings, works of increase, gain, creation	Maiden	Artemis (Gk.) Diana (Rom.) Diana (Etr.)
Full	Fruition, religious works, power, protection, intuition	Mother	Selene (Gk.) Luna (Rom.) Losna (Etr.)

---

31. Joanna Martine Woolfolk, *The Only Astrology Book You'll Ever Need* (Scarborough House, 1990), 145.

Table 2.1. Moon Phase Correspondences in Witchcraft			
Moon Phase	**Magical Activities**	**Triple Goddess Aspect**	**Goddesses**
Waning	Endings, works of decrease, banishing, separation, cursing	Crone	Hecate (Gk.) Trivia (Rom.) Manea (Etr.)

The information in Table 2.1 is adapted from Grimassi's *Hereditary Witchcraft: Secrets of the Old Religion*, Starhawk's *The Spiral Dance: A Rebirth of the Ancient Religion of the Great Goddess*, and personal notes. Here, Greek (Gk.), Roman (Rom.), and Etruscan (Etr.) goddesses are listed.

Phases are determined by the Moon's location relative to Earth and the Sun. A New Moon occurs when the Moon moves between Earth and the Sun. Since the Moon and Sun are on the same side of the sky, the far side completely blocks sunlight from reaching the near side, which remains in total darkness. As the Moon moves toward the opposite side of the sky, it waxes as a larger fraction of the near side becomes visible. A Full Moon occurs when Earth is between the Moon and Sun. Since the Moon and Sun are on opposite sides of the sky, the near side of the Moon becomes fully illuminated by the Sun's light. As the Moon moves toward the opposite side of the sky, it wanes as a smaller fraction of the near side becomes visible. When the Moon returns to its location between Earth and the Sun, the cycle begins anew.

Time and Other Correspondences

Each classical planet has dominion over a day of the week and alchemical metal.[32] In many paradigms it is auspicious to perform magical work governed by a particular planet on the day it rules. The Moon's day is Monday (Lat. *dies Lunae*). The alchemical metals are considered terrestrial manifestations of celestial forces. The Moon's alchemical metal is silver.

32. Yannis Almirantis, "The Paradox of the Planetary Metals," *Journal of Scientific Exploration* 19, no. 1 (2005): 31–42.

In ceremonial traditions the Moon is associated with *Yesod* (Heb. Foundation), the ninth sphere of the Qabala.[33] This foundation is the hidden infrastructure underlying physical reality. Psychologically, this sphere represents the unconscious mind, serves as a conduit for the personal self, and drives us to fulfill our needs. Correspondences of *Yesod* often relate to foundations and strength. The Moon is also associated with *Gimel*, the path connecting *Keter* (Crown) and *Tif'eret* (Beauty). It connects the pure spirit of transpersonal self to our personal self. In ancient script the letter *gimel* resembles a camel, the animal capable of crossing the abyss to make this journey. Correspondences of *Gimel* often relate to femininity and elemental water.

Lunar Mansions

Lunar mansions are comprised of segments of the sky the Moon passes through on its monthly (roughly twenty-eight-day) journey. They are thought to be Babylonian in origin but are present in some form across many cultures throughout history.[34,35,36] Western views of the mansions draw heavily from *Picatrix*, the Latin translation of *The Goal of the Sage* (Ara. *Ghayat al-Ḥakim*). Each night of the sidereal month, the Moon enters a new mansion. In many paradigms, when the Moon occupies a particular mansion, its governing head may be petitioned or talismans may be constructed for specific purposes.[37,38]

Fundamentals: Ceremonial Hierarchies

Each classical planet is associated with a Qabalistic sphere and path. Many magicians typically use the sphere hierarchies for spiritual purposes and the path hierarchies for practical purposes. This book focuses on the path hierarchies as presented in Crowley's

---

33. Aleister Crowley, "777 Revised" in *777 and Other Qabalistic Writings of Aleister Crowley*, ed. Israel Regardie (Samuel Weiser, 1999), 2–3, 5. Originally published in 1909 by The Walter Scott Publishing Co.

34. Stefan Weinstock, "Lunar Mansions and Early Calendars," *Journal of Hellenic Studies* 69, (1949): 48–69.

35. Philip Yampolsky, "The Origin of the Twenty-Eight Lunar Mansions," *Osiris* 9 (1950): 62–83.

36. Rupert Gleadow, *The Origin of the Zodiac* (Dover Publications, 2001), 152–74.

37. John Michael Greer and Christopher Warnock, trans., *The Picatrix: Liber Rubeus Edition* (Adocentyn Press, 2010–2011), 31–39.

38. Bardon, *Magical Evocation,* 277–89.

777 Revised, which are based on the planetary hierarchies given in Agrippa's *Three Books of Occult Philosophy*.[39],[40]

Each planetary hierarchy denizen occupies a particular Qabalistic world. These worlds represent different levels of the heavens and reflect the process of creating the universe. A complete Tree of Life is present in all four worlds, with the *Malkut* of one world manifesting the *Keter* of the next. Magicians may contact planetary hierarchy denizens to obtain knowledge, effect internal or external change, and more. They are typically called in a top-down fashion to refine the magician's request. The top-down Hebrew hierarchy for the Moon is shown in Table 2.2.

Table 2.2. The Moon Ceremonial Hierarchy		
Qabalistic World	**Level**	**Name**
Aṣilut	Divine names	*Hod, 'Elim*
Beri'a	Archangel	*Gabri'el*
Yeṣira	Intelligence of Intelligences Spirit of Spirits Spirit	*Malka' Betarshishim* *We'ad Beruaḥ Shaharim* *Shed Barshehm'ot Shartathan* *Ḥasmoda'y*
'Asiya	Magical tool	Bow and arrow

The information in Table 2.2 is adapted from Crowley's "777 Revised." See Appendix A for Hebrew spelling, pronunciation, etymologies, and more. *Shaday 'El Ḥay* is *Almighty Living God* in *Yesod*. The intelligence of intelligences is the collective consciousness of the various intelligences of the Moon. The spirit of spirits is the collective raw force of the various spirits of the Moon. Incense and sandals are associated with *Yesod*.

---

39. Crowley, "777 Revised," 18–19.
40. Agrippa, *Three Books*, 318–29.

The highest world, *'Olam 'Aṣilut* (Heb. World of Emanation), is divine and unchanging. It consists of pure principles and archetypes.[41] Universal qualities and divine names reside here.[42] Magicians vibrate divine names to resonate with particular aspects of the All in All. Each planet is associated with one or more divine names.

The second world is *'Olam Beri'a* (Heb. World of Creation). It is the first world created *ex nihilo* and thus the first separated from the Divine.[43] This is where archangels receive concepts and qualities emanated from *'Aṣilut*.[44] Archangels direct the manifestation of creation, and lesser angels and spirits are obedient to them. Each planet is associated with a particular archangel.

The third world is *'Olam Yeṣira* (Heb. World of Formation). This is the world of thoughts and ideas, where specific designs begin to take shape.[45] Planetary intelligences and spirits reside here.[46] The intelligences embody the consciousness of the planetary forces and direct the spirits' actions in *'Asiya*. The spirits embody the raw planetary forces. Each planet is associated with a particular intelligence and spirit.

The fourth world is *'Olam 'Asiya* (Heb. World of Action). This is the world of matter and physical manifestation, and the most tangible and dense of the four worlds. It consists of our physical world and its spiritual shadow.[47] We live here. Our planetary tools and the planetary metals reside here. Other denizens of *'Asiya* include intelligences and spirits.[48]

The Moon in Chaos Magic

The Moon may be integrated into magical practice in numerous ways. Various deities, egregores, or pop culture characters associated with the Moon may be invoked or evoked. Divination may be practiced via astrologically analyzing the Moon or through dreaming. Magical items associated with the Moon may be enchanted for purposes con-

---

41. Aryeh Kaplan, ed. and trans., *Sefer Yetzirah: The Book of Creation in Theory and Practice*, rev. ed. (Weiser Books, 1997), 41–43.

42. Lon Milo DuQuette, *The Chicken Qabalah of Rabbi Lamed Ben Clifford* (Weiser Books, 2001), 139.

43. Kaplan, *Sefer Yetzirah*, 43.

44. DuQuette, *Chicken Qabalah*, 139.

45. Kaplan, *Sefer Yetzirah*, 43.

46. DuQuette, *Chicken Qabalah*, 139.

47. Kaplan, *Sefer Yetzirah*, 43.

48. DuQuette, *Chicken Qabalah*, 139.

sistent with its nature. Exposing magical tools or other objects to moonlight serves to charge, cleanse, or consecrate them with lunar energy. Illumination rites aimed at gaining insight into the unconscious mind or cyclical knowledge may also be performed.

Rites for the Moon are provided in the "Active Work" box that starts on page 27. The attunement exercise familiarizes you with the force underlying each classical planet. The greeting rite formally introduces you to the planet and serves as a prelude to future magical work. The guided meditation allows you to explore the relationship between the exoteric (i.e., physical) and esoteric (i.e., metaphysical) properties of a planet. The guided meditations may be performed individually or in a group—feel free to record them beforehand. Finally, a monasticism is provided. The monasticism serves to strengthen your relationship with a classical planet in a manner consistent with its nature.

The Moon is receptive, acquiescent, malleable, mutable, cyclical, and surreptitious. It is also very sensitive and impressionable. These characteristics have been incorporated into the rites, which are intentionally rhythmic, and open-ended, and involve astral work.

Drawing Hexagrams

Some rites use ceremonial planetary hexagrams. It is best to commit them to memory. The lunar hexagrams are shown in Figure 2.2.

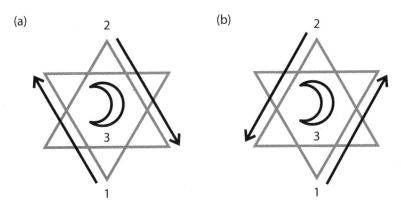

Figure 2.2. Lunar (a) invoking and (b) banishing hexagrams

Draw the planetary hexagrams with your magical tool or index finger in the numbered sequence shown. Visualize the hexagram shape in purple or silver and vibrate *ARARITA* as you draw. ARARITA (Heb. אראריתא) is an acronym of *'Eḥad Ro'sh*

'Eḥadoto Ro'sh Yiḥudo Temurato 'Eḥad ("One is His Beginning; One is His Individuality; His Permutation One"), a phrase from the *Sefer Hapliy'ah*.[49,50] Visualize the Moon's astronomical symbol in purple or silver and vibrate *Shaday 'El Ḥay* as you draw. When you have finished drawing the astronomical symbol while vibrating the divine name, your planetary hexagram is complete.

When drawing a hexagram in front of you, it is easiest to use your head, shoulders, hips, and lower pelvis as reference points. The top point will be located in front of your head, the upper middle points in front of your shoulders, the lower middle points in front of your hips, and the bottom point in front of your lower pelvis.

To draw an invoking lunar hexagram, the sequence of the first triangle is: lower pelvis, left shoulder, right shoulder, and back to your lower pelvis. The sequence of the second triangle is: head, right hip, left hip, and back to your head. Draw the planetary astronomical symbol in front of your chest. To draw a banishing lunar hexagram, the sequence of the first triangle is: lower pelvis, right shoulder, left shoulder, and back to your lower pelvis. The sequence of the second triangle is: head, left hip, right hip, and back to your head. Draw the planetary astronomical symbol in front of your chest.

---

49. Aleister Crowley, "Sepher Sephiroth," in *777 and Other Qabalistic Writings of Aleister Crowley*, ed. Israel Regardie (Samuel Weiser, 1999), 62.

50. *Sefer Hapliy'ah* [Book of Wonder], (Zupnik, Knoller & Hammerschmidt, 1883), 110.

Active Work
Moon Attunement

Go outside and gaze up at the Moon. If you live in an area where this is not practical, look through a window instead. As you gaze, carry out rhythmic breathing using any preferred method. Carefully observe the Moon's silvery white color, as well as the quality of light it reflects. Strongly visualize this light emanating down to Earth, softly enveloping you as you continue rhythmically breathing. Observe these lunar vibrations with all five of your senses, as well as astrally. As time passes, the vibrations grow stronger. Slowly adjust the rhythm of your body to match these vibrations. Feel them elevating, softening, and sensitizing you.

> November 1, 2021. *Lunar Attunement—Summary of Observations*. I attuned with the Moon each night for two lunar cycles. The manifestation of the lunar force varied with phase, zodiac sign, and other astrological conditions. Although its nature varied, I consistently felt more psychically sensitive and "in tune" with the astral plane afterward. Others reported similar results.

Moon Greeting Rite

The following rite should be performed when the Moon is visible in the sky. The Moon in Cancer or Taurus are preferable but not required.

Materials

- No materials are required.
- If you already have a lunar tool, you may ask the planetary spirit to bless it instead. Recall that the traditional ceremonial tool is the bow and arrow. Alternatively, you may use chunks of the planetary metals as "tools" if you prefer something discrete.

Statement of Intent

It is my will to access the lunar force.

Procedure

On a Monday night, face the Moon and attune with it as described earlier.

When ready, draw an invoking lunar hexagram in front of you so that the Moon as it appears in your field of vision is in the center of this hexagram. Visualize the Moon's light emanating down from the heavens, passing through your hexagram and enveloping you. Knock in the center of your hexagram nine times, as if you are knocking on a door. Place your open palms toward the Moon and say the following in your inner (astral) voice:

> *XIQUAL XOAC!*
> *Come long-winged Selēnē, the light in the dark!*
> *Come horned Luna, on your two-yoked chariot!*
> *Come Levana, the white one,*
> *Yareaḥ, who endures!*
> *In the divine names of Hod and 'Elim I greet you!*
> *Come Gabri'el, Archangel of the Moon,*
> *and reflect your divine light into the darkness!*
> *Grant me access to the lunar force*
> *so I may build a solid foundation!*

Close your eyes and inhale the lunar light enveloping you, until it fills your entire body. Take note of any astral impressions or intuitive messages you receive.

When ready, open your eyes and draw a triangle enclosing your hexagram. Visualize it in silver. Place your open palms slightly outside the triangle and proceed to evoke the planetary intelligence of intelligences. Say:

Malka' Betarshishim We'ad Beruaḥ Shaharim,
Intelligence of Intelligences of the Moon,
in the name of Gabri'el I evoke you!
Grant me access to the lunar force
so I may harness it for the Great Work of Magic!

If you do not sense its presence, gaze at the Moon and repeat the above until you do.

After you sense the planetary intelligence of intelligences' presence, proceed to evoke the planetary spirit of spirits and planetary spirit. With open palms still slightly outside the triangle, continue:

Shed Barshehm'ot Shartathan,
Spirit of Spirits of the Moon, in the name of
Malka' Betarshishim We'Ad Beruaḥ Shaharim
I evoke you!
Ḥasmoda'y, Spirit of the Moon,
in the names of Malka' Betarshishim We'Ad Beruaḥ Shaharim
and Shed Barshehm'ot Shartathan I evoke you!
Aid my efforts to obtain a lunar tool
that will assist me in the Great Work of Magic!

If you do not sense their presences, gaze at the Moon and repeat the above until you do. After you are finished communicating with them, thank them and send them on their way.

Banishing

Draw a banishing lunar hexagram over your invoking lunar hexagram and banish with laughter.

December 20, 2021. *Moon Greeting Rite.* The rite took about 15 minutes to perform. My lunar tool is a piece of silver jewelry that's been passed down through multiple generations of women in my family. The lunar light was diaphanous, malleable, soft, and gentle. Astrally, at one point it condensed and appeared as billowy silver smoke. The lunar hierarchy denizens arrived quickly and also seemed quite diaphanous in nature. The jewelry absorbed the lunar vibrations rapidly. The neighborhood dogs are typically quiet at night, but shortly after finishing the rite they all started howling!

Moon Guided Meditation

Find a warm, quiet place and sit in a comfortable position. Close your eyes. Take a deep breath and center yourself. With each rhythmic breath, you will feel calmer and more relaxed. Feel the tension in your toes. As you exhale, the tension dissipates until they are completely relaxed. This feeling of relaxation grows, spreading through your feet into your ankles. They are now completely relaxed. It continues, travelling up your legs and into your knees, which are now completely relaxed. Feel the lack of tension in your shins and calves. Any outside noises or distractions just serve to relax you further. Now your upper legs, hips, and waist are completely relaxed. As you continue to rhythmically breathe, your abdominal region, chest, and back are completely relaxed. Your relaxation grows further, moving into your shoulders, and then down into your arms, elbows, hands, fingers, and fingertips. Your entire body below your neck is now completely relaxed. This feeling of relaxation grows, filling your neck and face. Feel your chin, jaw, nose, cheeks, eyes, eyelids, forehead, and ears relax. Finally, feel your scalp relax. Your entire body is now completely relaxed.

In your mind's eye, visualize a Full Moon glowing above your head. It is about the size of a basketball and reflects a silvery white light. The light shines down, softly enveloping you as you continue rhythmically breathing. Observe the light with all five of your senses. See its gentle brightness, feel its warmth, smell it, and taste it. Does it emanate a sound? The Moon rings like a bell but emanates no sound when touched. As you continue breathing, the silvery white light accumulates within you and around you, filling your body and field of vision completely. You draw an invoking lunar hexagram in front of you. As you trace the symbol of the Moon while vibrating *Shaday 'El Ḥay* in your astral voice, the light inside you gently glows.

Slowly, the light in the surrounding environment disperses. Still unable to see anything, you smell and taste the faint odor of spent gunpowder. It is completely silent. As your eyes adjust to the dim light, an unfamiliar terrain comes into focus. It is littered with rocks, craters, and regolith of varying shades of gray. Occasionally a dull green rock punctuates the landscape. In the distance you see smoother, darker plains formed by ancient volcanic eruptions. As you scan the plains, your eyes are drawn to a group of unusual silhouettes that appear to be gathered on one of them. Intrigued, you make your way toward them to investigate more closely. As you walk, the ground beneath you abrasively crunches but produces no sound. Your feet kick up some of the fine, powdery regolith that floats upward as if in slow motion.

The gentle, steady glow you emanate lights the way as you get closer and closer to the silhouettes. The ground beneath you is now smoother and harder. It is a darker gray, almost black. As you gaze up into space you see hundreds of stars, their shine unhindered by an atmosphere. You also notice a larger object in the unfamiliar sky. It is covered in a swirling white, with hints of blue, brown, and green underneath. After a few more moments pass, you recognize this object—it is Earth. You are standing on the Moon.

As your eyes return to the lunar surface you see the silhouettes have encircled you. They are partially obscured by shadows, silently standing a few meters away. As you examine them, you note their varied appearances. Some glow with lighter hues of silvery white light, while some glow with darker hues. Some have visible faces, while others remain concealed. Some are tall. Some are short. Some resemble humans. Some do not. As they silently study you, you realize they are the governing heads overseeing the twenty-eight mansions of the Moon. One of these governing heads steps out of the circle and approaches you. It needs to tell you something important. You may talk with this governing head for as long as you'd like. After you are finished, you thank it and send it on its way.

You can visit the Moon any time you'd like—now you know the way here. The silvery white light again accumulates within you and around you, filling your body and field of vision completely. As you continue to rhythmically breathe, you draw a banishing lunar hexagram in front of you. As you trace the symbol of the Moon while vibrating *Shaday 'El Ḥay* in your astral voice, the light in the surrounding environment slowly disperses. The room where your physical body resides begins to return. You begin to feel your fingers and toes. As the last remnants of the silvery white light fade, you gradually feel the rest of your body. Slowly open your eyes and become reacquainted with your surroundings. Stand up when you are ready and document your experience in your magical diary.

November 6, 2021. *Moon Guided Meditation.* The messages participants received from the governing heads tended to be highly personal in nature. The geological description of the lunar surface was inspired by astronaut accounts of their experiences on the Moon.

Moon Monasticism

This monasticism serves to strengthen your relationship with the Moon. It should be performed for nine days, since this number is associated with *Yesod*. However, feel free to use another Moon-related number if it suits your fancy. Carry your Moon tool at all times during the monasticism—it serves as a constant reminder of the Moon and increases vigilance. After your monasticism is complete keep your Moon tool someplace special, such as an altar or favorite shelf. You may use it in future Moon work and reuse it if you perform the monasticism again.

The Lesser Observances are intended for someone who regularly has a busy schedule. The Extreme Observances are intended for someone who has extended free time. The Greater Observances are a mean between the two.

Beginning the Monasticism

On a Monday night, face the Moon and attune with it. The Moon in Cancer or Taurus are preferable but not required. Take your time and do not rush.

When ready, draw an invoking lunar hexagram in front of you so that the Moon as it appears in your field of vision is in the center of this hexagram. Knock in the center of your hexagram nine times, as if you are knocking on a door. Place your open palms toward the Moon and say the following in your inner (astral) voice:

*Levana, I greet you! It is my will to perform the [Lesser/
Greater/Extreme] Observances of the Moon for nine days.
This entails [state the relevant sections here]. May this
monasticism lay a solid foundation for my future work!*

Lesser Observances

- Carry your lunar tool at all times. If you can't carry it openly, keep it in your pocket or a bag and carry that with you.
- Observe the Moon for a few minutes each night while contemplating its impact on your life and the earth at large.
- Perform a nightly lunar rite that incorporates your tool.
- Lunar gravity produces the tidal rhythms on Earth. Make a conscious effort to "go blue" (help our oceans) and perform at least one "blue" action a day that is not already part of your normal repertoire. Visit the National Ocean Service's *How can you help our ocean?* for suggestions.
- In many paradigms the Moon rules over mothers and infants. Donate items such as baby formula, diapers, or clothing to a women's shelter or organization that helps single mothers. If you are unable to make a material donation you may make a monetary donation instead, so long as the value is in a multiple of nine.

Greater Observances

- Perform all the Lesser Observances.
- Perform a second nightly lunar rite that incorporates your tool. To give your second rite an energetic boost, align its purpose with the Moon phase.

- Relate all of your meditation and magical work to the Moon. For example, meditate on lunar symbols or perform divination via dream interpretation.
- A large portion of marine litter comes from plastics. To combat this, abstain from plastics that are single-use (e.g., plastic soda bottles, disposable cutlery …). If you cannot be completely plastic-free due to health reasons, reduce your plastic waste in other areas of life as much as possible.

Extreme Observances

- Perform all the Greater Observances.
- Perform a third nightly lunar rite that incorporates your tool.
- Increase your efforts to "go blue" as much as possible. Actions to help the ocean may be large or small but must be at the fore-front of your consciousness. Examples include using sustainable shopping bags, saying no to illegal marine life products, or participating in a beach cleanup. Volunteer opportunities are available at National Marine Sanctuaries, VolunteerMatch, and Points of Light. If you want to combine your "blue" efforts with tourism, there is always GoEco.

Concluding the Monasticism

Return to the place you began your monasticism and attune with the Moon. Take your time and do not rush.

When ready, draw a banishing lunar hexagram in front of you so that the Moon as it appears in your field of vision is in the center of this hexagram. Place your open palms toward the Moon and say the following in your inner (astral) voice:

Levana, I greet you! I performed the [Lesser/Greater/ Extreme] Observances of the Moon for nine days. This entailed [state the relevant sections here]. Though I conclude this monasticism, my foundation will hold!

Date Unknown. I'm not sure when this was originally written! One of my cats jumped on this notebook and threw up on it when I pulled out a bunch of notebooks. I was digging through them to look for a record of something else.

Moon Monasticism—Summary. I performed the Extreme Observances for 28 days. Most of my magic focused on stabilizing my foundation, reconnecting with my intuition, and clearing out subconscious rubbish. Many rites were performed in my astral temple or via dreamwork.

My most foundation-shaking experience during this period involved breaking down intuitive barriers I voluntarily constructed over two decades ago. During my undergraduate years I gave a fellow student a tarot reading. The cards conveyed that if things continued on their current course, she would die of a drug overdose. I was stunned. S. was a top student on a full scholarship. Two weeks later she passed away. After a serious automobile accident, S. was overprescribed pain medication. No one knew she developed an addiction. I had a *very* vivid dream about her the night she died. I learned of her death the following day and haven't been the same since. S. would have made a fantastic engineer.

Fast forward two decades. I'm in the middle of the Moon Monasticism. After leaving my mundane job for the day, I head to my other job (at a metaphysical store). Due to the aforementioned events, I avoid performing tarot readings for customers.

About an hour before we are scheduled to close, I look up at the Moon and attune with it. *Do not leave. Very soon you will help someone who is unknowingly going to help you.*

A few minutes before closing, a customer enters the store in tears. The manager and I close early to aid her without any distractions. At this point only myself, the manager, and the customer are in the store. The customer specifically requests a tarot reading, and the manager doesn't read Tarot. I remember _____ the window. ___ In that moment my instinct to help the customer overrode all of my psychological hang-ups and intuitive barriers. After some additional services, we sent the customer home with some psychic self-defense exercises to provide further relief.

Before leaving for the night, I attuned with the Moon again. *You want to build a solid foundation, but you're not using the entire foundation you have. That's not how this works.* Was there anything I could have done to prevent S.'s death? *Just because you can see something happening doesn't mean you can stop it. People ultimately make their own choices.* If I was older when S. passed away, I would have (hopefully) realized that.

Chapter 2
Homework

After taking notes on the chapter, magical practice should be commenced for thirty minutes each day for a minimum of one month. Perform the assignments in the order presented. Take your time and do not rush, especially on the Moon. It is your foundation. Remember to document your efforts in your magical diary.

- ☐ Meditate on the Moon for a minimum of ten minutes each day. How does it affect your life? How do you interact with it?

- ☐ Examine your natal chart to determine your Moon sign. In this sign, is the Moon's manifestation strong, weak, or somewhere in between? We will revisit the natal Moon in chapters 7 and 11.

- ☐ Approximately every two and a half days, the Moon enters a new sign. Visit a reputable website to determine the current Moon sign. In this sign, is the Moon's manifestation strong, weak, or somewhere in between? We will examine the signs more scrupolously in chapter 7.

- ☐ Attune with the Moon nightly for a period of one week.

- ☐ Investigate the effects of the lunar hexagrams. To accomplish this, draw one and passively observe the impact on yourself and the immediate environment. After a few minutes, record any observations, thoughts, inner feelings, and other details you deem important in your magical diary. Feel free to draw a banishing hexagram after an invoking hexagram to cancel it out.

- ☐ Perform the Moon Greeting Rite. After obtaining your lunar tool, purify and consecrate it by exposing it to moonlight.

- ☐ Perform the Moon Guided Meditation.

- ☐ Perform a Moon Monasticism before proceeding to the next chapter.

Chapter 2 Resources

AstroSeek. "Today's Current Planets." https://horoscopes.astro-seek.com /current-planets-astrology-transits-planetary-positions.

GoEco. https://www.goeco.org.

National Marine Sanctuaries. "Get Involved." http://sanctuaries.noaa.gov/involved.

National Ocean Service. "How Can You Help Our Ocean?" https://oceanservice.noaa .gov/ocean/help-our-ocean.html.

Points of Light. "Engage." https://engage.pointsoflight.org.

VolunteerMatch. https;//www.volunteermatch.org.

CHAPTER 3
Mercury Inspects

Mercury provides the intellectual and communicative basis necessary to work with the classical planets. As Mercury is never far removed from the Sun, our intellectual mind is never far removed from our personal self. Since the Moon has provided our foundation, our next stop is Mercury. Common Mercury symbols are shown in Figure 3.1. They are useful focal points in meditation and magical practice.

(a)　　　　　　　　(b)

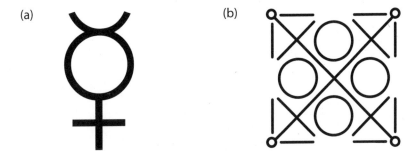

Figure 3.1. The (a) astronomical symbol and (b) planetary seal of Mercury

The Western View of Mercury

In the Greco-Roman model Mercury resides between the Moon and Venus.[51] Due to its close proximity to Earth and the Sun, Mercury may be wet or dry, and is capable of

---

51. Ptolemy, *Tetrabiblos*, 34–43, 78–81, 88–89.

quickly switching between these states. Thus, Mercury may be benefic or malefic, and masculine or feminine. Mercury is also diurnal (as a morning star) and nocturnal (as an evening star). Mercury's close proximity to the Moon and Sun is further reflected in the signs it rules—Gemini and Virgo. Each luminary rules one sign, whereas the other classical planets rule two. Gemini is adjacent to Cancer (ruled by the Moon), and Virgo is adjacent to Leo (ruled by the Sun). Mercury is exalted in Virgo and its fall is in Pisces.

In the Hermetic model Mercury affects the gases on Earth.[52] Mercury is also analogous to our mental body and the mental plane. In a nutshell, the mental plane is the realm of ideas, thought forms, and nonmaterial existence underlying physical reality. It is superimposed over the physical and astral planes, but consists of even higher vibrations. According to Franz Bardon, denizens of Mercury may be evoked in an orange or opalescent light.[53] This color of light emulates the Mercury zone's vibrations and is thus conducive to manifesting Mercurian beings.

Gk. *Hermēs* (Ἑρμῆς); Heb. *Kokav* (כוכב);
Lat. *Mercurius*; Ouranian Barbaric *THOGUT*

The Mercury Archetype

Mercury is our signal transducer. It represents our intellectual matrix, which manifests in our ability to exchange and interpret information. It also has ties to our sense of curiosity. Mercury oversees language and compulsory education, two important signal transducers. Exoterically, it is the translator who converts information into our various languages. Esoterically, it is the Divine Messenger who oversees movement in the terrestrial and celestial realms. Deities traditionally associated with Mercury include Thoth (Egyptian), Hermes (Greek), and Mercury (Roman). Keywords relevant to Mercury are as follows:

Signal Transduction

Our intellectual matrix is an important signal transducer. A functional transducer allows us to accurately send, receive, and interpret information. An unstable or overly rigid transducer may result in biased, distorted, or otherwise inaccurate information. It may also lead to an inability to grasp alternate worldviews.

52. Bardon, *Magical Evocation*, 292.

53. Bardon, *Magical Evocation*, 36, 128.

Intellectual Mind
The cognitive processes underlying the intellectual mind influence our logical faculties and decision-making skills. The Mercurian force may manifest through primary and secondary education, the scientific process, or research.

Thoughts
In many paradigms thoughts originate from the divine realm. Through meditation one may observe that we do not create our own thoughts, although it appears that way.

Communication
Communication is the act of transferring information. It requires a sender, receiver, and message. Messages may be conveyed verbally, nonverbally, in writing, or visually.

Movement
In addition to the movement of information (as communication), Mercury reigns over other forms of movement. This includes but is not limited to the movement of living beings (as travel), goods (as commerce or theft), and knowledge (as education).

Magic
Aleister Crowley defines magic as "the Science and Art of causing Change to occur in conformity with Will."[54] Yesterday's magic has often evolved into today's science. In modern practice, magic also falls under Uranus's domain.[55]

Western Mercury Magic
Mercury moves quickly through the sky, so the ancients associated this planet with speed and agility.[56] In many Western esoteric traditions Mercury is associated with mental, travel, communication, transmutation, trickster, and thinking magic. It is also generally associated with shamanic and alchemical works.

Mercury's day is Wednesday (Lat. *dies Mercurii*). The word *Wednesday* is derived from the Old English *Wōdnesdæg* (Woden's Day). The connection between the classical planet and day of the week is more obvious in languages such as Spanish (*miércoles*)

---

54. Aleister Crowley, *Magick: Liber ABA, Book 4*, 2nd ed., Hymanaeus Beta (Weiser Books, 1997), 126.

55. Carroll, *Liber Kaos*, 107–11.

56. Woolfolk, *The Only Astrology Book*, 181.

and French (*mercredi*). Mercury's alchemical metal is mercury. Note that elemental mercury (the shiny quicksilver found in old thermostats and thermometers) is toxic, and long-term exposure to its vapor causes irreversible neurological and organ damage. Safer, non-toxic alternatives that are magically useful include gallium (illusionists perform spoon-bending with a gallium spoon) and metal alloys.

In ceremonial traditions Mercury is associated with *Hod* (Heb. Splendor), the eighth sphere of the Qabala.[57] This splendor manifests in marvels that instill a sense of intellectual wonder in us. Psychologically, this sphere represents the intellectual mind, thoughts, and communication. Correspondences of *Hod* often relate to splendor and visions. Mercury is also associated with *Bet*, the path connecting *Keter* (Crown) and *Bina* (Understanding). It connects the pure spirit of transpersonal self to transpersonal love and awareness. In ancient script the letter *bet* resembles a house, the structure capable of bounding the internal from the external. Correspondences of *Bet* often relate to duality and haste. The top-down Hebrew hierarchy for Mercury is shown in Table 3.1.

Table 3.1. The Mercury Ceremonial Hierarchy		
Qabalistic World	**Level**	**Name**
'Aṣilut	Divine name	*'Azboga*
Beri'a	Archangel	*Mika'el*
Yeṣira	Intelligence Spirit	*Ṭiri'el* *Tafthartharath*
'Asiya	Magical tool	Wand, caduceus

The information in Table 3.1 is adapted from Crowley's "777 Revised." See Appendix A for Hebrew spelling, pronunciation, etymologies, and more. *'Elohim Ṣeba'ot* is *God of Hosts* in *Hod*. The names, versicles, and apron are associated with *Hod*.

Retrograde Motion

Mercury typically moves in a prograde (forward) direction along a narrow band, relative to the background of fixed stars. However, sometimes it appears to move in a ret-

<hr>

57. Aleister Crowley, "777 Revised," 2–3, 5.

rograde (backward) direction instead—this typically occurs three to four times a year and lasts for approximately three weeks. More distant planets exhibit fewer (but longer-lasting) retrograde periods.

Ptolemy employed epicycles to explain this phenomenon under the geocentric model accepted at the time.[58] Today, we know the planets orbit the Sun in a counter-clockwise direction when looking "down" from the Sun's North Pole. Apparent retrograde motion is an optical illusion caused by planets orbiting the Sun at different velocities. It is analogous to when a vehicle you are passing on the freeway appears to move backward for a few moments. Apparent retrograde motion also depends on rotational speed. When Mercury's orbital speed exceeds its rotational speed, the Sun appears to move backward in the Mercurian sky!

Mercury retrograde is one of the most discussed celestial events in modern Western astrology. Traditionally, retrograde motion is indicative of a weak or negatively manifesting planetary force.[59] Thus, Mercury retrograde is infamously associated with travel and communication mishaps. In modern astrology, if a planet is retrograde at the time of birth it is typically interpreted as a positively manifesting planetary force but one destined to appear later in life.[60] Alternatively, it may be interpreted as an internalized (instead of externalized) force. Overall, many magicians view retrograde periods as valuable opportunities to rest, perform introspection, and plan for the future.

Fundamentals: Magic Squares

Magic squares have a rich history and are believed to have esoteric properties in many paradigms.[61] In its traditional format, a magic square is an n x n grid (order n) with the integers inside (from 1 to n^2) arranged so the rows, columns, and diagonals yield the same sum (magic constant). Each magic square also yields an overall sum calculated by adding all its integers together. Magic squares of orders 3 through 9 are relevant to our magical work, as each is associated with a classical planet.[62] Esoterically, they represent planetary forces in a numerical format. Mercury is associated with the magic square of order *8* (Figure 3.2).

58. Ptolemy, *Ptolemy's Almagest*, trans. G. J. Toomer (Princeton University Press, 1998), 421–22.

59. Woolfolk, *The Only Astrology Book*, 342–43.

60. Woolfolk, *The Only Astrology Book*, 342–43.

61. Michael Daniels, "The Magic, Myth and Math of Magic Squares," filmed November 2014 at TEDxDouglas, Douglas, Isle of Man, video, 15:16, https://www.youtube.com/watch?v=-Tbd3dzlRnY.

62. Agrippa, *Three Books*, 318–29.

(a) Arabic Numerals

8	58	59	5	4	62	63	1
49	15	14	52	53	11	10	56
41	23	22	44	45	19	18	48
32	34	35	29	28	38	39	25
40	26	27	37	36	30	31	33
17	47	46	20	21	43	42	24
9	55	54	12	13	51	50	16
64	2	3	61	60	6	7	57

(b) Hebrew Numerals

ח	נח	נט	ה	ד	סב	סג	א
מט	יה	יד	נב	נג	יא	י	נו
מא	כג	כב	מד	מה	יט	יח	מח
לב	לד	לה	כט	כח	לח	לט	כה
מ	כו	כז	לז	לו	ל	לא	לג
יז	מז	מו	כ	כא	מג	מב	כד
ט	נה	נד	יב	יג	נא	נ	יו
סד	ב	ג	סא	ס	ו	ז	נז

(c) Seal   **(d) Intelligence**   **(e) Spirit**

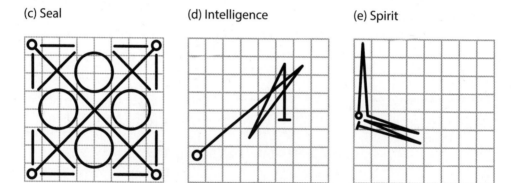

Figure 3.2. The Mercury magic square and associated sigils

The Mercury magic square (order = 8; magic constant = 260; overall sum = 2080) in Figure 3.2 is shown in (a) Arabic and (b) Hebrew numerical formats. Note that יה and יו are divine names, so are ordinarily written as טו and טז, respectively. The (c) planetary seal and sigils of the (d) planetary intelligence and (e) spirit are derived from the magic square. The beginning of a sigilized intelligence or spirit name is denoted by a circle, and the end is denoted by a dash. Hebrew letters with numerical values exceeding those in the magic square have been reduced.

Each classical planet is associated with a seal derived from its magic square.[63] The seals embody the totalities of the planetary forces. Sigils of planetary intelligences, spirits, and more may also be derived from magic squares. You may think of these

---

63. Agrippa, *Three Books*, 318–29.

seals and sigils as neurological circuits on planetary circuit boards. Additional sigils aimed at a particular purpose congruent with a planet's nature may also be derived from its magic square. For example, Mercury's magic square may be used to create sigils for clear communication, obtaining accurate divination results, or finding lost objects (Table 3.2).

Table 3.2. Mercurian Hebrew Phrases	
English	**Hebrew**
Clear communication	תקשורת ברורה
Accurate results	תוצאות מדויקות
Find my [lost item]!	מצא את ה[xxx] שלי
Quick thinking	חשיבה מהירה
Solve the problem!	פתור את הבעיה

An example sigil derived from the Mercury magic square is shown in Figure 3.3.

"Find my iPhone"
Meṣà 'et ha iPhone *sheli*

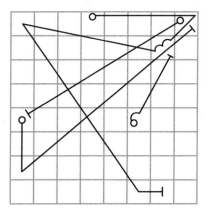

Figure 3.3. Sigil derived from the Mercury magic square

Finding a lost cell phone falls under Mercury's domain. The Hebrew phrase *Meṣa'* *'et ha* iPhone *sheli* ("Find my iPhone") may be drawn as a sigil on the Mercury magic square. The beginning of a sigilized word is denoted by a circle, and the end is denoted by a dash. A bump in a line segment indicates a cell is included on its way to another. Hebrew letters with numerical values exceeding those in the magic square have been reduced. Note that alternate sigil designs are possible.

October 22, 2021. *Mercury Magic Square Sigil.* The *Find my iPhone* sigil (Figure 3.3) worked successfully—the battery had died and one of my cats was "bread loafing" on top of it!

Mercury in Chaos Magic

Mercury may be integrated into magical practice in numerous ways. Various deities, egregores, or pop culture characters associated with Mercury may be invoked or evoked. Divination may be practiced via astrologically analyzing Mercury or through methods that involve language (e.g., bibliomancy, chresmomancy …). Magical items associated with Mercury may be enchanted for purposes consistent with its nature. All "found" objects also fall under this planet's domain. Illumination rites aimed at gaining insight into the intellectual mind or occult knowledge may also be performed.

Mercury is projective and receptive, transmutable, quick, clever, dual, and mobile. It is also very intellectual and analytical. These characteristics have been incorporated into the rites, which are intentionally vocal and fast-paced, and involve mental work. Ouranian Barbaric, a magical jargon used by chaos magicians, is also employed. Magical jargons and languages serve to bypass the conscious mind so magic may work more effectively. Some rites also use Mercury's ceremonial planetary hexagrams (Figure 3.4). It is best to commit them to memory.

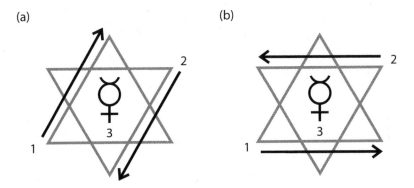

Figure 3.4. Mercury (a) invoking and (b) banishing hexagrams

Draw the planetary hexagrams with your magical tool or index finger in the numbered sequence shown. Visualize the hexagram shape in orange and vibrate *ARARITA* as you draw. Visualize Mercury's astronomical symbol in orange and vibrate *'Elohim Şeba'ot* as you draw. When you have finished drawing the astronomical symbol while vibrating the divine name, your planetary hexagram is complete.

Active Work
Mercury Attunement

Here we will attune with Mercury by imitating its movement in space. Find a clear area where you will not slip or bump into furniture. If you have limited mobility, feel free to modify the procedure to your liking or perform the exercise mentally.

1. Begin orbiting counterclockwise around an imaginary Sun by walking in an eccentric, elliptical path. Mercury's orbit resembles a Spirograph™ pattern, so your path should repeat the same shape with minimal overlap. Mercury also travels faster when closer to the Sun, so your speed should vary accordingly.

2. As you orbit around the imaginary Sun, spin counterclockwise one and a half times per revolution. Mercury rotates three times per two revolutions.

3. As you orbit and spin, visualize yourself glowing bright orange with a bright orange tail behind you. Mercury's orange, comet-like tail is caused by sodium ions.

4. As you orbit, spin, and visualize, chant *XIQUAL THOGUT* (Ouranian Barbaric: Manifest Mercury).

5. As you orbit, spin, visualize, and chant, resonate with this mental acuity. Observe the acuity with all five of your senses, as well as astrally. As time passes, the acuity grows stronger. Slowly adjust the rhythm of your body to match the vibrations underlying this acuity. Feel them intellectualizing, mobilizing, and hastening you.

November 13, 2022. *Mercury Attunement.* I consistently feel more mentally acute after performing the exercise. Others independently stated the mental overload from multitasking is a valuable springboard to attuning with the Mercurian force.

Mercury Greeting Rite

In this rite you will be manifesting Mercurian vibrations in a bounded circle, as opposed to drawing down its light directly, so planetary visibility is not required. When Mercury is visible in the sky it appears at dawn or dusk, near the horizon. If the planet is visible, you may face it and treat that direction as *metaphysical east* (i.e., perform the rite treating Mercury's direction as cardinal east) if you feel it is necessary. Mercury in Gemini or Virgo are preferable but not required.

Materials

- You will need a pen and paper to draw the Mercury magic square.
- If you already have a Mercury tool, you may ask the planetary spirit to bless it instead. Mercury's traditional ceremonial tool is the wand or caduceus. If you are a fan of planetary metals, recall that Mercury's *non-toxic* metals are gallium and metal alloys.

Statement of Intent

FACH DIBONGOF CHO COYANIOC CHO THOGUT.
(Ouranian Barbaric: I will to join together with Mercury.)

Procedure

The overall sequence of your movement throughout the rite is illustrated in Figure 3.5. The magic square of Mercury is also incorporated. Draw the square on a sheet of paper and place it where the center of your bounded circle will be.

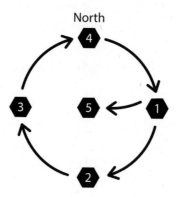

Figure 3.5. Mercury invocation

First, on a Wednesday at dawn or dusk, attune with Mercury.

Next, form your bounded circle. You will begin in the east and move in a clockwise (deosil) direction. Draw invoking Mercury hexagrams in the following locations: 1, east; 2, south; 3, west; and 4, north. After drawing a quarter circle to connect your northern and eastern hexagrams, walk into the center of the circle. The arrows in Figure 3.5 show your path of movement, starting at 1 and ending at 5.

1. When ready, face east. Take a deep breath and center yourself. Draw an invoking Mercury hexagram in front of you.
2. Walk to the south, drawing a quarter circle from your hexagram (about chest height) until you arrive in the south. Face south and draw an invoking Mercury hexagram in front of you.
3. Walk to the west, drawing a quarter circle from your hexagram until you arrive in the west. Face west and draw an invoking Mercury hexagram in front of you.

4. Walk to the north, drawing a quarter circle from your hexagram until you arrive in the north. Face north and draw an invoking Mercury hexagram in front of you.

5. Walk to the east, drawing a quarter circle from your hexagram until you arrive at the first hexagram you drew in the east. Your circle is now complete.

Walk into the center of your circle and face east behind Mercury's magic square. Visualize an opalescent orange light emanating down from the heavens, passing through your hexagrams and enveloping you.

Turn your attention toward the magic square of Mercury. Visualize the opalescent orange light saturating it. Vibrate 'Azboga eight times. Place your open palms toward the sky and say:

DHOLKEY, THOGUT! FACH DIBONGOF CHO
   COYANIOC.
(Ouranian Barbaric: Cheers, Mercury! I will to join together.)

Continue:

Mika'el, FACH HAVAWANG HEV! HUSA UHNGOL
   AHIKAYOWFA, THIWACH, EGELJACH CHO
   CHOYOFAQUE!
(Mika'el, I evoke you! Give me higher awareness, knowledge, clarity to do the Great Work!)

Inhale the opalescent orange light enveloping you, until it fills your entire body. Take note of any mental impressions or intellectual insights you receive.

When ready, use your index finger to draw a triangle enclosing Mercury's magic square. Visualize it in orange. Then, trace *Ṭiri'el*'s sigil inside the Mercury magic square, also visualizing it in orange. Place your open palms slightly outside the triangle and proceed to evoke the planetary intelligence. Say:

> *Ṭiri'el, FACH HAVAWANG HEV! COYANIOC UHNGOL*
> *CHO THOGUT!*
> (*Ṭiri'el,* I evoke you! Join me to Mercury!*)*

If you do not sense its presence, continue visualizing the opalescent orange light and repeat the above until you do.

After you sense the planetary intelligence's presence, proceed to evoke the planetary spirit. Trace *Tafthartharath*'s sigil inside the Mercury magic square. Visualize it in orange. With open palms still slightly outside the triangle, continue:

> *Tafthartharath, FACH HAVAWANG HEV! LARTIHÖ*
> *WADOCHASAG UHNGOL BOFENPOCH THOGUT*
> *FIRUHL!*
> (*Tafthartharath,* I evoke you! Please bring me a ritual Mercury tool!)

If you do not sense its presence, continue visualizing the opalescent orange light and repeat the above until you do. After you are finished communicating with them, thank them and send them on their way.

Banishing

To clear away the Mercurian vibrations, we will overwrite our invoking Mercury hexagrams with banishing Mercury hexagrams, starting in the east and moving in a counterclockwise direction (Figure 3.6). To conclude, stand over your Mercury magic square, clap, and laugh. You may keep the sheet of paper in your magical diary.

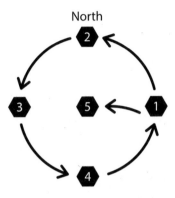

Figure 3.6. Mercury banishing

When banishing, you will begin in the east and move in a counter-clockwise (widdershins) direction. Draw banishing Mercury hexagrams in the following locations: 1, east; 2, north; 3, west; and 4, south. After drawing a quarter circle to connect your southern and eastern hexa-grams, walk into the center of the circle. The arrows in Figure 3.6 show your path of movement, starting at 1 and ending at 5.

November 9, 2022, dawn (☿ cazimi in ♏). *Mercury Greeting Rite.* The rite took about 20 minutes to perform. Although I felt scatterbrained, the planetary intelligence and spirit arrived almost instantaneously. They informed me I already had an item suitable for use as a Mercury planetary tool. The item was gifted to me a few days earlier, is thematically appropriate, and reminds me of how much running around I do in the name of magic! I placed the item in the triangle so the planetary intelligence and spirit could purify, consecrate, and infuse it with Mercurian vibrations. The intelligence and spirit were quick to depart. After drawing the banishing Mercury hexagrams and grounding I felt significantly less scatterbrained.

Mercury Guided Meditation

Find a quiet place and sit in a comfortable position. Close your eyes. Take a deep breath and center yourself. With each breath, you will feel calmer and more relaxed. Feel the tension in your toes. As you exhale, the tension dissipates until they are completely relaxed. This feeling of relaxation grows, spreading through your feet into your ankles. They are now completely relaxed. It continues, travelling up your legs and into your knees, which are now completely relaxed. Feel the lack of tension in your shins and calves. Any outside noises or distractions just serve to relax you further. Now your upper legs, hips, and waist are completely relaxed. As you continue to breathe, your abdominal region, chest, and back are completely relaxed. Your relaxation grows further, moving into your shoulders, and then down into your arms, elbows, hands, fingers, and fingertips. Your entire body below your neck is now completely relaxed. This feeling of relaxation grows, filling your neck and face. Feel your chin, jaw, nose, cheeks, eyes, eyelids, forehead, and ears relax. Finally, feel your scalp relax. Your entire body is now completely relaxed.

In your mind's eye, visualize Mercury glowing above your head. It is about the size of a basketball and reflects an opalescent orange light. The light shines down, swiftly enveloping you as you continue breathing. Observe the light with all five of your senses. See its stochastic shimmer, feel its varied temperature, smell it, and taste it. Does it emanate a sound? Mercury is tectonically active but produces no sound when it quakes. As you continue breathing, the opalescent orange light accumulates within you and around you, filling your body and field of vision completely. You draw an invoking Mercury hexagram in front of you. As you trace the symbol of Mercury while vibrating *'Elohim Ṣeba'ot* in your astral voice, the light inside you intricately glows.

The light in the surrounding environment quickly disperses. You are immediately blinded by hot, intense light—the Sun is more than three times larger and seven times brighter than it appears on Earth. As you lift your hand to shield your eyes, you smell and taste the faint odor of metal. It is completely silent. As you look away from the Sun, an unfamiliar terrain comes into focus. It is littered with rocks, craters, and regolith of varying shades of gray. Occasionally a fault scarp punctuates the landscape. In the distance you see towering cliffs and larger craters, their depth occluded by the darkness of night. Intrigued, you make your way toward them to investigate more closely. As you walk, the ground beneath you abrasively crunches but produces no sound. Your feet kick up some of the fine, powdery regolith that floats upward as if in slow motion.

As the light of the Sun fades, the opalescent orange glow you emanate lights the way as you walk deeper and deeper into the darkness. The searing heat transforms into a freezing cold. Faint glimmers of water ice glisten within larger craters. The battered gray landscape eventually disappears in the night. Unable to venture further, you gaze up into space and see hundreds of stars, their shine unhindered by an atmosphere. You also notice three additional celestial objects that pique your interest. After a few more moments pass, you recognize these objects—they are Venus, Earth, and the Moon. You are standing on Mercury.

As your eyes return to the Mercurian surface, you contemplate the dual nature of its daytime and nighttime sides. You decide to head back to the terminator (the line dividing day and night) to more fully experience this dual nature. The opalescent orange glow you emanate lights the way as you pass familiar craters, fault scarps, and other geological features. A sliver of zodiacal light eventually peeks out from beyond the horizon. As you stand at Mercury's terminator, you orient one half of your body toward its daytime side, and the other half toward its nighttime side. You outstretch your hands—one is searing hot, and the other is freezing cold. As you look toward Mercury's daytime side, you are blinded by the Sun and unable to see much else. Looking toward the nighttime side obscures the planetary surface in darkness, but you are able to see other celestial bodies among a backdrop of fixed stars. Mercury contains many dualities, and so do you.

You can visit Mercury any time you'd like—now you know the way here. The opalescent orange light again accumulates within you and around you, filling your body and field of vision completely. As you continue to breathe, you draw a banishing Mercury hexagram in front of you. As you trace the symbol of Mercury while vibrating *'Elohim Ṣeba'ot* in your astral voice, the light in the surrounding environment quickly disperses. The room where your physical body resides begins to return. You begin to feel your fingers and toes. As the last remnants of the opalescent orange light fade, you gradually feel the rest of your body. Slowly open your eyes and become reacquainted with your surroundings. Stand up when you are ready and document your experience in your magical diary.

September 18, 2021. *Mercury Guided Meditation.* Participants consistently reported a deeper understanding of how we contain various dualities inside ourselves. We are all masculine/feminine, projective/receptive, and so on in varying proportions. The geological description of the Mercurian surface was inspired by data from NASA's *Mariner 10* and *MESSENGER* missions.

Mercury Monasticism

This monasticism serves to strengthen your relationship with Mercury. It should be performed for eight days, since this number is associated with *Hod* and the magic square of Mercury. However, feel free to use another Mercury-related number if it suits your fancy. Carry your Mercury tool at all times during the monasticism—it serves as a constant reminder of Mercury and increases vigilance. After your monasticism is complete, keep your Mercury tool someplace special, such as an altar or favorite shelf. You may use it in future Mercurian work and reuse it if you perform the monasticism again.

Beginning the Monasticism

On a Wednesday at dawn or dusk, attune with Mercury. Mercury in Gemini or Virgo are preferable but not required. Take your time and do not rush.

When ready, draw the magic square of Mercury on a sheet of paper. You may reuse your paper from the Mercury Greeting Rite or make a new one. Draw the planetary seal of Mercury (Figure 3.1) inside the magic square. Gaze at the seal and vibrate ʾAzboga eight times. Place your open palms toward the sky and say:

> *DHOLKEY, THOGUT! FACH DIBONGOF CHO ONGO [ICHECBAJ/AXBIM/DECHAHCOHIFCHEH] THOGUT LEVIFITH YODIXINCH HAGLECHOJ HUTAYAX AXOL. HUSA UHNGOL AHIKAYOWFA, THIWACH, EGELJACH CHO CHOYOFAQUE!*

(Ouranian Barbaric: Cheers, Mercury! I will to do [Lesser/Greater/Extreme] Mercury magic over a time divisible by eight. Give me higher awareness, knowledge, clarity to do the Great Work!)

Lesser Observances

- Carry your Mercury tool at all times. If you can't carry it openly, keep it in your pocket or a bag and carry that with you.

- Contemplate how, like Mercury, you contain many dualities for a few minutes each dawn or dusk.

- Perform a Mercury rite that incorporates your tool each dawn or dusk.

- Esoterically, Mercury rules over elemental air and the atmosphere. Make a conscious effort to reduce air pollution and perform at least one clean air-related action a day that is not already part of your normal repertoire. Visit the American Lung Association's Clean Air website for suggestions.

- In many paradigms Mercury rules over merchants and young students. Donate items such as pencils, notebooks, or calculators to needy schoolchildren or an organization that helps struggling small businesses. If you are unable to make a material donation you may make a monetary donation instead, so long as the value is in a multiple of eight.

Greater Observances

- Perform all the Lesser Observances.

- Perform a second Mercury rite that incorporates your tool each dawn or dusk. To give your second rite an energetic boost, include a sigil derived from the Mercury magic square.

- Relate all your meditation and magical work to Mercury. For example, meditate on Mercury's magic square or practice vibrating Mercurian divine names.

- A large proportion of airborne particulates come from motor vehicle emissions, especially in urban areas. To combat this, carpool, bike, walk, or use public transportation as much as possible.

Extreme Observances

- Perform all the Greater Observances.
- Perform a third Mercury rite that incorporates your tool each dawn or dusk.
- Increase your efforts to reduce air pollution as much as possible. Actions to improve air quality may be large or small but must be at the forefront of your consciousness. Examples include planting trees, saying no to illegal trash burning, or participating in a community carpool. Volunteer opportunities are available at Arbor Day Foundation, VolunteerMatch, and Points of Light. If you want to combine your clean air efforts with tourism, there is always GoEco.

Concluding the Monasticism

Return to the place you began your monasticism and attune with Mercury. Take your time and do not rush.

When ready, gaze at the planetary seal of Mercury and vibrate 'Azboga eight times. Place your open palms toward the sky and say:

DHOLKEY, THOGUT! SYCUZ! FACH DIBONGOF DON-
GET BICOW VYRUCH. JESNUHS!
(Cheers, Mercury! It is done! I will return in the future. Thank you!)

You may keep the sheet of paper in your magical diary.

November 9, 2022, dusk (☿ cazimi in ♏). *Mercury Monasticism, Day 1.* I am performing the Extreme Observances of Mercury for eight days. [Details of the three rituals I performed at dusk follow.]

November 18, 2022. *Mercury Monasticism—Summary.* I concluded the Extreme Observances of Mercury yesterday at dusk. Most of my magic focused on improving communication skills, working accurately and quickly, and safe travel. Many rites were performed in an open-handed manner or on the fly.

During the monasticism period I won Employee of the Month at both jobs and was rewarded with Mercurian items! I received a fancy tablet from my mundane job and a magical item of my choosing from my other job. Further, my submission to a major conference in my field got accepted as a talk. It all happened so fast!

Chapter 3
Homework

After taking notes on the chapter, magical practice should be commenced for thirty minutes each day for a minimum of one month. Perform the assignments in the order presented. Take your time and do not rush, even though Mercury likes to do things in a hurry. Remember to document your efforts in your magical diary.

☐ Meditate on Mercury for a minimum of ten minutes each day. How does this planetary force manifest in your life? How do you interact with it?

☐ Examine your natal chart to determine your Mercury sign. In this sign, is Mercury's manifestation strong, weak, or somewhere in between? Is Mercury retrograde? We will revisit natal Mercury in chapters 7 and 11.

☐ Approximately every fourteen to thirty days, Mercury enters a new sign. Visit a reputable website to determine the current Mercury sign. In this sign, is Mercury's manifestation strong, weak, or somewhere in between? Is Mercury retrograde?

☐ Attune with Mercury at dawn or dusk for a period of one week.

☐ Investigate the effects of the Mercury hexagrams. To accomplish this, draw one and passively observe the impact on yourself and the immediate environment. After a few minutes, record any observations, thoughts, inner feelings, and other details you deem important in your magical diary. Feel free to draw a banishing hexagram after an invoking hexagram to cancel it out.

☐ Perform the Mercury Greeting Rite. After obtaining your Mercury tool, purify and consecrate it on the magic square of Mercury.

☐ Create a sigil from the Mercury magic square. You may launch your sigil during your monasticism.

☐ Perform the Mercury Guided Meditation.

☐ Perform a Mercury Monasticism before proceeding to the next chapter.

Chapter 3 Resources

American Lung Association. "Clean Air." https://www.lung.org/clean-air.

Arbor Day Foundation. "Take Action." https://www.arborday.org/takeaction.

AstroSeek. "Today's Current Planets." https://horoscopes.astro-seek.com /current-planets-astrology-transits-planetary-positions.

GoEco. https://www.goeco.org.

Points of Light. "Engage." https://engage.pointsoflight.org.

VolunteerMatch. https://www.volunteermatch.org.

CHAPTER 4
Venus Connects

Venus provides the emotional basis necessary to work with the classical planets. As Venus reflects the light of the Sun, our inner feelings reflect our personal self and drive us to fulfill our desires. Since the Moon has provided our foundation and Mercury has provided our intellectual and communicative basis, our next stop is Venus. Common Venus symbols are shown in Figure 4.1. They are useful focal points in meditation and magical practice.

(a)   (b)

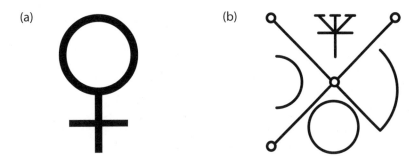

Figure 4.1. The (a) astronomical symbol and (b) planetary seal of Venus

The Western View of Venus

In the Greco-Roman model Venus resides between Mercury and the Sun.[64] Like the Moon, Venus is primarily wet and secondarily hot. Thus, like the Moon, Venus is

---

64. Ptolemy, *Tetrabiblos*, 34–43, 78–81, 88–89.

benefic, feminine, and nocturnal. Venus's fertile nature is further reflected in the signs it rules: Taurus and Libra. Taurus is sextile (60°) to Cancer (ruled by the Moon), and Libra is sextile to Leo (ruled by the Sun). When planets are sextile, their interaction is harmonious.[65] Venus is exalted in Pisces and its fall is in Virgo.

In the Hermetic model Venus affects the fertility on Earth.[66] It is also responsible for humanity's love and sympathy. According to Bardon, denizens of Venus may be evoked in a green light.[67] This color of light emulates the Venus zone's vibrations, so is conducive to manifesting Venusian beings.

> Gk. *Aphroditē* ('Αφροδίτη); Heb. *Nogah* (נגה);
> Lat. *Venus*; Ouranian Barbaric *CHALUQ(E)*

The Venus Archetype

Venus is our mediator. It represents our emotional matrix, which manifests in our ability to develop and maintain relationships. It also has ties to our sense of aesthetics. Venus oversees the romantic partner and social settings, two important mediators. Exoterically, it is the lover who gives and receives affection. Esoterically, it is the Divine Lover who propagates beauty and pleasure in the terrestrial and celestial realms. Deities traditionally associated with Venus include Hathor (Egyptian), Aphrodite (Greek), and Venus (Roman). Keywords relevant to Venus are as follows:

Mediation

Our emotional matrix is an important mediator. A solid mediator allows us to sympathize, empathize, and socialize. An unstable mediator may result in an inability to connect with others. It may also lead to chronic feelings of social awkwardness and rejection.

Inner Feelings

Whereas emotions are subconsciously generated physiological states, feelings are consciously experienced emotional responses.[68] The Venusian force may manifest through sympathy or be conveyed via artistic expression, such as dancing your feelings.

---

65. Ptolemy, *Tetrabiblos*, 72–73.

66. Bardon, *Magical Evocation*, 292.

67. Bardon, *Magical Evocation*, 36, 128.

68. Manuela Lenzen, "Feeling Our Emotions," *Scientific American Mind* 16, no. 1 (April 2005): 14–15.

Love

Our connections to others may take many forms. The ancient Greeks had four words designating different types of love: *agapē* (Gk. ἀγάπη; charitable love), *philia* (φιλία; friendship), *eros* (ἔρος; erotic love), and *storgē* (στοργή; familial love).

Relationships

Interpersonal relationships may manifest as acquaintances, friendships, romantic relationships, and more. Larger alliances such as professional organizations, business partnerships, and allied countries are also in Venus's domain.

Pleasure

Pleasurable activities give us a sense of happiness and enjoyment. This includes but is not limited to leisure activities (such as dining out and visiting museums), recreational activities (such as dancing and listening to music), and hobbies (such as gardening and painting).

Beauty

Venus has long been revered for its stunning appearance in the sky. This carries over esoterically, thus in many traditions Venus reigns over creative expression and aesthetics. This is also why Venus is associated with the arts.

Western Venus Magic

Venus has a stunning appearance in the sky, so the ancients associated this planet with love and beauty.[69] In many Western esoteric traditions Venus is associated with emotional, social, peacekeeping, artistic, gardening, and love magic. It is also generally associated with attractive and romantic works.

Venus's day is Friday (Lat. *dies Veneris*). The English word *Friday* is derived from the Old English *Frīgedæg* (Frige's Day). The connection between the classical planet and day of the week is more obvious in languages such as Spanish (*viernes*) and French (*vendredi*). Venus's alchemical metal is copper. The word *copper* is derived from the Latin *cuprum*, alluding to the Greek island of Cyprus. In ancient Greece, Cyprus was an important source of copper ore and major center of Aphrodite worship.[70]

---

69. Woolfolk, *The Only Astrology Book,* 187–88.

70. George Hill, *A History of Cyprus, Volume 1: To the Conquest by Richard Lion Heart* (Cambridge University Press, 1940), 1–14, 55–94.

In ceremonial traditions Venus is associated with *Neṣaḥ* (Heb. Victory), the seventh sphere of the Qabala.[71] This victory manifests in marvels that instill a sense of emotional wonder in us. Psychologically, this sphere represents feelings (e.g., love, hate, joy, sadness …). Correspondences of *Neṣaḥ* often relate to victory and love. Venus is also associated with *Dalet*, the path connecting *Ḥokma* (Wisdom) and *Bina* (Understanding). It connects transpersonal will and purpose to transpersonal love and awareness. In ancient script the letter *dalet* resembles a door, the structure capable of opening to invite others in. Correspondences of *Dalet* often relate to fertility and sensuality. The top-down Hebrew hierarchy for Venus is shown in Table 4.1.

Table 4.1. The Venus Ceremonial Hierarchy		
Qabalistic World	**Level**	**Name**
'Aṣilut	Divine name	AHA
Beri'a	Archangel	*H'ani'el*
Yeṣira	Intelligence Spirit	*Hagi'el* *Qedem'el*
'Asiya	Magical tool	Girdle

The information in Table 4.1 is adapted from Crowley's "777 Revised." See Appendix A for Hebrew spelling, pronunciation, etymologies, and more. *YHWH Ṣeba'ot* is *LORD of Hosts* in *Neṣaḥ*. The lamp and girdle are associated with *Neṣaḥ*.

Fundamentals: Sympathetic Correspondence

Each classical planet corresponds to a particular day of the week, alchemical metal, magic square, and more. These associations are derived from sympathetic correspondence—different components of the terrestrial realm are symbolically linked to different components of the celestial realm. Thus, they may serve as microcosmic representations of macrocosmic archetypes. The Hermetic axiom "As above, so below; as below, so above," alludes to this concept.[72]

---

71. Crowley, "777 Revised," 2–3, 5.

72. Three Initiates, *The Kybalion* (Yogi Publication Society, 1940), 28–30. Originally published in 1908 by Yogi Publication Society.

Sympathetic magic harnesses the connection between microcosm and macrocosm. Symbolically creating a desired outcome by means of sympathetic correspondence has long been a popular magical practice. For instance, Venusian items (such as green candles or rose petals) are frequently used in modern love spells. Many planetary rites in this book also employ sympathetic correspondence. A short list of correspondences traditionally associated with Venus is shown in Table 4.2.

Table 4.2. Venus Correspondences in Ceremonial Magic		
Attribute	**Sphere (*Neṣaḥ*)**	**Path (*Dalet*)**
Colors		
King Scale	Amber	Emerald green
Queen Scale	Emerald green	Sky blue
Prince Scale	Bright yellow-green	Early spring green
Princess Scale	Olive, flecked gold	Bright rose or cerise, rayed pale green
Animals	*IYNX*, raven, carrion birds	Sparrow, dove, swan, sow, birds
Plants	Rose, laurel	Myrtle, rose, clover, fig, peach, apple
Stones	Emerald	Emerald, turquoise
Incense	Benzoin, rose, red sandal	Sandalwood, myrtle, soft voluptuous odors

The information in Table 4.2 is adapted from Crowley's "777 Revised." Feel free to integrate the above correspondences into your personal practice if you feel they are useful. Regarding colors, the King, Queen, Prince, and Princess scales are associated with the worlds of ʾAṣilut, Beriʾa, Yeṣira, and ʿAsiya, respectively. The pantomorphic *IYNX* is an "emblem of universal being."[73] In Hermetic practice, cinnamon powder or cassia flowers may be used as a Venusian incense.[74]

73. Éliphas Lévi, *The History of Magic*, trans. A. E. Waite (Cambridge University Press, 2013), 77–78. Originally published in 1860 by Germer Baillière.

74. Bardon, *Magical Evocation*, 143.

Venus in Chaos Magic

Venus may be integrated into magical practice in numerous ways. Various deities, egregores, or pop culture characters associated with Venus may be invoked or evoked. Divination may be practiced via astrologically analyzing Venus or through methods that incorporate beauty. Magical items associated with Venus may be enchanted for purposes consistent with its nature. All so-called love potions also fall under this planet's domain. Illumination rites aimed at gaining insight into feelings or interpersonal relationships may also be performed.

Venus is receptive, connective, captivating, sensual, luxurious, and indulgent. It is also very emotional and social. These characteristics have been incorporated into the rites, which are intentionally fun, leisurely, and involve emotional work. Some use Venus's ceremonial planetary hexagrams (Figure 4.2). It is best to commit them to memory.

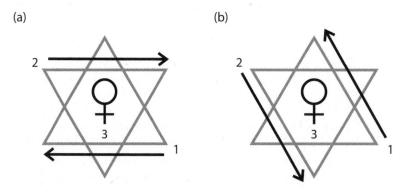

Figure 4.2. Venus (a) invoking and (b) banishing hexagrams

Draw the planetary hexagrams with your magical tool or index finger in the numbered sequence shown. Visualize the hexagram shape in green and vibrate *ARARITA* as you draw. Visualize the Venus astronomical symbol in green and vibrate *YHWH Ṣeba'ot* as you draw. When you have finished drawing the astronomical symbol while vibrating the divine name, your planetary hexagram is complete.

Active Work
Venus Attunement

Sit comfortably in a beautiful place, such as a backyard garden or room filled with art. If you don't have a beautiful place, find or make one. You may wear stylish clothes, play pleasant music, eat lavish food, or light luxurious incense if you'd like. As you lounge, take in your surroundings. Don't think; feel. Resonate with this harmonious, enjoyable beauty. Observe the beauty with all five of your senses, as well as astrally. As time passes, the beauty grows stronger. Slowly adjust the rhythm of your body to match the vibrations underlying this beauty. Feel them charming, soothing, and relaxing you.

> January 4, 2023, 9:27pm. *Venus Attunement.* The exercise was initially challenging because if my environment is even slightly dirty or cluttered, my anxiety increases to a level that is probably not normal. Thus, I wound up deep cleaning and decluttering my entire home! The sense of pleasure and satisfaction from relaxing in a clean, beautiful environment was a valuable springboard to attuning with the Venusian force.

Venus Greeting Rite

Here you will be manifesting Venusian vibrations in a dedicated area via sympathetic correspondence, so planetary visibility is not required. When Venus is visible in the sky it appears at dawn or dusk, near the horizon, and is typically the third brightest object behind the Sun and Moon. If Venus is visible, you may face it and treat that direction as *metaphysical east* if you feel it is necessary. Venus in Taurus, Libra, or Pisces are preferable but not required.

Materials

- A table or shelf to serve as a dedicated area for manifesting Venusian vibrations
- A physical representation of the astrological symbol or planetary seal of Venus
- Additional items of your choosing that bear connection to Venus via sympathetic correspondence
- If you already have a Venus tool, you may ask the planetary spirit to bless it instead. Recall that Venus's traditional ceremonial tool is the girdle, and its alchemical metal is copper.

Statement of Intent

It is my will to access the Venusian force.

Procedure

On a Friday night, attune with Venus.

When ready, stand in front of your altar and draw an invoking Venus hexagram over it. Visualize a beautiful green light emanating down from the heavens, passing through your hexagram and saturating your altar. The light also softly envelops you. Knock on your altar seven times, as if you are knocking on a door. Place your open palms toward the sky and say:

> *In the name of AHA I greet you, Venus! / I yearn to form a connection between us. / Come laughter-loving Aphroditē, giver of joy! / Come sea-born Venus, whether bold or coy! / Come Nogah, the bright one, Kokebet, the she-star! / I venerate you, stunning wanderer, admired from afar! / Alongside H'ani'el I will to cultivate harmony, love, and pleasure, / reach out to others, and spread joy beyond measure!*

Inhale the beautiful green light enveloping you, until it fills your entire body. Take note of any inner feelings or insights of the heart you receive.

When ready, draw a triangle enclosing the astrological symbol or planetary seal of Venus on your altar. Visualize it in green. Place your open palms slightly outside the triangle and proceed to evoke the planetary intelligence. Say:

> *I evoke you, Hagi'el, this auspicious evening! / Alongside H'ani'el, I send this greeting. / I yearn to work with Venus, flow in its ways. / May it brighten my inner feelings, nurture peaceful days!*

If you do not sense its presence, continue visualizing the beautiful green light and repeat the above until you do.

After you sense the planetary intelligence's presence, proceed to evoke the planetary spirit. With open palms still slightly outside the triangle, continue:

> *I evoke you, Qedem'el, this auspicious evening! / Alongside Hagi'el, I send this greeting. / Guide my heart toward a magical tool / to aid in my Venus magic, creative, fun, and pure!*

Banishing

Draw a banishing Venus hexagram over your invoking Venus hexagram and banish with laughter. Maintain your Venus altar for the duration of your planetary work in this chapter. Feel free to add, subtract, or upgrade items as necessary. It is not uncommon for altars to evolve and change as you do.

January 6, 2023. *Venus Greeting Rite*. My Venus altar incorporated the planetary symbol, a green candle, a polished copper bowl, a small chunk of polished copper, a flower-themed decorative box, love and attraction oil, and raw watermelon tourmaline.

The rite took about 25 minutes to perform. Venusian vibrations blossomed almost immediately after drawing the invoking hexagram. Astrally, the Venusian light appeared as a pale spring green reminiscent of newly sprouting plants. Upon arrival of the planetary spirit, a profound sense of peace, love, and happiness overcame me.

My Venus tool is a specific copper object the green light meandered toward during the rite. Upon further reflection, it alludes to my natal Venus placement. During its consecration, even more of the beautiful green light saturated the tool and its periphery, akin to an aura.

Venus Guided Meditation

Find a warm, quiet place and sit in a comfortable position. Close your eyes. Take a deep breath and center yourself. With each breath, you will feel calmer and more relaxed. Feel the tension in your toes. As you exhale, the tension dissipates until they are completely relaxed. This feeling of relaxation grows, spreading through your feet into your ankles. They are now completely relaxed. It continues, travelling up your legs and into your knees, which are now completely relaxed. Feel the lack of tension in your shins and calves. Any outside noises or distractions just serve to relax you further. Now your upper legs, hips, and waist are completely relaxed. As you continue to breathe, your abdominal region, chest, and back are completely relaxed. Your relaxation grows further, moving into your shoulders, and then down into your arms, elbows, hands, fingers, and fingertips. Your entire body below your neck is now completely relaxed. This feeling of relaxation grows, filling your neck and face. Feel your chin, jaw, nose, cheeks, eyes, eyelids, forehead, and ears relax. Finally, feel your scalp relax. Your entire body is now completely relaxed.

In your mind's eye, visualize Venus glowing above your head. It is about the size of a basketball and reflects a beautiful green light. The light shines down, softly enveloping you as you continue breathing. Observe the light with all five of your senses. See its gentle brightness, feel its warmth, smell it, and taste it. Does it emanate a sound? Sounds are deeper and travel faster on the Venusian surface. As you continue breathing, the beautiful green light accumulates within you and around you, filling your body and field of vision completely. You draw an invoking Venus hexagram in front of you. As you trace the symbol of Venus while vibrating *YHWH Ṣeba'ot* in your astral voice, the light inside you gently glows.

The light in the surrounding environment slowly disperses. You are met by a sea of stars shining amidst the black backdrop of space. It is completely silent. Your mind goes blank—you are awestruck. As you look around, a nearby white orb captures your attention. Mesmerized, you are pulled toward it as if compelled by an unseen magnetic force. As you draw closer and closer, you see hints of yellow swirl in otherwise featureless white clouds. Your feelings confirm your suspicions—you are looking at Venus. For a few moments, you admire its stunning beauty.

The unseen magnetic force begins to pull you through the Venusian sky. As the electric wind strips water from the upper atmosphere, you are whipped around at hurricane force speeds. The green light inside you forms a protective shield as sulfuric acid clouds swirl beneath you. Their corrosive rain smells like boiling battery acid and rotten eggs. The deeper down you are pulled, the greater the temperature and pressure become. As you taste the torrid heat of the lower atmosphere, the rain boils away. Still unable to see the Venusian surface, you observe the clouds give way to a sulfuric acid haze.

When you finally reach the surface, it is not what you expected. The entire planet is an infernal pressure cooker. As you look up at the hazy yellow sky, the smell and taste of the sulfuric acid rain lingers. In terms of light, it is like a partly cloudy day on Earth. The Sun is never visible through Venus's thick atmosphere, but if it was, it would rise in the west and set in the east due to the planet's retrograde spin. You outstretch your hands. The air is so thick and heavy that it feels like you are wading through water.

As you turn your attention toward the landscape, a scorched terrain comes into focus. It is littered with rocks, craters, and dirt of varying shades of gray. Occasionally a volcano punctuates the landscape. In the distance you see rugged mountains and larger volcanoes. Some of the mountaintops are coated in a shiny substance. The vast amount of refracted light tints everything orange, and makes the horizon appear closer than it actually is. Intrigued, you wade through the air to investigate more closely. A gentle breeze blows like a slow-moving river current, catching you by surprise. As you stumble over a large rock you let out a loud, high-pitched yelp, but the atmosphere transforms it into a small baritone squeak. The green light shields you, softening your impact upon the ground.

As you sit upright to regain your bearings, you are overwhelmed with numerous feelings—this is the part of Venus that few see. It is infernal, unforgiving, and spins in the opposite direction. It rains acid and snows metal. A gentle breeze is hot enough to melt lead. It is home to the immense temperatures and pressures under which many things collapse, but also make Venus the icon of beauty that it is.

You can visit Venus any time you'd like—now you know the way here. The beautiful green light again accumulates within you and around you, filling your body and field of vision completely. As you continue to breathe, you draw a banishing Venus hexagram in front of you. As you trace the symbol of Venus while vibrating *YHWH Ṣeba'ot* in your astral voice, the light in the surrounding environment slowly disperses. The room where your physical body resides begins to return. You begin to feel your fingers and toes. As the last remnants of the beautiful green light fade, you gradually feel the rest of your body. Slowly open your eyes and become reacquainted with your surroundings. Stand up when you are ready and document your experience in your magical diary.

Date Unknown. This entry was probably written in either late 2021 or early 2022. It is also roughly paraphrased. Thanks, cat vomit!

Venus Guided Meditation. The overall theme for the guided meditation theme struck me when J. L. cringed at my natal chart earlier today and said, "Well… pressure makes diamonds." The geological description of Venus was inspired by data from the Soviet *Venera* and ESA's *Venus Express* missions.

Venus Monasticism

This monasticism serves to strengthen your relationship with Venus. It should be performed for seven days, since this number is associated with *Neṣaḥ* and the magic square of Venus. However, feel free to use another Venus-related number if it suits your fancy. Carry your Venus tool at all times during the monasticism—it serves as a constant reminder of Venus and increases vigilance. After your monasticism is complete, keep your Venus tool someplace special, such as an altar or favorite shelf. You may use it in future Venusian work and reuse it if you perform the monasticism again.

Beginning the Monasticism

On a Friday night, attune with Venus. Venus in Taurus, Libra, or Pisces are preferable but not required. Take your time and do not rush.

When ready, stand in front of your altar and draw an invoking Venus hexagram over it. Knock on your altar seven times, as if you are knocking on a door. Place your open palms toward the sky and say:

> *I hail you, Nogah, this auspicious evening! / With the start of my monasticism, I send this greeting. / A stunning beauty, or a raging inferno, / I yearn to practice your magic, let my inner feelings flow. / May these [Lesser/Greater/Extreme] Observances cultivate harmony, love, and pleasure. / I will to grow my relationship with you, and spread joy beyond measure!*

Lesser Observances

- Carry your Venus tool at all times. If you can't carry it openly, keep it in your pocket or a bag and carry that with you.
- As the Lesser Benefic, Venus unifies and reconciles.[75] Participate in a fun social activity each night.
- Perform a nightly Venus rite that incorporates your tool.
- Venus's beauty has long captivated mankind. Beautify yourself by getting a makeover. It may involve updating your wardrobe, getting a new haircut, or starting a skincare routine. Don't neglect your inner beauty! Cultivate it by practicing kindness, gratitude, and compassion.

---

75. Chris Brennan, *Hellenistic Astrology: The Study of Fate and Fortune* (Amor Fati Publications, 2017), 184–90.

• In many paradigms Venus rules over artisans and entertainers. Donate items such as gourmet sweets, champagne, or flowers to a crafting guild, community theatre, or organization that supports the arts. If you are unable to make a material donation you may make a monetary donation instead, so long as the value is in a multiple of seven.

Greater Observances

• Perform all the Lesser Observances.

• Perform a second nightly Venus rite that incorporates your tool.

• Relate all your meditation and magical work to Venus. For example, meditate on sympathetic correspondences or perform divination to discover hidden beauty in the world.

• Environmental clutter negatively affects our health and well-being.[76] Beautify your environment by decluttering your home, office, or other personal space. Remove items that are not useful or do not bring you joy. If you are unsure where to begin, visit KonMari for suggestions.

Extreme Observances

• Perform all the Greater Observances.

• Perform a third nightly Venus rite that incorporates your tool.

• Increase your efforts to beautify the environment while making some new friends along the way. Volunteer at a neighborhood cleanup, community garden, or organization that helps local parks. If there is no group in your area, feel free to start your

---

76. Joseph Ferrari, "Why Clutter Stresses Us Out," interview by Kim Mills, *Speaking of Psychology*, February 22, 2023, audio, 35:35, https://www.apa.org/news/podcasts/speaking-of-psychology/clutter.

own! You can do simple things like picking up roadside litter, clearing debris in natural areas (such as hiking trails or campgrounds), or reporting public structures in disrepair (such as broken stoplights or downed power lines).

Concluding the Monasticism

Return to the place you began your monasticism and attune with Venus. Take your time and do not rush.

When ready, stand in front of your altar and draw a banishing Venus hexagram over it. Place your open palms toward the sky and say:

> *I hail you, Nogah, this final evening! / As I conclude this monasticism, I send this greeting. / A stunning beauty, or a raging inferno, / I yearned to practice your magic, let my inner feelings flow. / Though my monasticism now comes to an end, / our future work has yet to begin!*

January 6, 2023. *Venus Monasticism, Day 1.* I am performing the Extreme Observances of Venus for seven days and the Greater Observances of Venus for seven days immediately after. [Details of the three nightly rituals I performed follow.]

January 20, 2023. *Venus Monasticism—Summary.* I concluded the Greater Observances of Venus last night. Most of my magic focused on improving existing relationships, creating new ones, and improving my overall emotional well-being. Many rites incorporated items bearing sympathetic correspondence with Venus.

The monasticism took a dark turn fairly quickly. After going no contact with toxic people, I spent much of my leisure time at the local botanical garden. Mounting evidence suggests spending time in nature improves overall mental and emotional health, and I experienced this improvement firsthand.[77]

January 25, 2023. *Addendum.* I told a few new friends about the positive effects of spending time at the garden. Some went to visit the garden too! They consistently reported a greater sense of peace and emotional well-being.

May 14, 2024. *Addendum.* To this day, the garden remains an important source of beauty, peace, and joy.

77. Kirsten Weir, "Nurtured by Nature," *Monitor on Psychology* 51, no. 3 (2020): 50–56.

Chapter 4
Homework

After taking notes on the chapter, magical practice should be commenced for thirty minutes each day for a minimum of one month. Perform the assignments in the order presented. Do not dawdle, even though Venus likes to take her time. Remember to document your efforts in your magical diary.

- ☐ Meditate on Venus for a minimum of ten minutes each day. How does this planetary force manifest in your life? How do you interact with it?

- ☐ Examine your natal chart to determine your Venus sign. In this sign, is Venus's manifestation strong, weak, or somewhere in between? Is Venus retrograde? We will revisit natal Venus in chapters 7 and 11.

- ☐ Approximately every twenty-four days, Venus enters a new sign. Visit a reputable website to determine the current Venus sign. In this sign, is Venus's manifestation strong, weak, or somewhere in between? Is Venus retrograde?

- ☐ Attune with Venus nightly for a period of one week.

- ☐ Investigate the effects of the Venus hexagrams. To accomplish this, draw one and passively observe the impact on yourself and the immediate environment. After a few minutes, record any observations, thoughts, feelings, and other details you deem are important in your magical diary. Feel free to draw a banishing hexagram after an invoking hexagram to cancel it out.

- ☐ Use sympathetic correspondence to create a Venus altar. Ensure it is in a location that is practical to maintain for the remainder of your work in this chapter.

- ☐ Perform the Venus Greeting Rite. After obtaining your Venus tool, purify and consecrate it on your Venus altar.

- ☐ Perform the Venus Guided Meditation.

- ☐ Perform a Venus Monasticism before proceeding to the next chapter.

Chapter 4 Resources

AstroSeek. "Today's Current Planets." https://horoscopes.astro-seek.com
/current-planets-astrology-transits-planetary-positions.

KonMari. "Tidy Tips." https://konmari.com/category/tidy-tips.

CHAPTER 5
The Sun Projects

The Sun provides the consciousness necessary to work with the classical planets. As the planets in our solar system orbit the Sun, various parts of our psyche orbit our personal self. Since the Moon has provided our foundation, Mercury has provided our intellectual and communicative basis, and Venus has provided our emotional basis, our next stop is the Sun. Common Sun symbols are shown in Figure 5.1. They are useful focal points in meditation and magical practice.

(a)

(b)

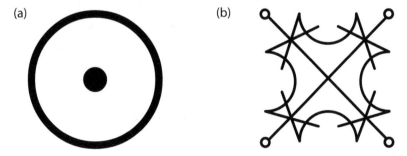

**Figure 5.1. The (a) astronomical symbol
and (b) planetary seal of the Sun**

The Western View of the Sun

In the Greco-Roman model the Sun resides between Venus and Mars.[78] Since the Sun is the source of heat, it is primarily hot and secondarily dry. Thus, the Sun is masculine and diurnal. It may also be benefic or malefic.

The Sun rules Leo. Ptolemy assigned the Moon to Cancer and the Sun to Leo because these signs were believed to be closest to Earth's zenith.[79] The other classical planets rule one lunar and one solar sign. The semicircle consisting of Aquarius, Pisces, Aries, Taurus, Gemini, and Cancer is considered lunar, while the semicircle consisting of Leo, Virgo, Libra, Scorpio, Sagittarius, and Capricorn is considered solar. The Sun is exalted in Aries and its fall is in Libra.

In the Hermetic model the Sun affects the life on Earth.[80] It maintains the matrices that bestow life to our physical, astral, and mental bodies. It is also responsible for life in all the planetary zones in general. The Hermetic universe is vitalistic—living beings are filled with a vital energy that nonliving things lack. This life force as a concept recurs in many paradigms and is known by many names: the *pneúma* of the ancient Greeks, the *ruaḥ* of the Hebrews, the *prāṇa* of the Hindus, and more.[81,82,83] In chaos magic it may be personified as Lévi's Baphomet, as described in the "Mass of Chaos."[84] According to Bardon, denizens of the Sun may be evoked in a yellow or gold light.[85] These colors of light emulate the Sun zone's vibrations, so are conducive to manifesting solar beings.

> Gk. *Hēlios* (Ἥλιος); Heb. *Shemesh* (שמש);
> Lat. *Sol*; Ouranian Barbaric *CHABOJ*

---

78. Ptolemy, *Tetrabiblos*, 34–43, 78–81, 88–89.

79. Ptolemy, *Tetrabiblos*, 78–81.

80. Bardon, *Magical Evocation*, 292.

81. Ernest DeWitt Burton, *Spirit, Soul, and Flesh* (University of Chicago Press, 1918), 170–71.

82. Burton, *Spirit, Soul, and Flesh*, 157.

83. Patrick Olivelle, ed., *The Early Upaniṣads: Annotated Text and Translation* (Oxford University Press, 1998), 121.

84. Peter J. Carroll, *Liber Null & Psychonaut: An Introduction to Chaos Magic* (Weiser Books, 1987), 131–32.

85. Bardon, *Magical Evocation*, 128.

The Solar Archetype

The Sun is our epicenter. It represents our central point of consciousness, which manifests in our ability to function as individuals. It also has ties to our sense of agency. The Sun oversees the father and higher self, two important epicenters. Exoterically, it is the biological father who directs and provides for the nuclear family. Esoterically, it is the Great Father who oversees life on Earth, directs the other planetary forces, and allows us to "shine." Deities traditionally associated with the Sun include Ra (Egyptian), Helios (Greek), and Sol (Roman). Keywords relevant to the Sun are as follows:

Epicenter

Our personal matrix is an important epicenter. A solid epicenter provides a sense of purpose, allowing parts of the whole to work together while maintaining their individuality. An unstable epicenter may result in a loss of equilibrium or overall direction. It may also lead to internal conflict.

Conscious Mind

The conscious mind encompasses everything within our awareness (e.g., sensory information, thoughts, feelings …). The solar force may manifest through self-awareness or be conveyed via independence, such as exercising our free will.

Personal Self

Our personal self is the part of us that recognizes we are individuals. Our temperament, background, life experiences, and more distinguish us from others. This is also why the Sun is associated with ego magic.

Purpose

The Sun's core drives nuclear fusion. Likewise, our divine consciousness drives our life trajectory. This "higher self" recurs in many paradigms and is known by many names: the *daimōn* of the Greeks, the *genius* of the Romans, the Holy Guardian Angel of Thelema, and more.[86,87,88]

---

86. Plotinus, *The Enneads*, ed. Lloyd P. Gerson (Cambridge University Press, 2017), 283–90.

87. *Horace: Satires, Epistles, Ars Poetica*, trans. H. Rushton Fairclough (William Heinemann, 1926), 408–09.

88. Aleister Crowley, *Magick: Liber ABA, Book 4*, xxxii–xxxiii.

Success

Working toward personal goals gives us a sense of self-determination. It also instills a sense of accomplishment, which contributes to a positive self-image.

Vitality

Without the Sun, life as we know it would not be possible. It warms our oceans, drives our weather patterns, and provides the energy necessary for plants to perform photosynthesis. This carries over esoterically, thus in many traditions the Sun reigns over health.

Western Sun Magic

In the sky, the Sun appears to be the same size as the Moon, so the ancients perceived both luminaries as powerful.[89] In many Western esoteric traditions the Sun is associated with illumination, personal improvement, self empowerment, success, health, and ego magic. It is also generally associated with spiritual and masculine works.

The Sun has long held significance in witchcraft. In many duotheistic traditions a solar god is the consort of a lunar triple goddess.[90] Since the Sun does not exhibit phases, there was probably not a tripartite solar god in antiquity. However, in some neopagan paradigms I have seen practitioners create symmetry by giving the solar god a lad-father-sage triplicity to complement the lunar goddess maiden-mother-crone triplicity.

In some practices the times of day represent different movements or tendencies of energy, and each is well suited for a particular type of magic (Table 5.1). The information in Table 5.1 is adapted from personal notes.

Table 5.1. Sun Correspondences in Witchcraft	
Time of Day	**Magical Activities**
Sunrise	Growth, beginnings, works of increase, confidence, equilibration
Noon	Vitality, works of illumination, power, protection, prosperity
Sunset	Endings, banishing, breaking bad habits, "ego buster" rites, divination

---

89. Woolfolk, *The Only Astrology Book*, 145.

90. Raven Grimassi, *Encyclopedia of Wicca & Witchcraft*, 2nd ed. (Llewellyn Publications, 2003), 444–45.

Time of day is determined by the Sun's location relative to Earth's horizon. Sunrise occurs when the upper edge of the Sun's disk crosses above the local horizon. As Earth rotates on its axis, the Sun appears to ascend in the sky. Local noon occurs when the Sun reaches its highest position in the sky that day (transiting the observer's local meridian). As Earth continues rotating, the Sun appears to descend in the sky. Sunset occurs when the upper edge of the Sun's disk crosses below the local horizon.

The Sun's day is Sunday (Lat. *dies Solis*). In some areas, the *Sun's day* became the *Lord's day* (*dies Dominica*) shortly after the advent of Christianity.[91] The Sun's alchemical metal is gold. If elemental gold is unavailable or too expensive where you live, the inorganic compound pyrite (fool's gold) is a more widely available, cheaper alternative that is magically useful.

In ceremonial traditions the Sun is associated with *Tif'eret* (Heb. Beauty), the sixth sphere of the Qabala.[92] This beauty is the hidden equilibrium underlying physical reality. Psychologically, this sphere represents the personal self and pure self-awareness. Correspondences of *Tif'eret* often relate to beauty and divinity. The Sun is also associated with *Resh*, the path connecting *Yesod* (Foundation) and *Hod* (Splendor). It connects our unconscious mind to our intellectual mind. In ancient script the letter *resh* resembles a human head, which may allude to chiefs, leaders, and other group "heads." Correspondences of *Resh* often relate to masculinity and vitality. The top-down Hebrew hierarchy for the Sun is shown in Table 5.2.

Table 5.2. The Sun Ceremonial Hierarchy		
Qabalistic World	**Level**	**Name**
'Aṣilut	Divine name	*'Eloah*
Beri'a	Archangel	*Rafàel*
Yeṣira	Intelligence Spirit	*Naki'el* *Sorath*
'Asiya	Magical tool	Lamen, bow and arrow

---

91. John Paul II, "Dies Domini—Apostolic Letter, John Paul II," (Libreria Editrice Vaticana, 1998).

92. Crowley, "777 Revised," 2–3, 5.

The information in Table 5.2 is adapted from Crowley's "777 Revised." See Appendix A for Hebrew spelling, pronunciation, etymologies, and more. *YHWH ʾEloah Wedaʿat* is *LORD God of Knowledge* in *Tifʿeret*. The lamen and Rosy Cross are associated with *Tifʿeret*.

The Sun and The Zodiac

The Greco-Roman zodiac is comprised of segments of the ecliptic the Sun passes through on its yearly (roughly 365-day) journey. It is thought to be Babylonian in origin but is present in some form across many cultures throughout history.[93,94] Western views of the zodiac draw heavily from Ptolemy's *Tetrabiblos*, which uses the tropical system. In it, the signs are oriented to the seasons in the Northern Hemisphere: the Sun enters Aries on the Spring Equinox, Cancer on the Summer Solstice, Libra on the Autumn Equinox, and Capricorn on the Winter Solstice.[95] The signs do not perfectly overlap their constellation counterparts—they are names for segments of the ecliptic. Approximately every thirty days, the Sun enters a new sign. In many paradigms, when the Sun occupies a sign, its governing head may be petitioned or talismans may be constructed for specific purposes.[96,97]

Solar Conjunctions

When two or more celestial objects appear in close proximity to each other, they are conjunct. Ptolemy briefly mentions solar conjunctions but does not discuss them in detail.[98] However, some of his contemporaries and successors do. Planets may conjunct the Sun three different ways: being *under the beams*, combust, or *in the heart*.

Under the Beams

Planets *under the beams* are not visible to the unaided eye, as they are concealed by the Sun's light. Originally, planets within 15° of the Sun were considered under the beams.[99]

---

93. John H. Rogers, "Origins of the Ancient Constellations," 9–28.

94. Gleadow, *Origin of the Zodiac*, 152–74.

95. Ptolemy, *Tetrabiblos*, 58–63.

96. Greer and Warnock, *Picatrix*.

97. Bardon, *Magical Evocation,* 328–36.

98. Ptolemy, *Tetrabiblos*, 112–15.

99. Brennan, *Hellenistic Astrology*, 200–1.

In Renaissance astrology the range was revised to 17°.[100] This concealed nature carries over esoterically, thus being under the beams is typically interpreted as a weak, hidden, or secretly manifesting planetary force.[101]

Combustion

In Medieval and Renaissance astrology, planets within 8° 30' of the Sun are considered combust.[102,103] Here, planets are in a more weakened state than those under the beams because they are scorched by the Sun.

In the Heart

Planets very close to the Sun are *in the heart*, and are not weakened by its beams. Originally, planets within 1° of the Sun were considered in the heart.[104] In Renaissance astrology the range was revised to 17'.[105] This close nature carries over esoterically, thus being in the heart is typically interpreted as a strongly manifesting planetary force that is irrevocably fused with the personal self.

Biblical commentator and philosopher Avraham Ibn-Ezra summarizes solar conjunctions brilliantly: "A planet under the light of the Sun is like a person in prison. / A combust planet is like a dying person. / A planet joined with the Sun is like a person sitting with the king in one chair."[106] Some astrological conditions are capable of mitigating a planet being weakened by the Sun—we will discuss them in chapter 11.

---

100. William Lilly, *Christian Astrology* (John Macock, 1659), 113.

101. Brennan, *Hellenistic Astrology*, 200–04.

102. Greer and Warnock, *Picatrix*, 295.

103. Lilly, *Christian Astrology,* 113.

104. Brennan, *Hellenistic Astrology*, 204–5.

105. Lilly, *Christian Astrology*, 113–14.

106. Avraham Ibn-Ezra, *The Beginning of Wisdom*, ed. Robert Hand, trans. Meira B. Epstein (ARHAT, 1998), 136–37.

Fundamentals: Day versus Night Charts

Astrological charts may be broadly classified as day charts or night charts.[107] If you were born during the daytime, you have a day chart. If you were born during the nighttime, you have a night chart. To determine your chart type, find the Ascendant-Descendant (Asc-Dsc) axis in your natal chart. If the Sun is above this axis you have a day chart, and if it is below it, you have a night chart. If you have a day chart, the Sun is your ruling light. If you have a night chart, the Moon is your ruling light.[108] It is not uncommon for people with night charts to relate more to their Moon sign than their Sun sign! You may think of twilight as a transitional period where power is being transferred from one sect to another.

The benefic or malefic temperament of a planet is further modulated according to sect.[109] Jupiter (the Greater Benefic) and Saturn (the Greater Malefic) belong to the diurnal sect, while Venus (the Lesser Benefic) and Mars (the Lesser Malefic) belong to the nocturnal sect. Generally, planets are more benefic in astrological charts of their sect, whereas out of sect planets have their benefic effects reduced. Thus, if you have a day chart, Jupiter will be more benefic than Venus (although both planets are benefic), and Saturn will be less malefic than Mars (although both planets are malefic). Likewise, if you have a night chart, Venus will be more benefic than Jupiter, and Mars will be less malefic than Saturn.

The Sun in Chaos Magic

The Sun may be integrated into magical practice in numerous ways. Various deities, egregores, or pop culture characters associated with the Sun may be invoked or evoked. Divination may be practiced via astrologically analyzing the Sun or through heliomancy. Magical items associated with the Sun may be enchanted for purposes consistent with its nature. Exposing magical tools or other objects to sunlight serves to charge, cleanse, or consecrate them with solar energy. Illumination rites aimed at gaining insight into the conscious mind or "higher self" may also be performed.

The Sun is projective, purposeful, resilient, radiant, equilibrating, and illuminating. It is also very autonomous and independent. These characteristics have been incor-

---

107. Vettius Valens, *Anthologies*, trans. Mark Riley, 25–26, accessed March 29, 2021, https://www.csus.edu/indiv/r/rileymt/Vettius%20Valens%20entire.pdf.

108. Valens, *Anthologies*, 25–26, 62.

109. Brennan, *Hellenistic Astrology*, 184–90.

porated into the rites, which are intentionally focused and goal-oriented, and involve personal work. Some also use the ceremonial planetary hexagrams. It is best to commit them to memory. The solar hexagrams are shown in Figure 5.2.

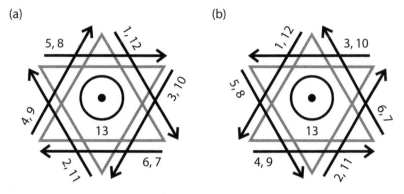

Figure 5.2. Solar (a) invoking and (b) banishing hexagrams

Draw the planetary hexagrams with your magical tool or index finger in the numbered sequence shown. The first and last lines of the invoking hexagram are drawn from the top point to the lower middle right point. The first and last lines of the banishing hexagram are drawn from the top point to the lower middle left point. Visualize the hexagram shape in yellow or gold and vibrate *ARARITA* as you draw. Visualize the Sun's astronomical symbol in yellow or gold and vibrate *YHWH 'Eloah Weda'at* as you draw. When you have finished drawing the astronomical symbol while vibrating the divine name, your planetary hexagram is complete.

Regarding safety, exercise common sense. Wear protective clothing or sunscreen. Do not look directly at the Sun—it is harmful to your eyes. Even short-term exposure may cause irreversible eye damage. Wearing sunglasses or looking through a camera lens does not mitigate this effect. If you are unable to stand in direct sunlight, you may stand in indirect sunlight and visualize the Sun in the appropriate direction instead. Alternatively, you may view images or video of the Sun online: NASA's Solar Dynamics Observatory and Stanford University's Solar Center are excellent resources.

Active Work
Sun Attunement

Go outside and stand in the Sun's rays. If you live in an area where this is not practical, stand in the sunlight shining through a window instead. As you stand, center yourself using any preferred method. Carefully observe the Sun's warm, radiant energy, as well as the quality of light it projects. Strongly visualize this light emanating down to Earth, completely saturating you, as you continue centered. Observe these solar vibrations with all five of your senses, as well as astrally. As time passes, the vibrations grow stronger. Slowly adjust the rhythm of your body to match these vibrations. Feel them blessing, equilibrating, and healing you.

> July 4, 2021. *Solar Attunement – Summary of Observations*. I attuned with the Sun each day on and off for three months. The manifestation of the solar force varied with time of day, zodiac sign, and other astrological conditions. Despite this variance, I consistently felt healthier, purer, and more balanced afterward. Others reported similar results.

Sun Greeting Rite

The following rite should be performed when the Sun is visible in the sky. Local noon is ideal; you can find your local (solar) noontime with the Global Monitoring Laboratory's NOAA Solar Calculator. The Sun in Leo or Aries are preferable but not required.

Materials
- No materials are required.
- If you already have a solar tool, you may ask the planetary spirit to bless it instead. Recall that the Sun's traditional ceremonial

tool is the lamen or bow and arrow, and its alchemical metal is gold (or pyrite).

Statement of Intent

It is my will to access the solar force.

Procedure

On a Sunday afternoon, face the Sun and attune with it.

When ready, draw an invoking solar hexagram in front of you so that the Sun as it would appear in your field of vision is in the center of this hexagram. Visualize the Sun's light emanating down from the heavens, passing through your hexagram and enveloping you. Knock in the center of your hexagram six times, as if you are knocking on a door. Place your open palms toward the Sun and say:

XIQUAL CHABOJ!
Come all-seeing Hēlios, the undying flame!
Come unconquered Sol, on your four-yoked chariot!
Come Ḥama, the hot one,
Shemesh, who bakes!
In the divine name of ʾEloah I greet you!
Come Rafaʾel, Archangel of the Sun,
and project your divine light into the darkness!
Grant me access to the solar force
so I may empower my higher self!

Close your eyes and inhale the solar light enveloping you, until it fills your entire body. Take note of any divine inspiration or spiritual insights you receive.

When ready, open your eyes and draw a triangle enclosing your hexagram. Visualize it in yellow or gold. Place your open palms slightly outside the triangle and proceed to evoke the planetary intelligence. Say:

Naki'el, Intelligence of the Sun,
in the name of Rafa'el I evoke you!
Grant me access to the solar force
so I may harness it for the Great Work of Magic!

If you do not sense its presence, continue standing in the Sun's rays and repeat the above until you do.

After you sense the planetary intelligence's presence, proceed to evoke the planetary spirit. With open palms still slightly outside the triangle, continue:

Sorath, Spirit of the Sun,
in the name of Naki'el I evoke you!
Aid my efforts to obtain a solar tool
that will assist me in the Great Work of Magic!

If you do not sense its presence, continue standing in the Sun's rays and repeat the above until you do. After you are finished communicating with them, thank them and send them on their way.

Banishing

Draw a banishing solar hexagram over your invoking solar hexagram and banish with laughter.

January 22, 2023. *Sun Greeting Rite.* The rite took about 15 minutes to perform. The solar light was radiant, revitalizing, purifying, and pervasive. Astrally, at one point it condensed and appeared as incandescent golden liquid. The solar hierarchy denizens arrived quickly and also seemed quite radiant in nature. To conclude I drew two banishing hexagrams instead of one, since the overall experience was very intense.

February 23, 2023. *Addendum.* My solar tool is a lamen blatantly associated with *Tif'eret*. It was gifted to me shortly before undertaking the bulk of my solar magical work—the givers were oblivious of this! The lamen absorbed the solar vibrations rapidly.

Sun Guided Meditation

Find a warm, quiet place and sit in a comfortable position. Close your eyes. Take a deep breath and center yourself. With each breath, you will feel calmer and more relaxed. Feel the tension in your toes. As you exhale, the tension dissipates until they are completely relaxed. This feeling of relaxation grows, spreading through your feet into your ankles. They are now completely relaxed. It continues, travelling up your legs and into your knees, which are now completely relaxed. Feel the lack of tension in your shins and calves. Any outside noises or distractions just serve to relax you further. Now your upper legs, hips, and waist are completely relaxed. As you continue to breathe, your abdominal region, chest, and back are completely relaxed. Your relaxation grows further, moving into your shoulders, and then down into your arms, elbows, hands, fingers, and fingertips. Your entire body below your neck is now completely relaxed. This feeling of relaxation grows, filling your neck and face. Feel your chin, jaw, nose, cheeks, eyes, eyelids, forehead, and ears relax. Finally, feel your scalp relax. Your entire body is now completely relaxed.

In your mind's eye, visualize the Sun glowing in the center of your chest. It is about the size of a basketball and projects a radiant gold light. The light shines outward, completely saturating you as you continue breathing. Observe the light with all five of your senses. See its pure brightness, feel its warmth, smell it, and taste it. Does it emanate a sound? The Sun dynamically vibrates but emanates no sound as it shines. As you continue breathing, the radiant gold light accumulates within you and around you, filling your body and field of vision completely. You draw an invoking solar hexagram over yourself. As you trace the symbol of the Sun while vibrating *YHWH ʾEloah Wedaʿat* in your astral voice, the light inside you intensifies.

Eventually the light becomes so hot and bright that it transforms into the brilliant white of pure energy. It radiates from your body, growing exponentially large, hot, and bright beyond comprehension. Still unable to see anything, you smell and taste the intense heat of nuclear fusion. It is completely silent. As you lift your hand to shield your eyes, you are overwhelmed by powerful convection waves. They come from all directions, completely disorienting you. The dualities of up and down, left and right, and day and night no longer exist.

Desperate to regain your bearings, you search for your center. As your attention turns inward, the light and heat swirl around you in the burning hot silence. There is no way to describe how immensely large, hot, and bright you have become. As you search deeper and deeper, you gradually find the core of your being, the divine spark of your life force. The more you focus on it the more centered you become, and the more your size, temperature, and luminosity become manageable. Fully centered, you slowly open your eyes.

You are met by the stark blackness of space. It is cold, empty, and lonely. Though you are surrounded by darkness, you burn bright within. You are a star, shining in space. After a few more moments pass, your light reaches the surrounding planets. First you see Mercury making haste in its orbit around you. Next you see Venus. Your light refracts in its thick atmosphere, producing a stunning glow. Next you see Earth and the Moon. One by one, the other planets appear. Though they are beautiful, you still feel alone—the planets reflect your light, as they do not have their own.

After a few more moments pass, you hear a booming voice from deep within, somewhere even deeper than the core of your being. It says, "Do not despair. Loneliness is not a lack of company. Loneliness is a lack of purpose. You were born to manifest the divine light within you. This light will instill you with purpose, and as you fulfill this purpose you will have the momentum of the other planetary forces behind you. You will also shine brighter. As your light reaches others, it will help them conquer their own despair, find purpose, and shine."

Beyond the solar system an orchestra of lights emerge, surrounding you completely. They are other stars—each one has a unique glow. As you look more closely, you recognize some of these stars. They are your family, friends, acquaintances, and more. Some may even be pets! There are also some unfamiliar stars that you haven't met yet. Just as they shine, so do you.

You can visit the Sun any time you'd like—now you know the way here. As you continue to breathe, you draw a banishing solar hexagram over yourself. As you trace the symbol of the Sun while vibrating *YHWH 'Eloah Weda'at* in your astral voice, the light begins condensing in the center of your chest. This divine solar light will remain with you for the rest of your life, and no one can ever take it away. Visualize this light to call upon it when needed. The room where your physical body resides begins to return. You begin to feel your fingers and toes. As the last remnants of the light condense, you gradually feel the rest of your body. Slowly open your eyes and become reacquainted with your surroundings. Stand up when you are ready and document your experience in your magical diary.

> March 5, 2023. *Sun Guided Meditation.* I consistently feel physically warmer after performing the exercise. Some participants even started sweating! The physical description of the Sun was inspired by data from NASA's Parker Solar Probe and Solar Dynamics Observatory.

Sun Monasticism

This monasticism serves to strengthen your relationship with the Sun. It should be performed for six days, since this number is associated with *Tif'eret* and the magic square of the Sun. However, feel free to use another Sun-related number if it suits your fancy. Carry your Sun tool at all times during the monasticism—it serves as a constant reminder of the Sun and increases vigilance. After your monasticism is complete, keep your Sun tool someplace special, such as an altar or favorite shelf. You may use it in future solar work and reuse it if you perform the monasticism again.

Beginning the Monasticism

On a Sunday afternoon, face the Sun and attune with it. Local noon is ideal. The Sun in Leo or Aries are preferable but not required.

When ready, draw an invoking solar hexagram in front of you so that the Sun as it would appear in your field of vision is in the center of this hexagram. Knock in the center of your hexagram six times, as if you are knocking on a door. Place your open palms toward the Sun and say:

Shemesh, I greet you! It is my will to perform the [Lesser/ Greater/Extreme] Observances of the Sun for six days. This entails [state the relevant sections here]. May this monasticism empower my higher self!

Lesser Observances

- Carry your solar tool at all times. If you can't carry it openly, keep it in your pocket or a bag and carry that with you.
- Stand in the Sun's rays for a few minutes each day while contemplating its impact on your life and the Earth at large.
- Perform a daily solar rite that incorporates your tool.
- Solar energy is a necessary prerequisite for life on Earth. Make a conscious effort to establish healthy habits and perform at least one healthy action a day that is not already part of your normal repertoire. Visit the National Institutes of Health's *Creating Healthy Habits* for suggestions.
- In many paradigms the Sun rules over fathers and male authority figures. Donate items such as vitamins, whole grain snacks, or motivational wall art to a men's leadership program or organization that helps single fathers. If you are unable to make a material donation you may make a monetary donation instead, so long as the value is in a multiple of six.

Greater Observances

- Perform all the Lesser Observances.
- Perform a second daily solar rite that incorporates your tool. To give your second rite an energetic boost, align its purpose with the time of day.

- Relate all your meditation and magical work to the Sun. For example, meditate on your higher self or perform illumination exercises to facilitate self-improvement.
- Diet and exercise significantly impact our overall health. Determine what practical steps you can take to improve them, and then follow through. It is generally more effective to start with a few small changes and then work up to larger ones. If you are unsure where to begin, consult with a licensed nutritionist or physician.

Extreme Observances

- Perform all the Greater Observances.
- Perform a third daily solar rite that incorporates your tool.
- Increase your efforts to live a healthy lifestyle as much as possible. Actions to improve your health may be large or small but must be at the forefront of your consciousness. Examples include getting daily exercise, participating in a personal development workshop, and avoiding substance abuse. Many community colleges and universities offer reasonably priced introductory self-improvement courses. Two reputable online options are the University of Pennsylvania's "Achieving Personal and Professional Success" and Yale University's "The Science of Well-Being."

Concluding the Monasticism

Return to the place you began your monasticism and attune with the Sun. Take your time and do not rush.

When ready, draw a banishing solar hexagram in front of you so that the Sun as it would appear in your field of vision is in the center of this hexagram. Place your open palms toward the Sun and say:

*Shemesh, I greet you! I performed the [Lesser/Greater/
Extreme] Observances of the Sun for six days. This entailed
[state the relevant sections here]. Though I conclude this
monasticism, my higher self remains empowered!*

March 5, 2023. *Sun Monasticism, Day 1.* I am performing the
Extreme Observances of the Sun for six days and the Greater
Observances for six days immediately after. [Details of the
three daytime rituals I performed follow.]

March 17, 2023. Sun Monasticism – Summary. I concluded
the Greater Observances of the Sun yesterday afternoon.
Most of my magic focused on achieving personal goals, self-
improvement, and good health. Many rites incorporated sunlight, the Solar Plexus (San. *Maṇipūra*), and heliomancy.

During the monasticism period I had a handful of specific
goals I wanted to accomplish. At times, it felt like my higher
self was leading me toward additional goals, especially during
the Extreme Observances. During the Greater Observances,
my doctor caught what could have turned into a serious health
issue early on!

Chapter 5
Homework

After taking notes on the chapter, magical practice should be commenced for thirty minutes each day for a minimum of one month. Perform the assignments in the order presented. Remember to document your efforts in your magical diary.

- ☐ Meditate on the Sun for a minimum of ten minutes each day. How does it affect your life? How do you interact with it?

- ☐ Examine your natal chart to determine your Sun sign. In this sign, is the Sun's manifestation strong, weak, or somewhere in between? Are any planets conjunct the Sun? We will revisit the natal Sun in chapters 7 and 11.

- ☐ Approximately every thirty days, the Sun enters a new sign. Visit a reputable website to determine the current Sun sign. In this sign, is the Sun's manifestation strong, weak, or somewhere in between?

- ☐ Examine your natal chart to determine if it is a day chart or a night chart. Which planet is your ruling light? Which planets are in sect? Out of sect? List your natal Venus, Mars, Jupiter, and Saturn from most to least benefic.

- ☐ Attune with the Sun daily for a period of one week.

- ☐ Investigate the effects of the solar hexagrams. To accomplish this, draw one and passively observe the impact on yourself and the immediate environment. After a few minutes, record any observations, thoughts, inner feelings, and other details you deem important in your magical diary. Feel free to draw a banishing hexagram after an invoking hexagram to cancel it out.

- ☐ Perform the Sun Greeting Rite. After obtaining your solar tool, purify and consecrate it by exposing it to sunlight.

- ☐ Perform the Sun Guided Meditation.

- ☐ Perform a Sun Monasticism before proceeding to the next chapter.

Chapter 5 Resources

AstroSeek. "Today's Current Planets." https://horoscopes.astro-seek.com/current-planets-astrology-transits-planetary-positions.

Global Monitoring Laboratory. "NOAA Solar Calculator." https://gml.noaa.gov/grad/solcalc.

National Institutes of Health. "Creating Healthy Habits." Published March 2018. https://newsinhealth.nih.gov/2018/03/creating-healthy-habits.

Solar Dynamics Observatory. "The Sun Now." https://sdo.gsfc.nasa.gov/data.

Stanford Solar Center. "View Current Solar Images." https://solar-center.stanford.edu/sun-today.html.

University of Pennsylvania. "Achieving Personal and Professional Success." https://online.wharton.upenn.edu/personal-and-professional-success.

Yale Univeristy. "The Science of Well-Being." https://www.coursera.org/learn/the-science-of-well-being.

CHAPTER 6
Mars Objects

Mars provides the raw energy and physical power necessary to work with the classical planets. Whereas Venus attracts our eyes in the sky, the vibrant red of Mars demands our attention. Since the Moon has provided our foundation, Mercury has provided our intellectual and communicative basis, Venus has provided our emotional basis, and the Sun has provided our consciousness, our next stop is Mars. Common Mars symbols are shown in Figure 6.1. They are useful focal points in meditation and magical practice.

(a)   (b)

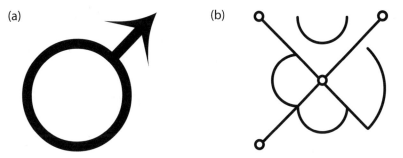

**Figure 6.1. The (a) astronomical symbol
and (b) planetary seal of Mars**

The Western View of Mars

In the Greco-Roman model Mars resides between the Sun and Jupiter.[110] Due to its proximity to the Sun, Mars is primarily dry and secondarily hot. Thus, Mars is malefic and masculine. Mars is also nocturnal. Ptolemy assigned Mars to the nocturnal sect (associated with wetness) to counterbalance its malefic temperament (caused by its primary dryness). Mars's antagonistic nature is further reflected in the signs it rules, Aries and Scorpio. Aries is square (90°) to Cancer (ruled by the Moon), and Scorpio is square to Leo (ruled by the Sun). When planets are square, their interaction is disharmonious.[111] Mars is exalted in Capricorn and in its fall in Cancer.

In the Hermetic model, Mars affects Earth's raw power.[112] It is responsible for humanity's impulsiveness and survival instincts. According to Bardon, denizens of Mars may be evoked in a red light.[113] This color of light emulates the Mars zone's vibrations, making it conducive to manifesting Martian beings.

Gk. *Arēs* (Ἄρης); Heb. *Ma'adim* (מאדים);
Lat. *Mars*; Ouranian Barbaric *RAFHAXET*

The Mars Archetype

Mars is our might. It represents our energetic matrix, which manifests in our ability to express raw physical power. It also has ties to our sense of self-assertion. Mars oversees comrades in arms and military institutions, two important conduits for might. Exoterically, it is the warrior who has courage under pressure and emerges victorious in battle. Esoterically, it is the Divine Warrior who wages war in the terrestrial and celestial realms. Deities traditionally associated with Mars include Horus and Montu (Egyptian), Ares (Greek), and Mars (Roman). Keywords relevant to Mars are as follows:

Might

Our energetic matrix is an important conduit for might. Constructive channeling directs raw energy purposefully toward a meaningful goal. Destructive channeling may result

---

110. Ptolemy, *Tetrabiblos*, 34–43, 78–81, 88–89.

111. Ptolemy, *Tetrabiblos*, 72–73.

112. Bardon, *Magical Evocation*, 292.

113. Bardon, *Magical Evocation*, 128.

in unwarranted or misdirected aggression. It may also lead to chronic feelings of anger and frustration.

Action

Venus attracts what she desires, whereas Mars goes out and gets what he desires. The Martian force may manifest through physical effort or be conveyed via enthusiasm (e.g., getting fired up).

Intensity

Our raw energy may amplify itself in many forms. This includes but is not limited to physical intensity (such as vigorous exercise and pain), mental intensity (such as tenacity and obsession), and emotional intensity (such as lust and wrath).

Conflict

Mars rules the manner in which we handle conflict. This may positively manifest through competitive sports, martial arts, and athletic games. This may negatively manifest through lashing out at others or violent behavior.

Courage

Courage allows us to assess risk and act accordingly. The ancient Greeks viewed *andreia* (Gk. ἀνδρεία; manliness/courage) as the mean between the extremes of *phobos* (φόβος; fear) and *tharsos* (θάρσος; boldness).[114]

Metalwork

Mars has long been associated with metal forging. Throughout history, metals have been transformed into weapons, armor, and more. The forging process requires strength of body and mind, as well as tenacity—all Martial traits.

Western Mars Magic

Mars has an intense red appearance in the sky, so the ancients associated this planet with elemental fire.[115] In many Western esoteric traditions Mars is associated with energy raising, physical empowerment, separation, combat, blood, and war magic. It is also generally associated with wrathful and vengeful works.

---

114. Aristotle, *Nicomachean Ethics*, trans. C. D. C. Reeve (Hackett Publishing Company, 2014), 46–51.

115. Woolfolk, *The Only Astrology Book*, 193.

Mars's day is Tuesday (Lat. *dies Martis*). The word *Tuesday* is derived from the Old English *Tīwesdæg* (Tiw's Day). The connection between the classical planet and day of the week is more obvious in languages such as Spanish (*martes*) and French (*mardi*). Mars's alchemical metal is iron. Today, we know the Red Planet gets its appearance due to iron compounds. Our blood is also red due to iron—it is a key component of hemoglobin, the dominant protein in red blood cells.

In ceremonial traditions Mars is associated with *Gebura* (Heb. Strength or Might), the fifth sphere of the Qabala.[116] This might is the raw power required to manifest physical reality. Psychologically, this sphere represents personal will and power. Correspondences of *Gebura* often relate to might and physical empowerment. Mars is also associated with *Pe*, the path connecting *Neṣaḥ* (Victory) and *Hod* (Splendor). It connects our feelings to our intellectual mind. In ancient script the letter *pe* resembles a human mouth, which may allude to the voice of the people. As *Mars Thingsus*, the Roman Mars protected public assemblies.[117] Correspondences of *Pe* often relate to intensity and elemental fire. The top-down Hebrew hierarchy for Mars is shown in Table 6.1.

Table 6.1. The Mars Ceremonial Hierarchy		
Qabalistic World	**Level**	**Name**
ʾAṣilut	Divine name	ʾAdonay
Beriʾa	Archangel	Kamἁel
Yeṣira	Intelligence Spirit	Grἁfiʾel Barṣabʾel
ʿAsiya	Magical tool	Sword

---

116. Crowley, "777 Revised," 2–3, 5.

117. E. A. Wallis Budge, *An Account of the Roman Antiquities Preserved in the Museum at Chesters Northumberland* (Gilbert & Rivington, 1903), 190–93.

The information in Table 6.1 is adapted from Crowley's "777 Revised." See Appendix A for Hebrew spelling, pronunciation, etymologies, and more. *'Elohim Gibor* is *Mighty God* in *Gebura*. In older texts, *Sama'el* is often attributed instead of *Kama'el*.[118] The sword, spear, scourge, and chain are associated with *Gebura*.

Fundamentals: Raw Energy and Planetary Spirits
The unprocessed energy embodied by the Martian archetype bears general similarity to the raw forces personified by the planetary spirits. You may think of your conscious mind as the *intelligence* guiding the *spirit* of your unprocessed energy. When this energy is not deliberately directed, it may manifest in disastrous or unruly ways. Likewise, it is usually a bad idea to work with a planetary spirit in the absence of its intelligence. Planetary spirits are notorious for their potential to wreak havoc when left to their own devices.

Mars in Chaos Magic
Mars may be integrated into magical practice in numerous ways. Various deities, egregores, or pop culture characters associated with Mars may be invoked or evoked. Divination may be practiced via astrologically analyzing Mars or through methods that incorporate weapons (e.g., dagger spinning, divining arrows …). Magical items associated with Mars may be enchanted for purposes consistent with its nature. All war trophies also fall under this planet's domain. Illumination rites aimed at gaining insight into personal will and power or the nature of conflict may also be performed.

Mars is projective, assertive, active, combative, untamed, and unapologetic. It is also very physical and intense. These characteristics have been incorporated into the rites, which are intentionally energetic, hard-hitting, and involve physical work. Some also use Mars's ceremonial planetary hexagrams (Figure 6.2). It is best to commit them to memory.

---

118. Kaplan, *Sefer Yetzirah*, 168.

(a)   (b)

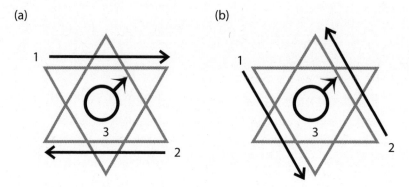

Figure 6.2. Mars (a) invoking and (b) banishing hexagrams

Draw the planetary hexagrams with your magical tool or index finger in the numbered sequence shown. Visualize the hexagram shape in red and vibrate *ARARITA* as you draw. Visualize the Mars astronomical symbol in red and vibrate *'Elohim Gibor* as you draw. When you have finished drawing the astronomical symbol while vibrating the divine name, your planetary hexagram is complete.

Active Work
Mars Attunement

Perform exercise or some other physical activity that is strenuous enough to make you break a sweat. You may turn up the heat, play motivational music, or think of something that makes you angry if you'd like. As you exert yourself, let your raw energy push you further. Do not worry about grace or tact. Resonate with this raw energy and physical power. Observe its might with all five of your senses, as well as astrally. As time passes, the might intensifies. Instinctually adjust the rhythm of your body to match the vibrations underlying this might. Feel them strengthening, empowering, and intensifying you.

> January 31, 2023. *Mars Attunement.* I consistently feel more physically empowered, ambitious, and bold after performing the exercise. Others independently stated the tenacity required to exert more physical energy than normal is a valuable springboard to attuning with the Martian force.

Mars Greeting Rite

This rite incorporates religious practices of ancient Rome's *cultus deorum.* Here, Mars is the father of Romulus, the founder of Rome. Mars was highly revered—originally an agricultural deity, he later evolved into a war god. Both agriculture and warfare were important in early Rome.

Since you will be manifesting Martian vibrations on a tablet of burning incense charcoal, planetary visibility is not required. If Mars is visible in the sky, you may face it and treat that direction as metaphysical east if you feel it is necessary. When visible in the sky, Mars's appearance varies due to how much sunlight it reflects, its proximity to Earth, and other factors. Mars in Aries, Scorpio, or Capricorn are preferable but not required.

Materials

- Matches
- A tablet of incense charcoal
- Tongs
- A fireproof container in which to burn your charcoal (a clay flowerpot filled halfway with sand works well)
- A small glass of wine
- A plate with a small serving of cooked red meat
- A head covering (such as a scarf or part of a toga)
- If you already have a Mars tool, you may ask the planetary spirit to bless it instead. Recall that Mars's traditional ceremonial tool is the sword and its alchemical metal is iron.

    Note: Feel free to substitute modern Mars-related offerings (e.g., red chili peppers, hot sauce …) if the traditional Roman offerings of wine and red meat are not practical. You may also optionally play Mars-related music, such as Holst's "Mars, the Bringer of War" from *The Planets, Op. 32* or Respighi's *Feste Romane, P. 157* throughout the rite.

Preparation

Ensure the area you are in is well ventilated. Incense charcoal is safe to use indoors. Do not use lump charcoal or briquettes as a substitute—their combustion produces a large amount of carbon monoxide, which can kill you. If you follow Roman *cultus deorum* practices, feel free to perform an ablution before commencing the rite at your *lararium*.

Statement of Intent

It is my will to greet (planet) Mars.

Procedure

On a Tuesday night, attune with Mars.

When you feel sufficiently physically energized, cover your head *capite velato* (leaving only the front of your face exposed)—this signifies piety and prevented ancient Romans from receiving bad omens during rituals.[119] Kiss the top of your right hand and briefly touch the side of your fireproof container, akin to an *adoratio* (adoration).[120] Light your incense charcoal and hold it with tongs so you do not burn yourself. Place the burning tablet in your fireproof container and draw an invoking Mars hexagram over it. Visualize a vibrant red light emanating down from the heavens that passes through your hexagram and saturates your charcoal. Vibrate 'Adonay five times. Place your open palms toward the sky and say:

> *Ave stella Martis!* (Lat. Hail [the deity] Mars's star!)
> *Come mighty Arēs, arbiter of arms!*
> *Come bellicose Mars, father of Romulus!*
> *Come Ma'adim, the red one,*
> *Kama'el, ardent archangel!*
> *May these offerings grant me strength of body and mind!*
> *Do ut des!* (I give so that you may give!)
> *Ave stella Martis!* (Hail [the deity] Mars's star!)

Sprinkle a few drops of wine on the burning charcoal, followed by a few bits of red meat. As they are consumed by the fire, take note of any bursts of physical energy or calls to action you receive.

---

119. *The Roman Questions of Plutarch*, trans. H. J. Rose (Clarendon Press, 1924), 123–24.

120. William Smith, ed., *A Dictionary of Greek and Roman Antiquities* (Taylor and Walton, 1842), 14.

When ready, draw a triangle enclosing your charcoal. Visualize it in red. Place your open palms slightly outside the triangle and proceed to evoke the planetary intelligence. Say:

Graʾfiʾel, Intelligence of Mars,
in the name of Kamaʾel I evoke you!
Grant me access to the Martian force
so I may harness it for the Great Work of Magic!
Do ut des! (I give so that you may give!)

Sprinkle a few more drops of wine on the burning charcoal, followed by a few more bits of red meat. If you do not sense its presence, continue visualizing the vibrant red light and repeat the above until you do.

After you sense the planetary intelligence's presence, proceed to evoke the planetary spirit. With open palms still slightly outside the triangle, continue:

Barṣabʾel, Spirit of Mars,
in the name of Graʾfiʾel I evoke you!
Aid my efforts to obtain a Mars tool
that will assist me in the Great Work of Magic!
Do ut des! (I give so that you may give!)

Sprinkle a few more drops of wine on the burning charcoal, followed by a few more bits of red meat. If you do not sense its presence, continue visualizing the vibrant red light and repeat the above until you do. After you are finished communicating with them, thank them and send them on their way.

Make one final offering as a precaution. Expiation was not uncommon in ancient Roman practice. Say:

If anything in this rite was unsatisfactory,
I make amends by these offerings.
Ave stella Martis! (Hail [the deity] Mars's star!)

Sprinkle a few more drops of wine on the burning charcoal, followed by a few more bits of red meat. Consume the remainder of the wine and meat. If you are unable to consume them due to health reasons, you may bury them outside later.

Banishing

Say, *Valete!* (Lat. Farewell!) *Go in peace!* Draw a banishing Mars hexagram over your invoking Mars hexagram. You may now uncover your head.

Let the charcoal burn out naturally. If you are in a hurry, you may smother it with sand. Whatever you do, *never* leave burning charcoal unattended! Make sure the ashes are completely extinguished and cool to the touch before disposal.

January 31, 2023. *Mars Greeting Rite.* Excluding the attunement, the rite took about 20 minutes to perform. I've used the same brand of incense charcoal for years, and have never seen offerings snap, crackle, and pop like that! During the evocation of the planetary intelligence, a piece of beef jerky loudly popped while jumping off the charcoal. During the evocation of the planetary spirit, additional pieces of beef jerky crackled and burnt rapidly. I also learned I'd have to actively seek out a suitable planetary tool, since Mars assists those who actively work toward their goals.

February 1, 2023. *Addendum.* Today I actively sought out a Mars tool. After a few hours of unsuccessful searching, I went for a walk to blow off steam. I eventually entered a local

Navajo store boasting a stunning collection of handmade pocketknives. Upon looking at one knife in particular, it hit me like a ton of bricks—this would be my Mars tool! I purchased the knife and performed a divination to confirm when I got home. The divination result was a *very* snarky: "Was it not obvious enough in the store?"

Mars Guided Meditation

Find a warm, quiet place and sit in a comfortable position. Close your eyes. Take a deep breath and center yourself. With each breath, you will feel calmer and more relaxed. Feel the tension in your toes. As you exhale, the tension dissipates until they are completely relaxed. This feeling of relaxation grows, spreading through your feet into your ankles. They are now completely relaxed. It continues, travelling up your legs and into your knees, which are now completely relaxed. Feel the lack of tension in your shins and calves. Any outside noises or distractions just serve to relax you further. Now your upper legs, hips, and waist are completely relaxed. As you continue to breathe, your abdominal region, chest, and back are completely relaxed. Your relaxation grows further, moving into your shoulders, and then down into your arms, elbows, hands, fingers, and fingertips. Your entire body below your neck is now completely relaxed. This feeling of relaxation grows, filling your neck and face. Feel your chin, jaw, nose, cheeks, eyes, eyelids, forehead, and ears relax. Finally, feel your scalp relax. Your entire body is now completely relaxed.

In your mind's eye, visualize Mars glowing above your head. It is about the size of a basketball and reflects a vibrant red light. The light shines down, boldly enveloping you as you continue breathing. Observe the light with all five senses. See its intrepid brightness, feel its warmth, smell it, and taste it. Does it emanate a sound? Sounds are softer and travel slower on the Martian surface. As you continue breathing, the vibrant red light accumulates within you and around you, filling your body and field of vision completely. You draw an invoking Mars hexagram in front of you. As you trace the symbol of Mars while vibrating *'Elohim Gibor* in your astral voice, the light inside you boldly glows.

The light in the surrounding environment quickly disperses and is overtaken by violently blowing butterscotch-colored dust. As you lift your hands to shield your face, you smell and taste the pungent odor of rust. The deep rumble of the wind permeates the cold, dry atmosphere. The fine dust particles are weakly electrostatic—they stick to you like styrofoam packing peanuts. Occasionally you feel a faint shock. After a few more moments pass, you realize you are in the midst of one of Mars's notorious dust storms. As it rages around you, unleashed and unchecked, you are reminded of *Barṣab'el*, the planetary spirit of Mars. Adrenaline rushes through your body. The red light inside you chaotically pulsates with the volatility of the storm. You impulsively freeze in place and slow your breathing. As you stand still, you sense the storm's intense raw energy and physical power. With each controlled breath, the light inside you gradually calms. So does the storm.

As the storm subsides, a rugged terrain comes into focus. The red light inside you now maintains a consistent rhythmic pulse. The battle-scarred landscape is filled with sand dunes, boulders, and smaller rocks of various sizes, all covered in a thin layer of dust. Occasionally an inactive volcano or crater punctuates the landscape. In the distance you see low-lying basins carved from ancient water, which are now vast deserts. In terms of light, it is like dawn or dusk on Earth. In this stillness you are reminded of *Gra'fi'el*, the planetary intelligence of Mars. Just as you managed your breathing, *Gra'fi'el* manages *Barṣab'el*. You brush away the fine dust sticking to your clothes. The particles eventually fall and settle on the ground.

You make your way toward a nearby flat rock. There, you can sit and observe the Martian sky. As you walk, the ground beneath you gently crunches—it appears to be a mixture of fine powder and larger rock fragments. You sit on the rock and turn your gaze upward. The dust particles lingering in the air give the sky a red-orange tint, akin to a sunset on Earth. The Sun is about half the size it appears on Earth. As it sets, the sky transforms from red-orange to deep blue. After a few more moments pass, Mars's two irregularly shaped satellites come into view. The closer, more quickly moving satellite appears about one third the size of Earth's Moon. As it travels across the Martian sky, the smaller, more slowly moving satellite rises. These satellites are named Phobos and Deimos, respectively. In the ancient Greek paradigm, *Phobos* (Gk. fear) and *Deimos* (terror) accompany their father *Arēs* into battle.

As your eyes return to the Martian surface, you jump back in surprise—a winged figure now towers in front of you! It is only a few centimeters away and is surrounded by a vibrant red light. As the figure outstretches its wings, your attention is drawn to the cup in its left hand. The cup's mouth glows intensely—it is filled with extremely concentrated red light. After a few moments pass, you realize you are standing before *Kama'el*, archangel of Mars. He smirks, amused at your shock. He slowly circles you, looking you up and down to inspect you by some unknown criteria. Even though he is intimidating, you stand still and do not flinch. He returns to face you and looks you squarely in the eyes. After examining you for a few more moments, he gives a nod of approval. He dips his right index finger into the cup, picking up some of the concentrated red light. It is as thick as blood. He begins to draw the symbol of Mars on your forehead. On contact, the light rapidly absorbs into your body, infusing it with might and vigor. Scenes of gladiatorial combat, courageous heroes, and long-forgotten wars rush through your mind. After he finishes drawing, you feel physically stronger and more energized than before. In the future, you may call upon this red light when you need a boost of physical energy or courage. Just as abruptly as *Kama'el* appeared, he disappears.

You can visit Mars any time you'd like—now you know the way here. The vibrant red light again accumulates within you and around you, filling your body and field of vision completely. While continuing to breathe, you draw a banishing Mars hexagram in front of you. As you trace the symbol of Mars while vibrating *'Elohim Gibor* in your astral voice, the light in the surrounding environment quickly disperses. The room where your physical body resides begins to return. You begin to feel your fingers and toes. As the last remnants of the vibrant red light fade, you gradually feel the rest of your body. Slowly open your eyes and become reacquainted with your surroundings. Stand up when you are ready and document your experience in your magical diary.

> February 13, 2023. *Mars Guided Meditation.* Participants consistently reported feeling more aware of the ebb and flow of their physical energy afterward, with the effect typically lasting a few days. The geological description of the Martian surface was inspired by data from NASA's Mars rovers. The description of archangel *Kama'el* was inspired by his stained-glass window at Saint Michael and All Angels Church in Brighton, England.

Mars Monasticism

This monasticism serves to strengthen your relationship with Mars. It should be performed for five days, since this number is associated with *Gebura* and the magic square of Mars. However, feel free to use another Mars-related number if it suits your fancy. Carry your Mars tool at all times during the monasticism—it serves as a constant reminder of Mars and increases vigilance. After your monasticism is complete, keep your Mars tool someplace special, such as an altar or favorite shelf. You may use it in future Mars work and reuse it if you perform the monasticism again.

Beginning the Monasticism

On a Tuesday night, attune with Mars. Mars in Aries, Scorpio, or Capricorn are preferable but not required.

When ready, cover your head *capite velato*. Kiss the top of your right hand and briefly touch the side of your fireproof container. Light a tablet of incense charcoal and place it in your fireproof container, as before. Draw an invoking Mars hexagram over it. Vibrate *'Adonay* five times. Place your open palms toward the sky and say:

> *Ave stella Martis!* (Lat. Hail [the deity] Mars's star!) *Be blessed by these offerings! It is my will to perform the [Lesser/ Greater/Extreme] Observances of Mars for five days. May they grant me strength of body and mind!*

Sprinkle a few drops of wine on the burning charcoal, followed by a few bits of cooked red meat. Say:

> *Do ut des!* (I give so that you may give!)

Lesser Observances

- Carry your Mars tool at all times. If you can't carry it openly, keep it in your pocket or a bag carried with you.
- As the Lesser Malefic, Mars separates and antagonizes.[121] To combat this stress, blow off steam through exercise or other physical activity each day.

---

121. Brennan, *Hellenistic Astrology*, 184–90.

- Perform a nightly Mars rite that incorporates your tool.
- Mars is notorious for its rugged environment. On Earth, make a conscious effort to be safety-minded wherever you go. Get trained in CPR, first aid, and defibrillator (AED) use if you are not already.
- In many paradigms Mars rules over soldiers and first responders. Donate items such as instant coffee, beef jerky, or pain relief cream to a public safety station or organization that helps veterans or deployed military. If you are unable to make a material donation, you may make a monetary donation instead, so long as the value is in a multiple of five. Mars also rules over blood, so blood donation is another option.

Greater Observances

- Perform all the Lesser Observances.
- Perform a second nightly Mars rite that incorporates your tool.
- Relate all your meditation and magical work to Mars. For example, meditate on the nature of raw, unprocessed energy or incorporate physical activity into your rites.
- Assess the security of your home and make any necessary improvements. Fortify points of entry, install or repair outdoor lighting, and determine if an alarm system is required. Post emergency numbers in a prominent location and make sure that everyone in your household is aware of them.

Extreme Observances

- Perform all the Greater Observances.
- Perform a third nightly Mars rite that incorporates your tool.
- Begin learning how to defend yourself by participating in a martial art or combat sport. If you are unsure which one to

choose, Brazilian jiu-jitsu, judo, and Western boxing are available in most major cities. Brazilian jiu-jitsu and judo emphasize grappling and groundwork, whereas Western boxing emphasizes striking. If you are vision impaired, judo is highly recommended. Alternatively, you may learn how to safely handle and shoot a firearm if they are legal in your country.

Concluding the Monasticism

Return to the place you began your monasticism and attune with Mars.

When ready, cover your head *capite velato*. Kiss the top of your right hand and briefly touch the side of your fireproof container. Light a tablet of incense charcoal and place it in your fireproof container, as before. Draw an invoking Mars hexagram over it. Vibrate *'Adonay* five times. Place your open palms toward the sky and say:

> *Ave stella Martis! (Lat. Hail [the deity] Mars's star!) Be blessed by these offerings! I performed the [Lesser/Greater/ Extreme] Observances of Mars for five days. Though it is done, my strength of body and mind remain! Do ut des!* (I give so that you may give!)

Sprinkle a few drops of wine on the burning charcoal, followed by a few bits of cooked red meat. Consume the rest, or bury it outside later.

February 7, 2023. *Mars Monasticism, Day 1.* I am performing the Extreme Observances of Mars for five days and the Greater Observances of Mars for five days immediately after. [Details of the three nightly rituals I performed follow.]

February 14, 2023. *Mars Monasticism, Day 8.* Throughout life, doing intense Mars work (especially within a short time-frame) consistently results in a super heavy period, whether it's that time of the month or not. Today was no exception…ugh. [Details of the three nightly rituals I performed follow.]

February 18, 2023. *Mars Monasticism—Summary.* I concluded the Greater Observances of Mars last night. Looking back, most of my magic focused on improving physical fitness, personal and household protection, and increasing overall assertiveness. Most rites incorporated physical activity.

Throughout the monasticism I noticed a marked increase in physical energy. Despite this, on a couple of nights I was almost too physically exhausted to perform my planetary rites! A few rites were also composed too impulsively or haphazardly— I wound up revising and reperforming them on subsequent nights. Overall, the monasticism reminded me that *managing* physical energy is just as important as *having* physical energy!

Chapter 6
Homework

After taking notes on the chapter, magical practice should be commenced for thirty minutes each day for a minimum of one month. Perform the assignments in the order presented. Take your time and do not rush, even though Mars likes to do things impulsively. Remember to document your efforts in your magical diary.

☐ Meditate on Mars for a minimum of ten minutes each day. How does this planetary force affect your life? How do you interact with it?

☐ Examine your natal chart to determine your Mars sign. In this sign, is Mars's manifestation strong, weak, or somewhere in between? Is Mars retrograde or conjunct the Sun? We will revisit natal Mars in chapters 7 and 11.

☐ Approximately every one and a half months, Mars enters a new sign. Visit a reputable website to determine the current Mars sign. In this sign, is Mars's manifestation strong, weak, or somewhere in between? Is Mars retrograde or conjunct the Sun?

☐ Attune with Mars nightly for a period of one week.

☐ Investigate the effects of the Mars hexagrams. To accomplish this, draw one and passively observe the impact on yourself and the immediate environment. After a few minutes, record any observations, thoughts, feelings, and other details you deem important in your magical diary. Feel free to draw a banishing hexagram after an invoking hexagram to cancel it out.

☐ Obtain a package of incense charcoal tablets, tongs, and a fireproof container in which to burn your charcoal if you do not have them already. You will also need a head covering (such as a scarf or part of a toga).

☐ Perform the Mars Greeting Rite. After obtaining your Mars tool, purify and consecrate it by passing it through incense charcoal smoke.

☐ Perform the Mars Guided Meditation.

☐ Perform a Mars Monasticism before proceeding to the next chapter.

Chapter 6 Resources

Artemis BJJ. "BJJ FAQ." Last modified December 26, 2017. https://www.artemisbjj .com/FAQ.

AstroSeek. "Today's Current Planets." https://horoscopes.astro-seek.com /current-planets-astrology-transits-planetary-positions.

ExpertBoxing. "The BEGINNER'S Guide to Boxing." https://expertboxing.com /the-beginners-guide-to-boxing.

Ferrari, Joseph. "Why Clutter Stresses Us Out." Interview by Kim Mills. *Speaking of Psychology*, February 22, 2023. Audio, 35:35. https://www.apa.org/news/podcasts /speaking-of-psychology/clutter.

Holst, Gustav. "Mars, the Bringer of War." In *The Planets, Op. 32*. Performed by BBC Symphony Orchestra. July 27, 2015. https://www.youtube.com/watch?v =cXOanvv4plU.

Judo Info. https://judoinfo.com.

Respighi, Ottorino. *Feste Romane, P. 157*. Performed by Chicago Youth Symphony Orchestras. November 20, 2016. https://www.youtube.com/watch?v=IyQdUStSLtY.

The Personal Planets in Astrology

In modern Western astrology, the Moon, Mercury, Venus, the Sun, and Mars are sometimes called the *personal* planets. They represent our psychological foundation, intellect, feelings, personal self, and raw energy and physical power, respectively. Before undertaking further magical work, we will examine the astrological properties of the personal planets more scrupulously.

The natal chart shows the positions of the classical planets at the moment of birth, with each one occupying a particular zodiac sign and house. In a nutshell, the planets indicate *what* is happening, the signs indicate *how* it is happening, and the houses indicate *where* it is happening.

Astrological Significations

The astrological significations of the classical planets are extrapolated from their hot/cold and wet/dry characteristics. They indicate *what* archetypal force is at play. Brief descriptions of the natal significations for each celestial body we have discussed so far are as follows:

The Moon

The Moon represents the unconscious mind. This includes our instincts, emotions, and drive to fulfill our needs. It is also generally associated with mothers (and females), cyclical change, and local or short-term travel.

Mercury

Mercury represents how you think and communicate. This includes our intellectual mind, cognitive processes, and sense of curiosity. It is also generally associated with rapid movement, irregularity, and fluctuation between dualities.

Venus

Venus represents how you connect with others. This includes our feelings, how we develop and maintain relationships, and our sense of aesthetics. It is also generally associated with unification, reconciliation, and attraction.

The Sun

The Sun represents the conscious mind. This includes our personal self (the "I"), ego, and sense of agency. It is also generally associated with fathers (and males), spiritual awareness, and illumination.

Mars

Mars represents how you express raw energy and physical power. This includes our intensity levels, conflict management, and assertiveness. It is also generally associated with separation, antagonism, and repulsion.

The Planets in Signs

The zodiac signs modulate *how* the planetary forces manifest. They represent different movements or tendencies of energy. In the Greco-Roman model each sign may be broadly classified as cardinal, fixed, or mutable.[122] Cardinal signs denote the beginning of a season, and embody more creative, active energy. Fixed signs denote the middle of a season, and embody more concrete, stable energy. Mutable signs denote the end of a season, and embody more flexible, adaptable energy.

Each sign also belongs to a particular trigon, which were later linked to the Aristotelian elements.[123,124,125] In Aristotelian physical theory the fire element is primarily hot

---

122. Ptolemy, *Tetrabiblos*, 64–67.

123. Ptolemy, *Tetrabiblos*, 82–87.

124. Dorotheus, *Carmen Astrologicum*, trans. David Pingree (Astrology Classics, 2005), 161–62.

125. Valens, *Anthologies*, 25.

and secondarily dry.[126] It is the most transformative element. The air element is primarily wet and secondarily hot. It is the most mobile element. The water element is primarily cold and secondarily wet. It is denser than the upward moving elements, and adaptable in shape. The earth element is primarily dry and secondarily cold. It is the densest element, and capable of maintaining its shape. A brief description of each sign is as follows:

Aries
Aries (♈) is a cardinal fire sign. It is the igniting energy of new beginnings, urgent action, and putting the pedal to the metal, so to speak. It is like the first spark of fire.

Taurus
Taurus (♉) is a fixed earth sign. It is the enduring energy of consistency, concrete routine, and slow, steady growth. It is like fertile soil.

Gemini
Gemini (♊) is a mutable air sign. It is the nimble energy of open-mindedness, social adaptability, and seeing both sides of a situation. It is like the wind.

Cancer
Cancer (♋) is a cardinal water sign. It is the nurturing energy of caregiving, emotional investment, and protecting the vulnerable. It is like the water of the womb.

Leo
Leo (♌) is a fixed fire sign. It is the radiant energy of nobility, illumination, and "being seen." It is like a steadily burning flame.

Virgo
Virgo (♍) is a mutable earth sign. It is the discerning energy of problem-solving, reflective analysis, and continuous improvement. It is like a grassy meadow that changes with the seasons.

---

126. Aristotle, *On Generation and Corruption*, 509–10.

Libra

Libra (♎) is a cardinal air sign. It is the balancing energy of diplomacy, compromise, and starting a dialogue. It is like a clear, crisp morning sky.

Scorpio

Scorpio (♏) is a fixed water sign. It is the penetrating energy of intense emotion, enduring inner feelings, and diving into the unknown. It is like still waters that run deep.

Sagittarius

Sagittarius (♐) is a mutable fire sign. It is the convective energy of divine inspiration, motivational speaking, and ideological advocacy. It is like wildfire.

Capricorn

Capricorn (♑) is a cardinal earth sign. It is the conservative energy of natural caution, navigating the lay of the land, and constructing long-term plans. It is like emerging mountains.

Aquarius

Aquarius (♒) is a fixed air sign. It is the imaginative energy of lofty ideals, exploring different paradigms, and thinking outside the box. It is like the clouds.

Pisces

Pisces (♓) is a mutable water sign. It is the dissolutive energy of natural empathy, going with the flow, and losing yourself in something greater. It is like raindrops falling into the ocean.

The zodiac signs rotate clockwise through the local sky, making a complete revolution approximately every 24 hours. The planets move counterclockwise through the zodiac along the ecliptic (Figure 7.1).

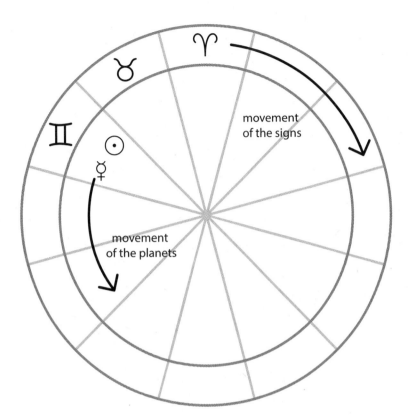

Figure 7.1. Zodiacal and planetary movements

The Planets in Houses

The houses show *where* the planetary forces, modulated by the signs they occupy, manifest in our lives. The whole sign system is the oldest house system.[127] Here, the local sky is divided into twelve segments of equal size, with each sign occupying one house. The signs rise in the first house and set in the seventh house.

In the Greco-Roman model each house may be broadly classified as angular, succedent, or cadent.[128,129] Angular houses are the most prominent in a chart, thus the planets occupying them play prominent roles in our lives. The first, fourth, seventh, and tenth

127. Robert Hand, *Whole Sign Houses: The Oldest House System* (ARHAT, 2000), 9–14.

128. Dorotheus, *Carmen Astrologicum*, 164, 224–31.

129. Valens, *Anthologies*, 27–34.

houses are angular. Succedent houses rise toward the angular houses and are increasing in prominence. Here, planetary forces are prominent, but not as prominent as those occupying angular houses. The second, fifth, eighth, and eleventh houses are succedent. Cadent houses follow the angular houses and are diminishing in prominence. Here, planetary forces are the least prominent. The third, sixth, ninth, and twelfth houses are cadent.

Each classical planet has an affinity for one particular house, where it is said to have its *joy* (Figure 7.2). When rejoicing, planetary forces are more benefic.[130] A brief description of each house is as follows:

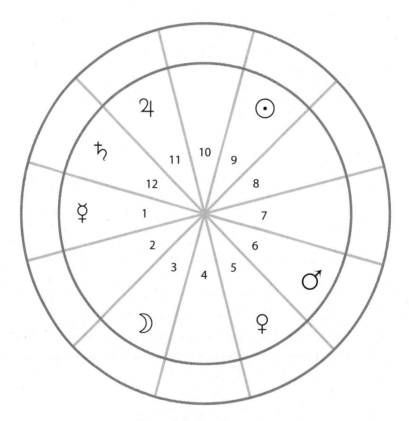

Figure 7.2. Planetary joys

---

130. Brennan, *Hellenistic Astrology,* 336–40.

Ascendant or Hour-Marker

The first house signifies who we are. This includes our physical appearance, temperament, and overall approach to life. Mercury rejoices here.

Gate of Hades

The second house signifies what we have. This includes our money, possessions, and what we value.

Goddess

The third house signifies our local community. This includes our siblings, compulsory education, and local or short-term travel. The Moon rejoices here.

Subterraneous

The fourth house signifies our origins. This includes our parents, domestic matters, and private lives.

Good Fortune

The fifth house signifies bodily delights. This includes our children, pleasurable activities, and creative pursuits. Venus rejoices here.

Bad Fortune

The sixth house signifies bodily afflictions. This includes health problems (e.g., illness, injury …), general labor, and subordinates. Mars rejoices here.

Descendant

The seventh house signifies who we are with. This includes our spouse, close friends, and other significant relationships.

Inactive Place or Idle Place

The eighth house signifies what others have. This includes death, inheritances, and the resources of others.

God

The ninth house signifies beyond our local community. This includes philosophical and spiritual matters, postsecondary education, and foreign or long-term travel. The Sun rejoices here.

Midheaven

The tenth house signifies what we do. This includes our career, social status, and public lives.

Good Daimōn

The eleventh house signifies mental and spiritual delights. This includes our friends, large groups, and our hopes and wishes. Jupiter rejoices here.

Bad Daimōn

The twelfth house signifies mental and spiritual afflictions. This includes our enemies, suffering, and isolation. Saturn rejoices here.

To make a diagram for your notes, feel free to copy the zodiac wheel shown in Figure 7.2 and write the relevant significations inside each house.

Cardinal Points

Astrological charts contain four cardinal points (Figure 7.3). They are the ascendant (Asc), descendant (Dsc), *medium coeli* (MC), and *imum coeli* (IC).

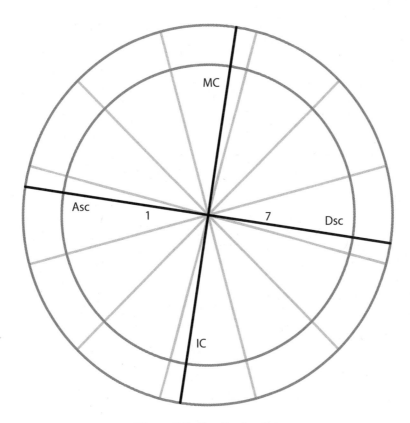

Figure 7.3. Cardinal points

In the Greco-Roman model, these points denote different sites in the local sky.[131],[132] Planets conjunct the cardinal points may also play more prominent roles in our lives. A brief description of each cardinal point is as follows.

Ascendant (Asc)

The ascendant (Asc) denotes the local eastern horizon. Planets conjunct the natal Asc are especially prominent in an individual, and it has long been considered an auspicious placement. The Asc dictates the first whole sign house.

---

131. Dorotheus, *Carmen Astrologicum*, 164, 224–31.

132. Valens, *Anthologies*, 97.

Descendant (Dsc)

The descendant (Dsc) denotes the local western horizon. It is located in the seventh whole sign house, opposite the Asc.

Medium Coeli (MC)

The *medium coeli* (MC) denotes the *middle sky* where the ecliptic intersects with the local meridian. Planets conjunct the natal MC are also prominent in an individual, and it has long been considered an auspicious placement, though not as auspicious as conjunct the Asc.

The MC is typically located in the tenth whole sign house. If your MC is located elsewhere, it imports tenth house significations into that house.

Imum Coeli (IC)

The *imum coeli* (IC) denotes the *bottom sky* opposite the MC. It is typically located in the fourth whole sign house. If your IC is located elsewhere, it imports fourth house significations into that house.

Example Delineations

The locales of the planets in particular signs and houses make our natal charts, and by extension us, unique. Five examples of how to apply the above information to interpret a natal chart are given below. Each placement is real—they are from the charts of five different people.

The Moon in Taurus in the Good Daimōn

The unconscious mind and instincts (the Moon) are modulated by enduring (Taurus) energy, making stability and long-term prosperity important foundational priorities of this individual. Since this manifests in this individual's mental and spiritual delights (eleventh house), belonging to a large group provides a sense of security and stability. In real life, this individual takes pride in her Cuban heritage. She credits the Cuban American community at large with providing the solid foundation that set her up for success later in life. She now serves as a role model for younger Cuban Americans.

Mercury in Pisces in the Descendant

Thinking and communication (Mercury) are modulated by dissolutive (Pisces) energy, predisposing this individual toward nonlinear thinking, keen intuition, and a vivid imagination. Since this manifests in his partnerships (seventh house), conversing about spirituality and other abstract topics are a key component of his significant relationships. Since the seventh house is angular, his need to converse with his closest companions is very noticeable. In real life, this individual sometimes struggles to communicate, but he shares a deep (and immediately obvious) bond with his wife and close friends.

Venus in Cancer in Good Fortune

Feelings and social relations (Venus) are modulated by nurturing (Cancer) energy, predisposing this individual to connect with others on an emotional level. Since this manifests in her bodily delights (fifth house), she takes pleasure in caring for others and creative pursuits. Although Venus is under the beams, the planet is in its joy and her natal chart is a night chart, producing largely benefic effects. In real life, this individual is a devoted wife and mother. Her unmarried twin sister (who has the same placement) is a beloved and highly acclaimed children's art teacher.

The Sun in Leo in Goddess

The conscious mind and ego (the Sun) are modulated by radiant (Leo) energy, making nobility and "shining light" on matters important personal priorities of this individual. Since this manifests in his interactions with the local community (third house), being a model citizen constitutes a large part of his personal identity. Further, his natal Sun is conjunct the IC, suggesting that childhood experiences in his local community were more influential in shaping his character than parents or other fourth-house influences. In real life, this individual was heavily involved in Boy Scouts throughout his formative years. When reflecting on his successful career, he praised the Boy Scouts for molding his character and facilitating his personal and professional success.

Mars in Libra in the Bad Daimōn

Raw energy and physical power (Mars) are modulated by balancing (Libra) energy, predisposing this individual to set personal needs aside to maintain social balance. Since this manifests in her mental and spiritual afflictions (twelfth house), she struggles to advocate for herself while maintaining that balance. Since Mars is retrograde and her natal chart is a day chart, the malefic effects of Mars are amplified. In real life, repressed anger and unresolved conflicts cause this individual much distress. However, professional involvement in dance provides an effective outlet to blow off steam and improve self-assertiveness.

Before undertaking further planetary work, here are some things to consider:

- Meditate on each personal planet's domicile, exaltation, and fall signs. How might these signs lead to stronger or weaker expression?
- Are any additional signs awkward for particular planets? For example, the Moon in Capricorn might be uncomfortable because the Moon is receptive, acquiescent, and mutable, whereas Capricorn is more unwavering, conservative, and cautious.
- Meditate on how each personal planet might manifest in the different houses.
- Reflect on the house each personal planet rejoices in. Why might these particular locales facilitate more benefic planetary expression?
- Meditate on how each personal planet might manifest when conjunct the cardinal points.

Planetary Ingression

The natal chart is a snapshot of the heavens at the moment of birth. Since the planets are in continuous motion, their locales change over time. Occasionally a planet may ingress (enter) into a new sign. The personal planets have shorter orbital periods than the *social* planets (Jupiter and Saturn), thus they ingress more frequently.

In the whole sign system, when a planet enters a new sign it also enters a new house. Thus, in addition to being modulated by a new sign, the planet now affects a different area of life. Some magicians may notice the shift in energy accompanying an ingression.

Chapter 7
Homework

After taking notes on the chapter, magical practice should be commenced for thirty minutes each day for a minimum of one month. Perform the assignments in the order presented. Remember to document your efforts in your magical diary.

- ☐ Meditate on the signs your personal planets reside in for a minimum of ten minutes each day. How do the signs modulate these planetary forces?

- ☐ Examine your natal chart to determine what house, in addition to what sign, each personal planet resides in. How do the planetary forces manifest in these specific areas of your life? Are any planets rejoicing or near a cardinal point? We will revisit the personal planets in chapter 11.

- ☐ Taking into account natal sign, house, and other factors (e.g., sect, retrograde motion, solar conjunctions …), delineate how each personal planet manifests in your life.

- ☐ Visit a reputable website to determine the current signs of the personal planets. In these signs, is manifestation strong, weak, or somewhere in between? Are there any recent or upcoming ingressions?

Chapter 7 Resources

AstroSeek. "Today's Current Planets." https://horoscopes.astro-seek.com /current-planets-astrology-transits-planetary-positions.

CHAPTER 8
Planetary Invoking, Banishing, and Balancing

So far, we have explored the personal planets, internalized them, and determined how they affect our lives. We have also interacted with them magically. Before we proceed to the social planets, we will practice invoking and banishing the planetary forces we have worked with thus far via the Lesser and Greater Rituals of the Hexagram.

The Golden Dawn's Supreme Ritual of the Hexagram may be found in the *R. R. et A. C.*'s "Ritual Document C," originally written in the 1890s. As time passed, numerous variations and permutations of this ritual evolved. Two of the most common variants practiced today are the Lesser Ritual of the Hexagram and the Greater Ritual of the Hexagram.

Lesser Ritual of the Hexagram

The Lesser Ritual of the Hexagram (LRH) is a staple in Western esotericism. Many ceremonial magicians perform a banishing LRH to clear their working area of unwanted vibrations from above the sublunar realm. The invoking LRH is a useful prelude to other magical work—it fills the working area with specific planetary vibrations and invokes divine light. You may think of these rituals as the magical equivalents of cleaning or decorating your home before guests come over.

If you regularly perform the Lesser Banishing Ritual of the Pentagram (LBRP), you may do so before the LRH—it clears your working area of any psychological and environmental junk in the sublunar realm.

Many variations of the LRH exist today, and magicians from diverse backgrounds and preparations have modified it to their liking. The overall format can be subdivided into three sections, discussed sequentially below: the Qabalistic Cross, Analysis of the Keyword, and hexagram drawing.

Qabalistic Cross

The magician creates a Tree of Life within the body by performing a modified Sign of the Cross while saying a modified version of the last lines of the Lord's Prayer.[133] It may be embellished with visualizations, such as a glowing cross superimposed on the body. The word *'Amen* (Heb. So be it!) is an acronym of *'El Melek Ne'eman* (God, Faithful King) and has a rich history.[134]

Analysis of the Keyword

The magician invokes divine power through *I. N. R. I.*, an acronym for the Latin *IESUS NAZARENUS REX IUDÆORUM* (Jesus the Nazarene, King of the Jews). In addition to the Latin, it was also inscribed in Greek and Hebrew on Jesus's cross.[135] Transliterating *I. N. R. I.* into Hebrew produces the letters *Yod* (י), *Nun* (נ), *Resh* (ר), and *Yod* (י). In many ceremonial traditions, these letters have distinct astrological meanings.[136] *Yod* corresponds to the sign of Virgo and represents the fertile energy of nature. *Nun* corresponds to the sign of Scorpio and represents the transformative energy of death. *Resh* corresponds to the Sun and represents rebirth and renewal of life. Thus, *I. N. R. I.* represents the cycling of energy from fertile nature to transformation and death, to rebirth and renewal, and back to fertile nature.

The letters *I. N. R. I.* also correspond to certain Egyptian deities via their astrological associations. Virgo alludes to Isis, the wife of Osiris and goddess of fertility and nature.[137] Scorpio alludes to Apophis, the giant serpent who tried to devour the Sun.[138] Set, the god of destruction and darkness, once assumed his form in a conflict with Ra.[139]

---

133. "The Lord's Prayer," *The Jewish Encyclopedia* 8, 183–84.

134. "Amen," *The Jewish Encyclopedia* 1, 491–92.

135. John 19:19–20 KJV 1611.

136. Aleister Crowley, *777 Revised*, 2–3.

137. Lewis Spence, *Ancient Egyptian Myths and Legends* (Dover Publications, 1990), 80–84.

138. Spence, *Myths and Legends*, 130–35.

139. Spence, *Myths and Legends*, 65–66, 99–103.

Set was later identified with the Greek Typhon. Sol alludes to Osiris, the god of death and resurrection.[140] After Set killed and dismembered Osiris, Isis collected the pieces of his body to resurrect him. Many deities who undergo the death-rebirth process are likened to the Sun, which rises, sets, and then rises again.

Isis, Apophis, and Osiris are also associated with certain ceremonial gestures (Figure 8.1). It is best to commit them to memory.

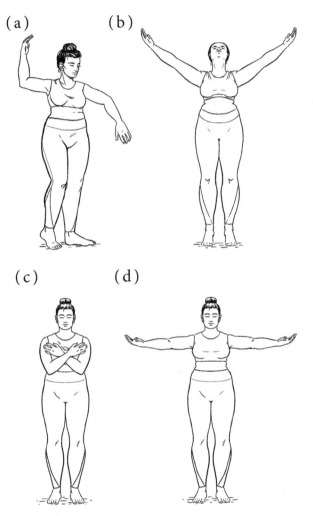

(a)   (b)

(c)   (d)

Figure 8.1. Hexagram ritual gestures

---

140. Spence, *Myths and Legends*, 63–80.

Table 8.2. Elemental hexagrams			
Invoking			
Fire	Earth	Air	Water

START

Table 8.2. Elemental hexagrams

	Banishing			
	Fire	Earth	Air	Water
☽				
☿				
♀				
☉		See Figure 5.2		
♂				

In Figure 8.1, each Egyptian deity is associated with one or more gestures. They are: (a) The Sign of Osiris Slain, (b) L – The Sign of the Mourning of Isis, (c) V – The Sign of Apophis and Typhon, and (d) X – The Sign of Osiris Risen. The gestures allude to different configurations on the Tree of Life.

The first letters of the names Isis, Apophis, and Osiris may be combined to form the acronym IAO (Gk. ΙΑΩ), a Greek divine name used in place of *YHWH* by some Jews during the Second Temple period.[141] It may be vibrated by intoning the individual letters (IPA: /i.ɑ.oʊ/). The Latin word for light is *LUX* (/luːks/).

Hexagram Drawing

The magician invokes or banishes planetary forces via drawing particular elemental hexagrams (Figure 8.2) in each cardinal direction while vibrating ARARITA, an acronym first seen in chapter 2.

Draw the invoking or banishing elemental hexagrams of each personal planet with the planetary tools you acquired in previous chapters or your index finger in the numbered sequence shown. You may visualize the hexagram shapes in an appropriate planetary color. Vibrate *ARARITA* as you draw. In the LRH, the additional step of drawing a planetary astronomical symbol while vibrating a divine name is omitted.

Elemental magic practitioners will immediately notice the LRH hexagrams are not drawn in their typical cardinal directions—this is because you are working with macrocosmic (planetary) forces, not microcosmic (elemental) ones. Here, the elemental hexagrams mirror the relative positions of the cardinal signs of the zodiac. You may think of yourself as standing in the center of the zodiac wheel with Aries to your east, Capricorn to your south, Libra to your west, and Cancer to your north.

Procedure: Lesser Ritual of the Hexagram

A modified version of the banishing ritual presented in Crowley's *Liber O* is as follows.[142] If you do not have a magical tool, use your index finger to draw the cross and hexagrams instead. Pronunciation is conveyed in the International Phonetic Alphabet and is based on current understanding of Biblical Hebrew phonology, as covered in the *Encyclopedia of Hebrew Language and Linguistics, Vol. 3.*

---

141. Frank Shaw, *The Earliest Non-Mystical Jewish Use of Iaω* (Peeters, 2014).

142. Crowley, *Magick: Liber ABA*, 613–26.

Note that the Supreme Ritual of the Hexagram includes the Qabalistic Cross at the beginning, whereas Crowley's LRH replaces it with an Analysis of the Keyword. Here, the Qabalistic Cross has been included. If you performed the LBRP beforehand you may omit the Qabalistic Cross here, since it is performed at the end of the LBRP. Vibration of IAO and LUX have also been included. In the *Liber O* LRH, only ARARITA is vibrated.

Qabalistic Cross

Stand and face east. If you have a magical tool, hold it in your right hand.

1. Touch your magical tool (or index finger) to your head and say ʾAta (Heb. / ʔaˈtɔː/; you are).
2. Touch it to your chest and say *Malkut* (/malˈkuːt̪/; kingdom).
3. Touch it to your right shoulder and say *Ugebura* (/u.gɛ̆.buːˈrɔː/; and strength/ might).
4. Touch it to your left shoulder and say *Ugedula* (/u.gɛ̆.d̪uːˈlɔː/; and greatness).
5. Clasp your hands in front of you and say *Le ʿolam* (/lɛ̆.ʕoˈlɔːm/; forever).
6. Point your magical tool up and say ʾAmen (/ʔɔːˈmen̪/; So be it!).

Analysis of the Keyword

Still facing east, hold your magical tool upright in front of your chest. You may drop your left arm to your side.

1. Say:

    I. N. R. I.

    Vibrate:

    Yod, Nun, Resh, Yod.

    Say:

    Virgo, Isis, Mighty Mother.

    Scorpio, Apophis, Destroyer.

    Sol, Osiris, Slain and Risen.

    Isis, Apophis, Osiris.

Vibrate:

IAO.

2. Make the Sign of Osiris Slain and say *The Sign of Osiris Slain.*
3. Make L—The Sign of the Mourning of Isis and say *The Sign of the Mourning of Isis.*
4. Make V—The Sign of Typhon and Apophis and say *The Sign of Apophis and Typhon.*
5. Make X—The Sign of Osiris Risen and say *The Sign of Osiris Risen.*
6. Make the L V X signs again while saying *L V X.*
7. Outstretch your arms in the shape of a cross and visualize yourself saturated with divine light.

Vibrate:

LUX.

Say:

The Light of the Cross.

Hexagram Drawing

Still facing east, take a few steps forward. You will be drawing a circle of divine light punctuated by hexagrams in each cardinal direction.

1. Draw a banishing fire hexagram in front of you while vibrating *ARARITA.*
2. Draw a quarter circle toward the south.
3. Face south. Draw a banishing earth hexagram in the south while vibrating *ARARITA.*
4. Draw a quarter circle toward the west.
5. Face west. Draw a banishing air hexagram in the west while vibrating *ARARITA.*
6. Draw a quarter circle toward the north.
7. Face north. Draw a banishing water hexagram in the north while vibrating *ARARITA.*
8. Draw a quarter circle back to the east to complete it.

Analysis of the Keyword

Perform the Analysis of the Keyword one more time.

Additional Notes and Variations

The invoking LRH is performed using the procedure above, but invoking elemental hexagrams are drawn instead of banishing elemental hexagrams. Even though banishing is typically performed in a counterclockwise direction, the banishing form of the LRH has you move clockwise because you are invoking divine light via Analysis of the Keyword.

Feel free to modify the rite to your liking. Many modern variants give visualization procedures, since in the Supreme Ritual of the Hexagram and LRH none are given.

To invoke or banish a specific planetary force, you may use the planetary tools you acquired in previous chapters. If you are an enthusiast of the planetary metals, holding a chunk of the appropriate metal in your hand as a tool is another option.

Individual invocation experiences vary, but they are generally consistent with the nature of each planet. Effects tend to be similar (but more subtle) than those produced by the GRH. When performing banishing rites in general, you typically don't feel anything, and this rite is no exception.

Greater Ritual of the Hexagram

The Greater Ritual of the Hexagram (GRH) is also commonly practiced in Western esotericism. Many ceremonial magicians perform the banishing GRH to rid their working area of unwanted planetary vibrations and the invoking GRH to fill it with specific ones. You may think of them as the magical equivalents of opening the front door of your home to invite guests in or see them out.

Structure

The GRH as presented in Crowley's *Liber O* does not come with cookbook-style instructions like the LRH.[143] However, it specifies only the earth hexagrams are used. In Hermetic practice, the earth element is a combination of the other elements and gives them a solid, concrete form.[144] After drawing the earth hexagram shape while vibrating *ARARITA*, the planet's astronomical symbol is drawn in the center of the hexagram

---

143. Crowley, *Magick: Liber ABA*, 613–26.

144. Bardon, *Magical Evocation*, 29.

while vibrating the appropriate Qabalistic sphere's divine name. These should seem familiar—they're the planetary hexagrams you drew in previous chapters!

Procedure: Greater Ritual of the Hexagram

Although many variants exist, most magicians I know perform the GRH using the LRH protocol, but with only earth hexagrams. The banishing GRH performed in this way is as follows. If you do not have a magical tool, use your index finger to draw the cross and hexagrams instead.

Qabalistic Cross
Perform the Qabalistic Cross as in the LRH procedure above.

Analysis of the Keyword
Perform the Analysis of the Keyword as in the LRH procedure above.

Drawing Hexagrams
Still facing east, take a few steps forward. You will again draw a circle of divine light punctuated by hexagrams in each cardinal direction.

1. Draw a banishing earth hexagram in front of you while vibrating *ARARITA [DIVINE NAME]*.
2. Draw a quarter circle toward the south.
3. Face south. Draw a banishing earth hexagram in the south while vibrating *ARARITA [DIVINE NAME]*.
4. Draw a quarter circle toward the west.
5. Face west. Draw a banishing earth hexagram in the west while vibrating *ARARITA [DIVINE NAME]*.
6. Draw a quarter circle toward the north.
7. Face north. Draw a banishing earth hexagram in the north while vibrating *ARARITA [DIVINE NAME]*.
8. Draw a quarter circle back to the east to complete it.

Analysis of the Keyword
Perform the Analysis of the Keyword one more time.

Additional Notes

The invoking GRH may be performed using the procedure above, but invoking earth hexagrams are drawn instead of banishing earth hexagrams.

Individual invocation experiences are generally consistent with the nature of each planet. For many magicians, the effects of the GRH are more noticeable than the LRH.

As an example, for the Moon, I typically sense the environment is more ethereal and impressionable in nature. For Mercury, the environment is more dynamic, and I commonly experience racing thoughts. For Venus, the environment typically evokes feelings of love and happiness. For the Sun, I typically sense the environment is cleaner and more radiant. I also commonly experience an increase in body temperature. For Mars, the atmosphere sometimes feels restless but at other times is like the calm before the storm. For Jupiter, the atmosphere usually feels larger and loftier. For Saturn, the atmosphere is consistently thicker and heavier. Everything also seems to move more slowly.

Again, when performing banishing rites in general, you typically don't feel anything; this rite is no exception.

Chapter 8
Homework

After taking notes on the chapter, magical practice should be commenced for thirty minutes each day for a minimum of one month. Perform the assignments in the order presented. Remember to document your efforts in your magical diary.

- ☐ Investigate the effects of the elemental hexagrams for each personal planet. To accomplish this, draw one and passively observe the effect on yourself and the immediate environment. After a few minutes, record any observations, thoughts, feelings, and other details you deem important in your magical diary. Feel free to draw a banishing hexagram after an invoking hexagram to cancel it out.
- ☐ Perform the banishing and invoking forms of the LRH for each personal planet. You may use the planetary tools you acquired in previous chapters. Feel free to perform a banishing ritual after an invoking ritual to cancel it out.
- ☐ Perform the banishing and invoking forms of the GRH for each personal planet. You may use the planetary tools you acquired in previous chapters. Feel free to perform a banishing ritual after an invoking ritual to cancel it out.

Chapter 8 Resources

Crowley, Aleister. *Magick: Liber ABA, Book 4*. 2nd ed. Edited by Hymanaeus Beta. Weiser Books, 1997, 613–26.

CHAPTER 9
Jupiter Protects

So far, we've explored the personal planets, internalized them, and determined how they impact our lives. We have also interacted with them magically. Now we will continue to Jupiter, which provides the aspiration necessary to work with the classical planets. Common Jupiter symbols are shown in Figure 9.1. They are useful focal points in meditation and magical practice.

(a) (b)

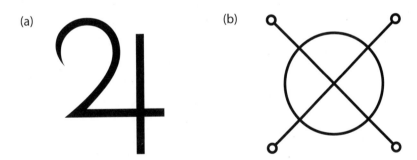

Figure 9.1. The (a) astronomical symbol and (b) planetary seal of Jupiter

The Western View of Jupiter

In the Greco-Roman model Jupiter resides between Mars and Saturn.[145] This locale makes Jupiter primarily hot, secondarily wet, and capable of producing fertilizing winds.

---

145. Ptolemy, *Tetrabiblos*, 34–43, 78–81, 88–89.

Thus, Jupiter is benefic, masculine, and diurnal. Jupiter's fertile nature is further reflected in the signs it rules, Pisces and Sagittarius. Pisces is trine (120°) to Cancer (ruled by the Moon), and Sagittarius is trine to Leo (ruled by the Sun). When planets are trine, their interaction is harmonious.[146] Jupiter is exalted in Cancer and in its fall is in Capricorn.

In the Hermetic model Jupiter affects the lawfulness on Earth.[147] It is also responsible for humanity's morality and spiritual growth. According to Bardon, denizens of Jupiter may be evoked in a blue light.[148] This color of light emulates the Jupiter zone's vibrations, so is conducive to manifesting Jupiterian beings.

Gk. *Zeus* (Ζεύς); Heb. *Ṣedeq* (צדק); Lat. *Iuppiter*; Ouranian Barbaric *GEZMEQ*

The Jupiter Archetype

Jupiter is our integrator. It represents our philosophical matrix, which manifests in our ability to internalize abstract concepts. It also has ties to our sense of generosity. Jupiter oversees government and religious institutions, two important integrators. Exoterically, it is the king who magnanimously governs and enriches his kingdom. Esoterically, it is the Divine King who oversees law and order in the terrestrial and celestial realms. Deities traditionally associated with Jupiter include Amun-Ra (Egyptian), Zeus (Greek), and Jupiter (Roman). Keywords relevant to Jupiter are as follows:

Expansion

Our philosophical matrix is an important integrator. A solid integrator provides a sense of inclusion, optimism, and opportunity. An unstable integrator may result in narrow-mindedness or an inability to see the big picture. It may also lead to chronic feelings of greed or stagnation.

Abstract Mind

The mental processes underlying the abstract mind allow us to make connections to the world at large. They also influence our sense of power.[149] The Jupiterian force may manifest through postsecondary education, the legal process, or foreign travel.

---

146. Ptolemy, *Tetrabiblos*, 72–73.

147. Bardon, *Magical Evocation*, 292.

148. Bardon, *Magical Evocation*, 128.

149. Pamela K. Smith, Daniël H. J. Wigboldus, and Ap Dijksterhuis, "Abstract Thinking Increases One's Sense of Power," *Journal of Experimental Social Psychology* 44, no. 2 (2008): 378–85.

Royalty

Throughout history, royals have served as heads of state and oversee the well-being of their kingdom. Many have ties to religious institutions in offices that historically held administrative power. Likewise, in many paradigms Jupiter is linked with chief deities who serve as king of the gods.

Inclusion

Jupiter grants the ability to say *yes*. This may positively manifest as fulfilling civic or religious duties, embracing diversity, and "broadening your horizons." This may negatively manifest as too much of a good thing or being so open-minded that your brains fall out.

Wealth

Wealth is more than an abundance of assets. It provides the power and security to do what you want when you want. In many cultures generosity is associated with wealth—in times of crisis wealthy citizens would assist the government in helping the less fortunate.[150]

Luck

The ancient Greeks viewed *tychē* (Gk. τύχη; luck) as a form of chance that can happen to people capable of making decisions.[151] It may yield either benefic or malefic results.

Western Jupiter Magic

Jupiter has a bright yellow-brown appearance in the sky, which may be why the ancients linked it with benefic significations.[152] In astrology, Jupiter represents our generosity and tolerance. It is also generally associated with our wealth, luck, and opportunity. In many Western esoteric traditions Jupiter is associated with protective, legal, religious, amplification, luck, and wealth magic. It is also generally associated with political and aspirational works.

Jupiter's day is Thursday (Lat. *dies Iovis*). The word *Thursday* is derived from the Old English *Þunresdæg* (Thunor's Day). The connection between the classical planet and day of the week is more obvious in languages such as Spanish (*jueves*) and French

---

150. Moonsil Lee Kim, "Food Distribution for the People: Welfare, Food, and Feasts in Qin/Han China and in Rome," in *Rulers and Ruled in Ancient Greece, Rome, and China*, eds. Hans Beck and Griet Vankeerberghen (Cambridge University Press, 2021), 225–68.

151. Aristotle, *Physics*, trans. C. D. C. Reeve (Hackett Publishing Company, 2018), 28–31.

152. Brennan, *Hellenistic Astrology*, 186.

(*jeudi*). Jupiter's alchemical metal is tin. Perhaps this is due to the tin cry—bending a bar of room temperature tin produces a crackling sound reminiscent of thunder. Jupiterian deities often rule over the sky and thunder.

In ceremonial traditions Jupiter is associated with *Ḥesed* (Heb. Love or Mercy), the fourth sphere of the Qabala.[153] This mercy yields the magnanimity required to manifest physical reality. Psychologically, this sphere represents personal love and awareness. Correspondences of *Ḥesed* often relate to mercy and righteousness. Jupiter is also associated with *Kaf*, the path connecting *Ḥesed* and *Neṣaḥ* (Victory). It connects personal love and awareness to our inner feelings. In ancient script the letter *kaf* resembles an open human palm, the structure capable of giving and receiving wealth. Correspondences of *Kaf* often relate to royalty and wealth. The top-down Hebrew hierarchy for Jupiter is shown in Table 9.1.

Table 9.1. The Jupiter Ceremonial Hierarchy		
Qabalistic World	**Level**	**Name**
'Aṣilut	Divine name	*'Abà, 'El 'Ab*
Beri'a	Archangel	*Ṣadqi'el*
Yeṣira	Intelligence Spirit	*Yohfi'el* *Hismàel*
'Asiya	Magical tool	Scepter

The information in Table 9.1 is adapted from Crowley's "777 Revised." See Appendix A for Hebrew spelling, pronunciation, etymologies, and more. *'El* is *God* in *Ḥesed*. In older texts, *Barak'el* is often attributed instead of *Ṣadqi'el*.[154] The Hebrew spelling yielding the above Romanization of *Yohfi'el* is from Agrippa. The wand, scepter, and crook are associated with *Ḥesed*.

Fundamentals: Planetary Charity

Planetary charity has origins in Indian astrology. Donating material goods, time, or money serves to mitigate the potential negative effects of weak or poorly placed planets in the natal chart. The key factors that make planetary charity work are an intent to honor the planet, making a donation relevant to the planet, donating at a time auspicious

153. Crowley, "777 Revised," 2–3, 5.

154. Kaplan, *Sefer Yetzirah*, 168.

to the planet, and donating graciously without expecting anything in return. Regarding intent, it is better to not perform planetary charity at all rather than vowing to do so and then not following through. Many magicians I know have stories of vowing to honor a planet, failing to do so, and then experiencing unfortunate events shortly thereafter. The vast majority of said unfortunate events blatantly fell under the planet's domain, and some even occurred during the planetary day or hour!

You have already been practicing a "Western" version of planetary charity during your monasticisms. If you have been performing them diligently, this is why your life is improving in areas governed by particular planets. Your Westernized charity may be as simple as reciting an Orphic Hymn before making an online donation at an auspicious time, or as elaborate as an extensive ritual honoring the planet before leaving home to embark on a volunteer activity. Here's anexample of a Western planetary charity for Jupiter:

> *On a Thursday shortly after sunrise, I declare it is my will to honor Jupiter through planetary charity—I vow to make a monetary donation to a particular Jupiter-related organization for four consecutive Thursdays. Each Thursday, just after sunrise, I read aloud the Orphic Hymn to Jupiter and then make an online donation to this organization immediately after. The value of the monetary donation is always in a multiple of four. I donate on the Thursday I make the vow and on the following three Thursdays.*

Since Jupiter rules over large institutions (e.g., governments, organized religions …), donating to a legal fund or religious establishment are reasonable options. Jupiter also rules over postsecondary education, so donating to a college or university is another possibility.

You may use the above example as a general template for your own planetary charity. If you are wondering why the vow and donations are performed shortly after sunrise, planetary hours will be discussed in chapter 10. The Orphic Hymns are available online at the Sacred Texts website, and the original Greek is available at the Hellenic-Gods website.

Jupiter in Chaos Magic

Jupiter may be integrated into magical practice in numerous ways. Various deities, egregores, or pop culture characters associated with Jupiter may be invoked or evoked.

Divination may be practiced via astrologically analyzing Jupiter or through methods that incorporate wealth (e.g., tossing coins, gemstone lithomancy …). Magical items associated with Jupiter may be enchanted for purposes consistent with its nature. All good luck charms also fall under this planet's domain. Illumination rites aimed at gaining insight into personal love and awareness or the nature of wealth may also be performed.

Jupiter is projective, expansive, noble, regal, tolerant, and inclusive. It is also very generous and jolly. These characteristics have been incorporated into the rites, which are intentionally cheerful, integrative, and involve exploratory work. Some also use Jupiter's ceremonial planetary hexagrams (Table 9.2). It is best to commit them to memory.

Table 9.2. Jupiter Invoking Hexagrams			
Fire	**Earth**	**Air**	**Water**

Table 9.2. Jupiter Banishing Hexagrams			
Fire	**Earth**	**Air**	**Water**

Draw the planetary hexagrams with your magical tool or index finger in the numbered sequence shown. To draw the earth hexagrams used in the Jupiter GRH, visualize the hexagram shape in blue and vibrate *ARARITA* as you draw, and then visualize the Jupiter astronomical symbol in blue and vibrate *'El* as you draw.

Active Work
Jupiter Attunement

Sit down in a fine chair within your home, office, or other personal space. Your posture should mimic a monarch on a throne. Gaze around as you survey your kingdom, so to speak. Observe your surroundings for no less than fifteen minutes. As you gaze, feel the lightness of the atmosphere on your skin. Feel the expansiveness of your domain and how unfettered you are. Resonate with this regal, buoyant expansiveness. Observe the expansiveness with all five of your senses, as well as astrally. As time passes, the expansiveness grows stronger. Slowly adjust the rhythm of your body to match the vibrations underlying this expansiveness. Feel them uplifting, broadening, and amplifying you.

> June 15, 2022. *Jupiter Attunement.* During the attunement, the tendency to think beyond myself (e.g., about general household maintenance, homeowner association concerns, ways to enrich my cats …) was a valuable springboard to attuning with the Jupiterian force.

Jupiter Greeting Rite

While not necessary, if Jupiter is visible in the sky, you may face its general direction and treat it as metaphysical east. Jupiter in Pisces, Sagittarius, or Cancer are preferable but not required.

Materials

- No materials are required.
- If you already have a Jupiter tool, you may ask the planetary spirit to bless it instead. Recall that Jupiter's traditional ceremonial tool is the scepter, and its alchemical metal is tin.

- Optional: Burning incense associated with Jupiter (such as saffron, amber, or lignum aloes)—incenses traditionally associated with Jupiter smell rich and pleasant.[155,156,157]
- Optional: Jupiter-related music (such as Holst's "Jupiter, the Bringer of Jollity" from *The Planets*, *Op. 32* or Beethoven's "Ode to Joy" from *Symphony No. 9 in D minor, Op. 125*)

Statement of Intent

It is my will to access the Jupiterian force.

Procedure

On a Thursday during the daytime, attune with Jupiter.

When ready, perform an invoking Jupiter GRH. Visualize a royal blue light emanating down from the heavens that passes through your hexagrams and envelops you. Knock in the center of your circle four times, as if you are knocking on a door. Place your open palms toward the sky and say:

XIQUAL GEZMEQ!
Come thundering Zeus, monarch of the sky!
Come guardian Iuppiter, with your royal scepter!
Come Ṣedeq, the righteous,
Kokav Baʿal, lordly star!
In the divine names of ʾAbaʾ and ʾEl ʾAb I greet you!
Come Ṣadqiʾel, Archangel of Jupiter,
and bless me with mercy and generosity!

---

155. Bardon, *Magical Evocation*, 143.

156. Aleister Crowley, "777 Revised," 13.

157. Greer and Warnock, *Picatrix*, 141.

Grant me access to the Jupiterian force
so I may protect those less fortunate!

Close your eyes and inhale the royal blue light enveloping you, until it fills your entire body. Take note of any religious inspiration or philosophical insights you receive.

When ready, use your index finger to draw a triangle on the ground in the center of your circle. Visualize it in blue. Place your open palms slightly outside the triangle and proceed to evoke the planetary intelligence. Say:

Yohfi'el, Intelligence of Jupiter,
in the name of Ṣadqi'el I evoke you!
Grant me access to the Jupiterian force
so I may harness it for the Great Work of Magic!

If you do not sense its presence, continue visualizing the royal blue light and repeat the above until you do.

After you sense the planetary intelligence's presence, proceed to evoke the planetary spirit. With open palms still slightly outside the triangle, continue:

Hisma'el, Spirit of Jupiter,
in the name of Yohfi'el I evoke you!
Aid my efforts to obtain a Jupiter tool
that will assist me in the Great Work of Magic!

If you do not sense its presence, continue visualizing the royal blue light and repeat the above until you do. After you are finished communicating with them, thank them and send them on their way.

Banishing

Perform a banishing Jupiter GRH and then banish with laughter.

> June 16, 2022. *Jupiter Greeting Rite.* Excluding the attunement, the rite took about 20 minutes to perform. On occasion I felt peculiar chills shoot through me—they immediately reminded me of lightning strikes. Images of vast, flashing thunderclouds stayed in the background of my conscious mind throughout the rite. I also eventually felt physically, astrally, and mentally larger and loftier. At one point it seemed like I would float away at any moment! Like Jupiter, the intelligence and spirit are grand, expansive, and regal. When concluding the rite, I almost felt too "lofty" to recall *very* basic banishing skills.
>
> August 18, 2022. *Addendum.* My Jupiter tool was gifted to me at my mundane job. When Jupiter was culminating, my colleague H. gave me an amethyst crystal shaped like a scepter. Upon touching it, I immediately sensed the planetary spirit. In many paradigms, amethyst is associated with Jupiter.[158,159] I was almost too stunned to thank H.!

Jupiter Guided Meditation

Find a warm, quiet place and sit in a comfortable position. Close your eyes. Take a deep breath and center yourself. With each breath, you will feel calmer and more relaxed. Feel the tension in your toes. As you exhale, the tension dissipates until your toes are completely relaxed. This feeling of relaxation grows, spreading through your feet into your ankles. They are now completely relaxed. It continues, trav-

---

158. Crowley, "777 Revised," 10.

159. Grimassi, *Encyclopedia of Wicca & Witchcraft*, 396.

elling up your legs and into your knees, which are now completely relaxed. Feel the lack of tension in your shins and calves. Any outside noises or distractions just serve to relax you further. Now your upper legs, hips, and waist are completely relaxed. As you continue to breathe, your abdominal region, chest, and back are completely relaxed. Your relaxation grows further, moving into your shoulders, and then down into your arms, elbows, hands, fingers, and fingertips. Your entire body below your neck is now completely relaxed. This feeling of relaxation grows, filling your neck and face. Feel your chin, jaw, nose, cheeks, eyes, eyelids, forehead, and ears relax. Finally, feel your scalp relax. Your entire body is now completely relaxed.

In your mind's eye, visualize Jupiter glowing above your head. It is about the size of a basketball and reflects a royal blue light. The light shines down, regally enveloping you as you continue breathing. Observe the light with all five of your senses. See its merry brightness, feel its warmth, smell it, and taste it. Does it emanate a sound? Jupiter emits radio waves that cannot be perceived by human ears. As you continue breathing, the royal blue light accumulates within you and around you, filling your body and field of vision completely. You draw an invoking Jupiter earth hexagram in front of you. As you trace the symbol of Jupiter while vibrating 'El in your astral voice, the light inside you regally glows.

The light in the surrounding environment slowly disperses, revealing a complex array of massive cyclones beneath your feet. White clouds with a tinge of brown swirl counterclockwise amidst a layer of icy blue, producing a hypnotic marbling effect. Mesmerized, you watch the grand dance of colors for a few more moments. Eventually, you realize you are hovering above Jupiter's North Pole. The blue light inside you expands, shielding you from the radiation of Jupiter's enormous magnetosphere.

As the blue light regally glows, feelings of cheer swell within you. Looking beyond Jupiter, you are able to identify some of its larger satellites. Io orbits closely. Its pale yellow and white surface is punctuated by smaller, darker-hued spots of green, brown, orange, and red. Io has many mountains and active volcanoes. Further out you see Europa. Its smooth, bright surface is white with yellow-brown splotches, and is intricately crisscrossed by numerous darker brown ridges. Current evidence suggests the presence of a liquid water ocean beneath Europa's surface. Further out you spot Ganymede, the largest satellite in our solar system. Its overall appearance resembles the Moon but with brown-hued undertones. Like the Moon, Ganymede has a surface that's a mosaic of geological areas of varying ages. Beyond Ganymede is Callisto. Callisto bears similarity to Ganymede in appearance but is completely plastered with cracks and craters. Current evidence suggests it is the oldest, most heavily impacted surface in our solar system.

Still hovering above Jupiter's North Pole, you feel as if you are in the center of a miniature solar system. While vast lightning storms illuminate Jupiter's upper atmosphere, numerous satellites merrily orbit about. For a few moments you remain completely still and silent, taking in the grandeur of it all. The blue light inside you expands even more, amplifying your feelings of cheer and warmth.

You turn your attention back to Jupiter, where a royal blue light now emanates from the array of cyclones. The light gathers above the array and eventually condenses into the likeness of a winged figure a few kilometers in diameter. After a few more moments pass, the winged figure unwaveringly moves toward you as if to greet you. As it approaches, you are able to make out the details of its rich robes and cloak amidst the blue light. Upon seeing the dagger in the winged figure's left hand, you realize you are being approached by Ṣadqi'el, archangel of Jupiter. The vibrations of love and mercy he emanates are on a grander scale than any you've previously experienced.

Ṣadqi'el gently grasps you in his large hands, pulling you in closer. He slowly ascends, steadily flying higher above Jupiter's North Pole. As you both come to a halt, more satellites come into view. After a few more moments pass, Ṣadqi'el says, "Just as Jupiter protects its satellites, you can protect those you love. *Yohfi'el*, Intelligence of Jupiter, I call you! In the name of *'El*, I command you reveal these individuals." While you are still in the archangel's hands, a complex satellite system materializes around you. Some satellites glow with lighter hues of blue light, while some glow with darker hues. Some are close, others are distant. Some are large. Some are small. Some are weathered. Some are not.

Ṣadqi'el continues, "Let me tell you a secret about the letter *kaf* (כ)." He smiles warmly and traces the letter above you with his dagger. "*Hisma'el*, Spirit of Jupiter, I call you! *Yohfi'el* and I command you reveal this secret." Royal blue light particles slowly condense above your head. As they merrily dart about, some meander toward your fingers and palms. Intrigued, you cup your hands to investigate them more closely. The particles react to this gesture and accumulate in your hands.

Ṣadqi'el lets out a jovial laugh. "I see you already sense this secret. Allow me to explain. Your hands are in the shape of the letter *kaf*. Just as it bends, sometimes you must bend to accommodate others. Sometimes you must also bend to accommodate divine will. Look at the light that has accumulated in your hands. If they did not bend, you could not receive, and, ultimately, you could not give."

The light particles continue darting about in your hands. "The light particles enjoy being in your hands! You are wise for not holding them too tightly—it is in their nature to move. If you held them too tightly, it would hinder their movement as well as their growth. Money also likes to move. Just as with the light particles, if you hold on to money too tightly, it hinders its movement and growth."

Ṣadqi'el continues, "The satellites orbiting you are magically linked to those you love. You may give them the blue light that has collected in your hands to protect them. Do not worry about running out—*Hisma'el* will ensure you receive all you need to give."

One by one you touch each satellite, intuitively giving it the appropriate amount of blue light. The satellites react to the particles in various ways. Dim ones glow brighter. Weary ones become energized, orbiting more confidently. Weathered ones appear refreshed. Some even acquire protective shields. The more blue light you give, the more you receive. Upon interacting with the final satellite, you give the last of the light particles remaining in your hands—precisely the amount needed. The archangel smiles in approval. He waves his dagger once more, and the satellites orbiting you go back into hiding.

You can visit Jupiter any time you'd like—now you know the way here. The royal blue light again accumulates within you and around you, filling your body and field of vision completely. As you continue to breathe, you draw a banishing Jupiter earth hexagram in front of you. As you trace the symbol of Jupiter while vibrating *'El* in your astral voice, the light in the surrounding environment slowly disperses. The room where your physical body resides begins to return. You begin to feel your fingers and toes. As the last remnants of the royal blue light fade, you gradually feel the rest of your body. Slowly open your eyes and become reacquainted with your surroundings. Stand up when you are ready and document your experience in your magical diary.

June 19, 2022. *Jupiter Guided Meditation.* Participants consistently reported more harmonious interactions with others, increased emphasis on matters beyond the personal self, and a greater sense that they can make a difference in the world.

It also was much easier to see the big picture. The physical descriptions of Jupiter and its satellites were inspired by data from NASA's *Galileo* and *Juno* missions.

Jupiter Monasticism

This monasticism serves to strengthen your relationship with Jupiter. It should be performed for four days or four weeks, since this number is associated with *Ḥesed* and the magic square of Jupiter. However, feel free to use another Jupiter-related number if it suits your fancy. Carry your Jupiter tool at all times during the monasticism—it serves as a constant reminder of Jupiter and increases vigilance. After your monasticism is complete, keep your Jupiter tool someplace special, such as an altar or favorite shelf. You may use it in future Jupiterian work and reuse it if you perform the monasticism again.

Beginning the Monasticism

On a Thursday during the daytime, attune with Jupiter. Jupiter in Pisces, Sagittarius, or Cancer are preferable but not required.

When ready, perform an invoking Jupiter GRH. Visualize a royal blue light emanating down from the heavens that passes through your hexagrams and envelops you. Knock in the center of your circle four times, as if you are knocking on a door. Place your open palms toward the sky and say:

> *Ṣedeq, I greet you! It is my will to perform the [Lesser/ Greater/Extreme] Observances of Jupiter for four [days/ weeks]. This entails [state the relevant sections here]. May this monasticism amplify my mercy and generosity!*

Lesser Observances

- Carry your Jupiter tool at all times. If you can't carry it openly, keep it in your pocket or a bag and carry that with you.
- As the Greater Benefic, Jupiter includes and accepts.[160] To cultivate a jovial spirit, perform a random act of kindness each day.
- Perform a daily Jupiter rite that incorporates your tool.
- It has long been believed that Jupiter protects Earth from comets and asteroids.[161] Likewise, royals protect their kingdoms from harm. Make a conscious effort to protect your household "kingdom" by managing it effectively. This may involve meal planning, delegating chores, or scheduling preventative maintenance. If you are unsure where to begin, visit the Household Management 101 website for suggestions.
- In many paradigms Jupiter rules over government workers and religious clergy. Donate items such as lucky charms, religious items, or sacred texts to a ministry or organization that helps social welfare. If you are unable to make a material donation you may make a monetary donation instead, so long as the value is in a multiple of four. Jupiter also rules over postsecondary education, so donating to a college or university is another option.

Greater Observances

- Perform all the Lesser Observances.
- Perform a second daily Jupiter rite that incorporates your tool.

---

160. Brennan, *Hellenistic Astrology*, 184–90.

161. Kevin R. Grazier, "Jupiter: Cosmic Jekyll and Hyde," *Astrobiology* 16, no. 1 (2016): 23–38.

- Relate all of your meditation and magical work to Jupiter. For example, meditate on your religious aspirations or paradigm shift to broaden your horizons.
- Establish a household budget to lay the groundwork for long-term prosperity. If you already have a household budget, revisit it and make modifications where necessary. The more wealth you have, the more you can give. If you do not have a licensed financial counselor or are unsure where to begin, Ramsey Solutions, NerdWallet, and The Motley Fool are excellent starting places.

Extreme Observances
- Perform all the Greater Observances.
- Perform a third daily Jupiter rite that incorporates your tool.
- In addition to the household budget, establish a long-term financial plan to ensure prosperity, security, and peace of mind. A long-term financial plan should allow you to cover emergencies, reach savings goals, and accomplish anything else you deem important. If you do not have a licensed financial counselor or are unsure where to begin, Ramsey Solutions, Suze Orman, and Rich Dad are excellent starting places.

Concluding the Monasticism

Return to the place you began your monasticism and attune with Jupiter. Take your time and do not rush.

When ready, perform a banishing Jupiter GRH. Place your open palms toward the sky and say:

> *Ṣedeq, I greet you! I performed the [Lesser/Greater/ Extreme] Observances of Jupiter for four [days/weeks].*

This entailed [state the relevant sections here]. Though I conclude this monasticism, my mercy and generosity remain!

April 13, 2023. *Jupiter Monasticism, Day 1.* I am performing the Extreme Observances of Jupiter for 16 (4×4) days. [Details of the three daytime rituals I performed follow.]

April 14, 2023. *Jupiter Monasticism, Day 2.* [Details of the three daytime rituals I performed follow.]

During the third Jupiter rite today, my amethyst broke cleanly in half! I strongly feel I should give one piece to F. S. and will try to do so on the final day. Since both amethyst pieces are functional on their own, I will treat them as a pair in subsequent rites.

April 29, 2023. *Jupiter Monasticism—Summary.* I concluded the Extreme Observances of Jupiter yesterday. Looking back, most of my magic focused on spiritual aspirations, accumulating wealth, and good luck. Many rites were performed with incense or under the open sky. Since one amethyst piece was a gift, I performed additional rituals I would not have done otherwise to provide extra benefits to the recipient.

Chapter 9
Homework

After taking notes on the chapter, magical practice should be commenced for thirty minutes each day for a minimum of one month. Perform the assignments in the order presented. Remember to document your efforts in your magical diary.

☐ Meditate on Jupiter for a minimum of ten minutes each day. How does this planetary force manifest in your life? How do you interact with it?

☐ Examine your natal chart to determine your Jupiter sign and house. Produce a broad delineation, using the examples in chapter 7 as a guide. We will revisit natal Jupiter in chapter 11.

☐ Approximately every twelve months, Jupiter enters a new sign. Visit a reputable website to determine the current Jupiter sign. In this sign, is Jupiter's manifestation strong, weak, or somewhere in between? Is Jupiter retrograde or conjunct the Sun?

☐ Attune with Jupiter daily for a period of one week.

☐ Investigate the effects of the Jupiter hexagrams. To accomplish this, draw one and passively observe the impact on yourself and the immediate environment. After a few minutes, record any observations, thoughts, inner feelings, and other details you deem important in your magical diary. Feel free to draw a banishing hexagram after an invoking hexagram to cancel it out.

☐ Examine your natal chart to determine which planets we have explored thus far are good candidates for Western planetary charity. Ideal candidates are typically not in domicile or exalted, and are retrograde or combust. If this subject interests you, the Renaissance Astrology website is an excellent resource for further information.

☐ Perform the Jupiter Greeting Rite. After obtaining your Jupiter tool, purify and consecrate it in a warm, humid environment.

☐ Perform the Jupiter Guided Meditation.

☐ Perform a Jupiter Monasticism before proceeding to the next chapter.

Chapter 9 Resources

AstroSeek. "Today's Current Planets." https://horoscopes.astro-seek.com /current-planets-astrology-transits-planetary-positions.

Beethoven, Ludwig van. "Ode to Joy." In *Symphony No. 9 in D minor*. Performed by Folsom Symphony and Sacramento Master Singers with American River College Chamber Choir. March 25, 2012. https://www.youtube.com/watch?v =hdWyYn0E4Ys.

HellenicGods. "The Orphic Hymns in Ancient Greek Online." https://www .hellenicgods.org/the-orphic-hymns-in-ancient-greek-online.

Holst, Gustav. "Jupiter, the Bringer of Jollity." In *The Planets, Op. 32*. Performed by NDR Radiophilharmonie. September 13, 2014. https://www.youtube.com /watch?v=3aXsQQ-ueBk.

Household Management 101. https://www.household-management-101.com.

The Motley Fool. "Budgeting 101: How to Start Budgeting for the First Time." http:// www.fool.com/investing/2018/04/21/budgeting-101-how-to-start-budgeting-for-the -first.aspx.

NerdWallet. "Budgeting 101: How to Budget Money." https://www.nerdwallet.com /article/finance/how-to-budget.

Ramsey Solutions. "How to Create a Budget." https://www.ramseysolutions.com /budgeting/guide-to-budgeting/how-to-create-a-budget.

———. "The 7 Baby Steps." https://www.ramseysolutions.com /dave-ramsey-7-baby-steps.

Renaissance Astrology. "Planetary Charity: Improving Your Relationship with the Planets." https://www.renaissanceastrology.com/planetarycharity.html.

Rich Dad. "Rich Dad Media Network." https://www.richdad.com/shows /shows-landing.

Sacred Texts. "The Hymns of Orpheus, translated by Thomas Taylor [1792]." https:// sacred-texts.com/cla/hoo/index.htm.

SuzeOrman. "What are your goals?" https://www.suzeorman.com/start-here.

CHAPTER 10
Saturn Corrects

Saturn provides the discipline necessary to work with the classical planets. As Saturn resides at the boundary between the other classical planets and the fixed stars, our restrictions and limitations reside at the boundary between the microcosmic self and the macrocosm. So far, the Moon has provided our foundation, Mercury has provided our intellectual and communicative basis, Venus has provided our emotional basis, the Sun has provided our consciousness, Mars has provided raw energy, and Jupiter has provided aspiration. Our last stop among the classical planets is Saturn. Common Saturn symbols are shown in Figure 10.1. They are useful focal points in meditation and magical practice.

(a) (b)

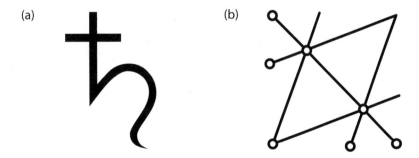

Figure 10.1. The (a) astronomical symbol and (b) planetary seal of Saturn

The Western View of Saturn

In the Greco-Roman model Saturn resides between Jupiter and the fixed stars.[162] Due to its distance from Earth and the Sun, Saturn is primarily cold and secondarily dry. Thus, Saturn is malefic and masculine. Saturn is also diurnal. Ptolemy assigned Saturn to the diurnal sect (associated with heat) to counterbalance its malefic temperament (caused by its primary coldness). Saturn's antagonistic nature is further reflected in the signs it rules, Capricorn and Aquarius. Capricorn is in opposition (180°) to Cancer (ruled by the Moon), and Aquarius is in opposition to Leo (ruled by the Sun). When planets are in opposition, their interaction is disharmonious.[163] Saturn is exalted in Libra and its fall is in Aries.

In the Hermetic model Saturn affects the structure of life on Earth.[164] It is also responsible for humanity's karma and overall destiny. According to Bardon, denizens of Saturn may be evoked in a purple light.[165] This color of light emulates the Saturn zone's vibrations and is thus conducive to manifesting Saturnian beings.

Gk. *Kronos* (Κρόνος); Heb. *Shabeta'y* (שבתאי);
Lat. *Saturnus*; Ouranian Barbaric *CHUFDOX*

The Saturn Archetype

Saturn is our restrictor. It represents our structural matrix, which manifests in our ability to function on a daily basis. It also has ties to our self-control. Saturn oversees space and time, two important restrictors. Exoterically, it is the sage who has earned wisdom through effort and experience. Esoterically, it is the Celestial Taskmaster overseeing consequences in the terrestrial and celestial realms. Deities traditionally associated with Saturn include Sobek and Mako (Egyptian), Kronos (Greek), and Saturn (Roman). Keywords relevant to Saturn are as follows:

Restriction

Our structural matrix is an important restrictor. A solid restrictor provides a sense of definition, limits, and boundaries. An unstable or overly rigid restrictor may result in

162. Ptolemy, *Tetrabiblos*, 34–43, 78–81, 88–89.

163. Ptolemy, *Tetrabiblos*, 72–73.

164. Bardon, *Magical Evocation*, 292–93.

165. Bardon, *Magical Evocation*, 128.

excessive inhibition or the inability to function on a daily basis. It may also lead to chronic feelings of isolation and oppression.

Structure

An orderly life improves our performance, productivity, and overall health.[166] Whereas Jupiter embodies the spirit of the law, Saturn embodies its letter. The Saturnian force may manifest through daily routine or be conveyed via discipline, such as adhering to a prescribed medication regimen.

Consequences

Our actions impact the future. In many paradigms Saturn is linked with agricultural deities—you reap what you sow. This is also why Saturn is associated with karma.

Exclusion

Saturn grants the ability to say *no*. It may positively manifest as creating and maintaining healthy boundaries, abstaining from illicit behavior, and getting enough alone time. It may negatively manifest as excessive isolation or blind adherence to conformity.

Destruction

Saturn reigns over corruption (as opposed to generation) and endings. This is also why Saturn is associated with death magic. Further, in many cultures Saturn bears connection to time, a force that devours all things.[167]

Necessity

The ancient Greeks viewed *anankē* (Gk. ἀνάγκη; necessity/constraint) as inevitable, unavoidable, and inescapable—not even deities could resist it.[168] We cannot survive without food, water, basic clothing, and shelter.

Western Saturn Magic

Saturn has a dark yellow-brown appearance in the sky, which may be why the ancients linked it with malefic significations.[169] In astrology, Saturn represents limitations and

---

166. Katherine R. Arlinghaus and Craig A. Johnston, "The Importance of Creating Habits and Routine," *American Journal of Lifestyle Medicine* 13, no. 2 (2019): 142–44.

167. Ovid, *Metamorphoses*, trans. Stanley Lombardo (Hackett Publishing Company, 2010), 424.

168. Plato, *Protagoras*, ed. Nicholas Denyer (Cambridge Univerity Press, 2008), 148, 165–66.

169. Brennan, *Hellenistic Astrology*, 186.

self-control. It is also generally associated with our boundaries, sacrifices, and sense of discipline. In many Western esoteric traditions Saturn is associated with space-time, agricultural, karmic, banishing, binding, and death magic. It is also generally associated with curses and malevolent works.

Saturn's day is Saturday (Lat. *dies Saturni*). In Abrahamic cultures, Saturday is often regarded as the last day of the week and a time for rest.[170] Saturn's alchemical metal is lead. Note that elemental lead (found in old paint chips, pipes, and fishing sinkers) is toxic, and long-term exposure to it causes irreversible neurological and organ damage. Even short-term exposure in high doses may cause death. Safer non-toxic alternatives that are magically useful include bismuth and tungsten, which may be found in modern lead-free fishing sinkers.

In ceremonial traditions Saturn is associated with *Bina* (Heb. Understanding), the third sphere of the Qabala.[171] This understanding yields the constraint required to bound physical reality. Psychologically, this sphere represents transpersonal love and awareness. Correspondences of *Bina* often relate to understanding and the divine feminine (i.e., magnetic principle). Saturn is also associated with *Taw*, the path connecting *Yesod* (Foundation) and *Malkut* (Kingdom). It connects our unconscious mind to our physical body and the material world of the five senses. In ancient script the letter *taw* resembles a pair of crossed sticks, which may allude to intersections, crossroads, and other boundaries. Correspondences of *Taw* often relate to manifestation and death. The top-down Hebrew hierarchy for Saturn is shown in Table 10.1.

Table 10.1. The Saturn Ceremonial Hierarchy		
Qabalistic World	**Level**	**Name**
ʾAṣilut	Divine name	*ʾAb, Yah*
Beriʾa	Archangel	*Ṣafqiʾel*

---

170. Leofranc Holford-Strevens, *The History of Time: A Very Short Introduction* (Oxford University Press, 2005), 64–85.

171. Crowley, "777 Revised," 2–3, 5.

Table 10.1. The Saturn Ceremonial Hierarchy		
Qabalistic World	**Level**	**Name**
Yeṣira	Intelligence Spirit	*ʾAgiʾel* *Zazʾel*
ʿAsiya	Magical tool	Sickle

The information in Table 10.1 is adapted from Crowley's "777 Revised." See Appendix A for Hebrew spelling, pronunciation, etymologies, and more. *YHWH ʾElohim* is *LORD God* in *Bina*. In older texts, *Kapṣiʾel* is often attributed instead of *Ṣafqiʾel*.[172] The yoni, outer robe of concealment, and cup are associated with *Bina*.

Fundamentals: Planetary Hours

In addition to ruling a day of the week, each classical planet rules particular hours of the day and night. Planetary hours are not the *equal* hours used in modern timekeeping; they are *unequal* or *seasonal* hours whose length is determined by the duration of local daylight (Figure 10.2). The use of unequal hours dates back to ancient Egypt, Greece, and Rome, and is also alluded to in the Bible.[173,174] Our modern equal hours comprised of sixty minutes each did not become popular until well after the fourteenth century, when mechanical clocks were introduced.[175]

172. Kaplan, *Sefer Yetzirah*, 168.

173. Holford-Strevens, *The History of Time*, 1–6.

174. John 11:9 KJV 1611.

175. Holford-Strevens, *The History of Time*, 6.

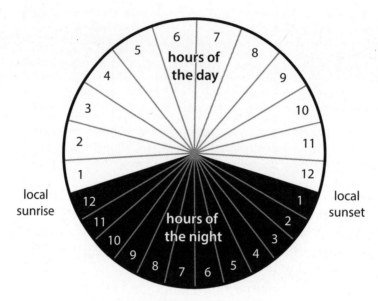

Figure 10.2. Planetary hour divisions

A day-night cycle (Gk. νυχθήμερον) begins at sunrise and ends at sunrise the next day. Hours of the day begin at sunrise and end at sunset, whereas hours of the night begin at sunset and end at sunrise the next day. These periods of daylight and darkness can be further subdivided into twelve unequal hours.

Since the duration of local daylight is longer in summer and shorter in winter, planetary hours of the day are longer in the summer and shorter in the winter. Likewise, hours of the night are shorter in the summer and longer in the winter. At higher latitudes, the difference becomes more dramatic.

Each day of the week is named after the classical planet ruling the first hour of the day. The planets ruling subsequent hours follow the so-called *Chaldean order*, which is: Saturn, Jupiter, Mars, the Sun, Venus, Mercury, and the Moon. (See Table 10.2 for details.)

Planetary hours are auspicious times to perform planet-specific meditations, rituals, charity, and more. Many magicians consider the overlap of the planetary day and hour the purest expression of time. Traditionally, planetary hours were frequently employed in ceremonial practice. Many modern magicians are also fond of using planetary hours—they are smaller (and thus more specific) increments of time.

Generally, when working with planetary hours the entirety of a longer rite does not have to be completed entirely within that hour—just the bulk and most critical parts of it. For instance, when performing the Saturn Greeting Rite it is fine to begin shortly after sunrise on Saturday morning. If your rite runs ten minutes into the next planetary hour, it will not negatively impact your magical work. Keep in mind that if you have made it this far, you have achieved decent results without taking into account planetary hours whatsoever.

Calculating Planetary Hours

Use the following steps to calculate the planetary hours for a particular day or night.

1. Determine the sunrise and sunset times for the day-night cycle of interest. For planetary hours of the day, find the times of local sunrise and sunset. For hours of the night, find the times of local sunset and then sunrise the next calendar day. You can find your local sunrise and sunset times via the Global Monitoring Laboratory's NOAA Solar Calculator.

2. Determine the total number of minutes in the planetary day or night. For hours of the day, sum the total number of minutes from local sunrise to sunset. For hours of the night, sum the total number of minutes from local sunset to sunrise the next calendar day.

3. Divide the total number of minutes in the planetary day or night by 12. The quotient is the length of each unequal hour during that particular planetary day or night, in minutes.

4. Now that you know the length of an unequal hour, identify their start and end times. It is easiest to begin at the first hour and move sequentially through the planetary day or night, filling in the times. Use Table 10.2 to determine the planetary ruler of each hour of the day or night.

Table 10.2. Planetary Hour Rulers							
Hour	**Sat.**	**Sun.**	**Mon.**	**Tue.**	**Wed.**	**Thu.**	**Fri.**
Day Hours							
1	♄	☉	☽	♂	☿	♃	♀
2	♃	♀	♄	☉	☽	♂	☿
3	♂	☿	♃	♀	♄	☉	☽
4	☉	☽	♂	☿	♃	♀	♄
5	♀	♄	☉	☽	♂	☿	♃
6	☿	♃	♀	♄	☉	☽	♂
7	☽	♂	☿	♃	♀	♄	☉
8	♄	☉	☽	♂	☿	♃	♀
9	♃	♀	♄	☉	☽	♂	☿
10	♂	☿	♃	♀	♄	☉	☽
11	☉	☽	♂	☿	♃	♀	♄
12	♀	♄	☉	☽	♂	☿	♃

Table 10.2. Planetary Hour Rulers							
Hour	**Sat.**	**Sun.**	**Mon.**	**Tue.**	**Wed.**	**Thu.**	**Fri.**
Night Hours							
1	☿	♃	♀	♄	☉	☽	♂
2	☽	♂	☿	♃	♀	♄	☉
3	♄	☉	☽	♂	☿	♃	♀
4	♃	♀	♄	☉	☽	♂	☿
5	♂	☿	♃	♀	♄	☉	☽
6	☉	☽	♂	☿	♃	♀	♄
7	♀	♄	☉	☽	♂	☿	♃
8	☿	♃	♀	♄	☉	☽	♂
9	☽	♂	☿	♃	♀	♄	☉
10	♄	☉	☽	♂	☿	♃	♀
11	♃	♀	♄	☉	☽	♂	☿
12	♂	☿	♃	♀	♄	☉	☽

Day hours begin at local sunrise, and night hours begin at local sunset. In Hellenistic astrology, the planetary week begins on Saturday.[176]

176. Holford-Strevens, *The History of Time*, 64.

Example Calculation

An example calculation is as follows. Here, we will determine the planetary hours of the day for Scottsdale, Arizona, on Friday, June 20, 2025—the Summer Solstice.

1. According to the NOAA Solar Calculator, local sunrise occurs at 05:18 and local sunset occurs at 19:41.

2. Using these local sunrise and sunset times, we can determine the planetary day lasts 14 h 22 min (862 min total). Since hours of the night begin at sunset, the minute of sunset is not included.

3. 862 min / 12 planetary hours = 71.8 min. Thus, each hour of the day is 1 h, 11 min, 48 sec long (Rounded: 1 h, 12 min).

4. Since we know the planetary hours of the day begin at 05:18 and end right before 19:41, and that each hour lasts approximately 1h, 12 min, now it's just a matter of determining the start and end times for each hour.

5. Use Table 10.2 to determine the planetary rulers of each hour of the day on Friday. If you are following along, your final result should resemble Table 10.3.

Table 10.3. Planetary Hours of the day on Friday, June 20, 2025, in Scottsdale, Arizona			
Day Hour	**Start Time**	**End Time**	**Ruler**
1	05:18	06:30	♀
2	06:30	07:42	☿
3	07:42	08:54	☽
4	08:54	10:06	♄
5	10:06	11:18	♃

Table 10.3. Planetary Hours of the day on Friday, June 20, 2025, in Scottsdale, Arizona			
Day Hour	**Start Time**	**End Time**	**Ruler**
6	11:18	12:30	♂
7	12:30	13:42	☉
8	13:42	14:54	♀
9	14:54	16:06	☿
10	16:06	17:17	☽
11	17:17	18:29	♄
12	18:29	19:41	♃

Local sunrise and sunset times are from the NOAA Solar Calculator. Scottsdale, Arizona does not observe Daylight Saving Time (DST). Local sunrise is at 05:18. Local sunset is at 19:41. Each planetary hour lasts approximately 1 h 12 min.

If you dislike performing calculations by hand, there are many free calculators available online. Although they are convenient, be sure to verify that the correct local sunrise, local sunset, and time zone are shown.

Saturn in Chaos Magic

Saturn may be integrated into magical practice in numerous ways. Various deities, egregores, or pop culture characters associated with Saturn may be invoked or evoked. Divination may be practiced via astrologically analyzing Saturn or through methods that incorporate death (e.g., necromancy, bone reading …). Magical items associated with Saturn may be enchanted for purposes consistent with its nature. All cursed objects also fall under this planet's domain. Illumination rites aimed at gaining insight into transpersonal love and awareness or the death process may also be performed.

Saturn is projective, heavy, strict, stern, impartial, and solitary. It is also very no-nonsense and practical. These characteristics have been incorporated into the rites, which are intentionally somber, serious, and highly structured. Some also use Saturn's ceremonial planetary hexagrams (Figure 10.3). It is best to commit them to memory.

Table 10.3. Saturn invoking hexagrams			
Fire	Earth	Air	Water

Table 10.3. Saturn banishing hexagrams			
Fire	Earth	Air	Water

Draw the planetary hexagrams with your magical tool or index finger in the numbered sequence shown. To draw the earth hexagrams used in the Saturn GRH, visualize the hexagram shape in black and vibrate *ARARITA* as you draw, and then visualize the Saturn astronomical symbol in black and vibrate *YHWH ʾElohim* as you draw.

Active Work
Saturn Attunement

Lie down in a cold, dark, quiet place where you will not be disturbed. Your posture should mimic a corpse in a coffin. Close your eyes. Practice motionlessness and silence for no less than fifteen minutes. As you lie still, feel the pressure of the atmosphere weighing you down. Feel the force of gravity and how heavy you are. Resonate with this thick, burdensome silence. Observe the silence with all five senses as well as astrally. As time passes, the silence grows stronger. Slowly adjust the rhythm of your body to match the vibrations underlying this silence. Feel them slowing, burdening, and binding you.

> July 11, 2021. *Saturn Attunement.* I consistently feel heavy, slow, and lethargic after attuning with Saturn. This makes my actions more deliberate afterward, since everything seems to require more effort. Others reported similar results.

Saturn Greeting Rite

While not necessary, if Saturn is visible in the sky, you may face its general direction and treat it as metaphysical east. Saturn in Capricorn, Aquarius, or Libra are preferable but not required.

Materials

- No materials are required.
- If you already have a Saturn tool, you may ask the planetary spirit to bless it instead. Saturn's traditional ceremonial tool is the sickle. If you are a fan of the planetary metals, recall that Saturn's *non-toxic* metals are bismuth and tungsten.

- Optional: Burning incense associated with Saturn (such as asafetida, gum arabic, or pulverized black poppy seeds)—incenses traditionally associated with Saturn smell unpleasant.[177,178,179]
- Optional: Additional forms of non-toxic and safe sensory unpleasantness.

Statement of Intent

It is my will to access the Saturnian force.

Procedure

Attune with Saturn during its planetary day and hour.

When ready, perform an invoking Saturn GRH. Visualize a thick black light emanating down from the heavens, passing through your hexagrams and enveloping you. Knock in the center of your circle three times, as if you are knocking on a door. Place your open palms toward the sky and say:

XIQUAL CHUFDOX!
Come all-father Kronos, who strikes the mind!
Come reaping Saturnus, with your harvesting sickle!
Come Shabeta'y, the restful one,
Kokav Shabeth, steady star!
In the divine names of 'Ab' and Yah I greet you!
Come Ṣafqi'el, Archangel of Saturn,
and bless me with diligence!
Grant me access to the Saturnian force
so I may make the most of my time!

---

177. Crowley, "777 Revised," 13.

178. Greer and Warnock, *Picatrix*, 141.

179. Bardon, *Magical Evocation*, 144.

Close your eyes and inhale the thick black light enveloping you, until it fills your entire body. Take note of any occult wisdom or karmic insights you receive.

When ready, use your index finger to draw a triangle on the ground in the center of your circle. Visualize it in black. Place your open palms slightly outside the triangle and proceed to evoke the planetary intelligence. Say:

> ʾAgiʾel, Intelligence of Saturn,
> in the name of Ṣafqiʾel I evoke you!
> Grant me access to the Saturnian force
> so I may harness it for the Great Work of Magic!

If you do not sense its presence, continue visualizing the thick light and repeat the above until you do.

After you sense the planetary intelligence's presence, proceed to evoke the planetary spirit. With open palms still slightly outside the triangle, continue:

> Zazʾel, Spirit of Saturn,
> in the name of ʾAgiʾel I evoke you!
> Aid my efforts to obtain a Saturn tool
> that will assist me in the Great Work of Magic!

If you do not sense its presence, continue visualizing the thick black light and repeat the above until you do. After you are finished communicating with them, thank them and send them on their way.

Banishing

Perform a banishing Saturn GRH and then banish with laughter.

June 18, 2022. *Saturn Greeting Rite*. The rite took about 30 minutes to perform. The overall tone was serious and solemn. My actions were slower and more deliberate than usual. I felt cold pins and needles throughout the rite, especially at its most critical points—the sensations completely stopped after banishing. Regarding the planetary intelligence and spirit, I recited each evocation three times before sensing a presence. The planetary intelligence conveyed it disliked my incense burner's placement inside the triangle—it was too hot. The planetary spirit was incredibly dense, heavy, and also not a fan of the incense burner's locale.

January 5, 2023. *Addendum*. My Jupiter and Saturn tools manifested much later than my other planetary tools—perhaps this bears connection to their relatively slower orbital periods. I encountered my Saturn tool (which was randomly sitting on the ground) on Jupiter's day in Saturn's hour. It is blatantly associated with *Bina*—a snowflake-themed cup with pearls and all![180,181] Most of the snowflakes strongly resemble chaos stars…

Saturn Guided Meditation

Find a cool, quiet place to sit in a comfortable position. Close your eyes. Take a deep breath and center yourself. With each breath, you will feel calmer and more relaxed. Feel the tension in your toes. As you exhale, the tension dissipates until they are completely relaxed. This feeling of relaxation grows and spreads through your feet into your ankles. They are now completely relaxed. It continues, travelling up your legs and into your knees, which are now completely relaxed.

---

180. Crowley, "777 Revised," 106.
181. Crowley, "777 Revised," 10.

Feel the lack of tension in your shins and calves. Any outside noises or distractions just serve to relax you further. Now your upper legs, hips, and waist are completely relaxed. As you continue to breathe, your abdominal region, chest, and back are completely relaxed. Your relaxation grows further, moving into your shoulders, and then down into your arms, elbows, hands, fingers, and fingertips. Your entire body below your neck is now completely relaxed. This feeling of relaxation grows to fill your neck and face. Feel your chin, jaw, nose, cheeks, eyes, eyelids, forehead, and ears relax. Finally, feel your scalp relax. Your entire body is now completely relaxed.

In your mind's eye, visualize Saturn glowing above your head. It is about the size of a basketball and reflects a thick black light. The light shines down, firmly enveloping you as you continue breathing. Observe the light with all five senses. See its stern brightness, feel its coolness, smell it, and taste it. Does it emanate a sound? As seismic waves discharge deep inside Saturn, its ring system rings like a bell but emanates no sound as it vibrates. As you continue breathing, the thick black light accumulates within and around you, filling your body and field of vision completely. You draw an invoking Saturn earth hexagram in front of you. As you trace the symbol of Saturn while vibrating *YHWH 'Elohim* in your astral voice, the light inside you firmly glows.

The light in the surrounding environment slowly disperses, revealing an enormous hexagonal jet stream beneath your feet. Its icy blue wind spins counterclockwise, sweeping smaller golden inner swirls clockwise. In the center of the jet stream lies a massive hurricane with an eye 50 times bigger than the average hurricane on Earth. After a few more moments pass, you realize you are hovering above Saturn's North Pole. The black light inside you shields you from Saturn's harsh exosphere and the cold emptiness of space.

As the black light firmly glows, a feeling of solitude envelops you. You are at the boundary between the classical planets and rest of the universe. From this vantage point, time flows slower. The Sun is easily recognizable—it is about nine and a half times smaller and a hundred times dimmer than it appears on Earth but is still too bright to look at directly. You are also able to identify some of the other classical planets. Jupiter and its Galilean moons merrily orbit about. Mars is a pale red dot. Earth is a pale blue dot, while Venus shines like a beacon.

You turn to look out at the fixed stars. They feel even more distant than when observed from Earth. Beyond Saturn's satellites, it is desolate. As you continue gazing out at the fixed stars, you get an eerie feeling that you are not alone. You turn your attention back to the jet stream—a thick black light now emanates from its center. After a few more moments pass, a dark figure surrounded by the same thick black light emerges. It is a few kilometers in diameter and unwaveringly moves toward you. You deduce this is one of Saturn's astral denizens coming to investigate—they must rarely get visitors this far out. As the figure closes in, you are able to make out the profile of a winged being.

The winged being towers over you. The dim sky and thick black light obscure any prominent features, but you are certain the winged being is angelic in nature. It firmly grasps you in its large hands, pulling you in close. Chills run down your spine as you suddenly realize you are in the hands of *Ṣafqi'el*, archangel of Saturn.

Ṣafqi'el ascends slowly to fly higher above Saturn's North Pole with you in tow. As you both come to a halt, relishing in the quiet stillness, Saturn's iconic ring system comes into full view. After a few more moments pass, *Ṣafqi'el* says, "Just as Saturn is bounded by rings, you too have boundaries. Some boundaries are beneficial, while some are detrimental. *'Agi'el*, Intelligence of Saturn, I call you! In the name of *YHWH 'Elohim*, I command you reveal the boundaries I speak of." While you are still in the archangel's hands, a complex ring system materializes around you. Some rings glow with lighter hues of black light while others glow with darker hues. Some are close, others distant. Some are thick. Some are thin. Some are comforting. Some are not.

Ṣafqi'el continues, "The light-hued rings represent boundaries that are beneficial to you, while the dark-hued rings represent boundaries that are detrimental to you." You reach out and touch a few rings, one by one. As you touch a ring, the particular boundary it represents is revealed. Many of your beneficial boundaries revolve around themes of self-control, inner discipline, and adhering to your moral code. Many of the detrimental boundaries surrounding you revolve around themes of blind adherence, aversion to the unfamiliar, and baseless fears. Ṣafqi'el continues, "Saturn's ring system changes over time. It will look very different in a few hundred million years. Your boundaries may also change, and fortunately in a much shorter amount of time. Zaz'el, Spirit of Saturn, I call you! 'Agi'el and I command you to permit evolution of these personal boundaries."

A much thicker, more concentrated black light slowly materializes in your hands. With this light, you may strengthen or weaken the rings surrounding you, and thus your boundaries. You can also create new rings. The concentrated black light diligently assists you as you strengthen, weaken, create, and destroy the rings surrounding you. As you touch one particular ring you pause, unsure of what to do. Ṣafqi'el notices your hesitation and whispers, "If you argue for your limitations, you get to keep them." After a few more moments pass, the rings surrounding you go back into hiding. The concentrated black light in your hands slowly disperses.

You can visit Saturn any time you'd like—now you know the way here. The thick black light again accumulates within and around you, filling your body and field of vision completely. As you continue to breathe, you draw a banishing Saturn earth hexagram in front of you. As you trace the symbol of Saturn while vibrating YHWH 'Elohim in your astral voice, the light in the surrounding environment slowly disperses. The room where your physical body resides begins to return. You begin to feel your fingers and toes. As the last remnants of the thick black light fade, you gradually feel the rest of your body. Slowly open your eyes and become reacquainted with your surroundings. Stand up when you are ready and document your experience in your magical diary.

> February 11, 2023 (♄ in term in ♒). *Saturn Guided Meditation.* I consistently feel a greater sense of self-awareness regarding my limitations as well as a renewed sense of self-discipline afterward. Others also felt a stronger sense of self-control. The physical description of Saturn was inspired by data from the international Cassini-Huygens mission.

Saturn Monasticism

This monasticism serves to strengthen your relationship with Saturn. It should be performed for three days or three weeks, since this number is associated with *Bina* and the magic square of Saturn. However, feel free to use another Saturn-related number if it suits your fancy. Carry your Saturn tool at all times during the monasticism—it serves as a constant reminder of Saturn and increases vigilance. After your monasticism is complete, keep your Saturn tool someplace special, such as an altar or favorite shelf. You may use it in future Saturnian work and if you perform the monasticism again.

Beginning the Monasticism

Attune with Saturn during its planetary day and hour. Saturn in Capricorn, Aquarius, or Libra are preferable but not required. Take your time and do not rush.

When ready, perform an invoking Saturn GRH. Visualize a thick black light emanating down from the heavens, passing through your hexagrams and enveloping you. Knock in the center of your circle three times as if you are knocking on a door. Place your open palms toward the sky and say:

> *Shabeta'y, I greet you! It is my will to perform the [Lesser/ Greater/Extreme] Observances of Saturn for three [days/ weeks]. This entails [state the relevant sections here]. May this monasticism manifest discipline!*

Lesser Observances

- Carry your Saturn tool at all times. If you can't carry it openly, keep it in your pocket or a bag and carry that with you.
- As the Greater Malefic, Saturn excludes and rejects.[182] Rest and recharge by spending a few minutes in quiet solitude each day.
- Perform a daily Saturn rite that incorporates your tool.
- Saturn is bounded by a prominent set of stunning rings. Likewise, creating and maintaining boundaries is a learnable skill. Make a conscious effort to apply boundaries that are beneficial to your life. Visit the Psychology Today website for suggestions.
- In many paradigms Saturn rules over the elderly and homeless. Donate items such as socks, underwear, or blankets to a homeless shelter or organization that helps needy senior citizens. If you are unable to make a material donation you may make a monetary donation instead, so long as the value is in a multiple of three.

---

182. Brennan, *Hellenistic Astrology*, 184–90.

Greater Observances

- Perform all the Lesser Observances.
- Perform a second daily Saturn rite that incorporates your tool.
- Relate all your meditation and magical work to Saturn. For example, incorporate motionlessness and silence into your meditation or perform divination to discover your manner of death.
- Saturn has long been associated with time. To better manage your time, implement tools such as time audits, electronic reminders, and to-do lists. If you are unsure where to begin, the University of Kentucky's *The Successful Person's Guide to Time Management* and University of Georgia's *Time Management: 10 Strategies for Better Time Management* are excellent resources.

Extreme Observances

- Perform all the Greater Observances.
- Perform a third daily Saturn rite that incorporates your tool.
- Marcus Aurelius states, "Since it is possible that thou mayest depart from life this very moment, regulate every act and thought accordingly."[183] Think long and hard about what kind of legacy you want to leave. Will you leave money for your descendants, start a community program, add knowledge to your field, or something else? Once you decide what your legacy will be, start building it. This clarity will renew your sense of purpose and allow you to manage time and other resources more effectively. From now on, live the way you want to be remembered.

---

183. Marcus Aurelius, *Meditations*, trans. George Long (Barnes & Noble Books, 2003), 10.

Concluding the Monasticism

Return to the place you began your monasticism and attune with Saturn during its planetary hour. Take your time and do not rush.

When ready, perform a banishing Saturn GRH. Place your open palms toward the sky and say:

> *Shabeta'y, I greet you! I performed the [Lesser/Greater/ Extreme] Observances of Saturn for three [days/weeks]. This entailed [state the relevant sections here]. Though I conclude this monasticism, my discipline remains!*

April 29, 2023. *Saturn Monasticism, Day 1.* I am performing the Extreme Observances of Saturn for nine (3×3) days. [Details of the three daytime rituals I performed follow.]

Also, I might have cancer. I recently underwent a bunch of tests. F— sitting around feeling sorry for myself. I'm completing this monasticism. I love magic and will practice until the day I die.

May 8, 2023. *Saturn Monasticism—Summary.* I concluded the Extreme Observances of Saturn yesterday. Most of my magic focused on maintaining discipline, improving time management, and leaving a legacy. Many rites incorporated sensory deprivation or contemplation. Compared to the other planetary monasticisms, with Saturn I had to more vigilantly plan ahead to ensure my second rite was performed during its planetary hour. I was also super careful with my cup!

Throughout the monasticism, I periodically experienced the Vision of Sorrow, and today was no exception! Imagine diving into a vast, black ocean that contains an understanding of all that was, all that is, and all that will be. Upon contact with the water, latent feelings of solitude and gloominess emerge. I still haven't sufficiently processed these experiences.

May 9, 2023. Today I got the call that I don't have cancer. The call came during Saturn's hour. I was forced to think longer and harder about my mortality during this monasticism than ever before. Looking back, I wouldn't have changed a thing—I performed the monasticism wholeheartedly at a critical time.

Chapter 10
Homework

After taking notes on the chapter, magical practice should be commenced for thirty minutes each day for a minimum of one month. Perform the assignments in the order presented. Do not lag, even though Saturn likes to take its time. Remember to document your efforts in your magical diary.

- ☐ Meditate on Saturn for a minimum of ten minutes each day. How does this planetary force manifest in your life? How do you interact with it?

- ☐ Examine your natal chart to determine your Saturn sign and house. Produce a broad delineation, using the examples in chapter 7 as a guide. We will revisit natal Saturn in chapter 11.

- ☐ Approximately every two and a half years, Saturn enters a new sign. Visit a reputable website to determine the current Saturn sign. In this sign, is Saturn manifestation strong, weak, or somewhere in between? Is Saturn retrograde or conjunct the Sun?

- ☐ Attune with Saturn daily for a period of one week.

- ☐ Investigate the effects of the Saturn hexagrams. To accomplish this, draw one and passively observe the impact on yourself and the immediate environment. After a few minutes, record any observations, thoughts, feelings, and other details you consider important in your magical diary. Feel free to draw a banishing hexagram after an invoking hexagram to cancel it out.

- ☐ In some paradigms the planets ruling the day and hour of birth are believed to significantly impact the course of an individual's life. Determine the planets ruling the day and hour of your birth (Table 10.2).

- ☐ Perform the Saturn Greeting Rite. After obtaining your Saturn tool, purify and consecrate it in a cold, dry environment.

- ☐ Perform the Saturn Guided Meditation.

- ☐ Perform a Saturn Monasticism before proceeding to the next chapter.

Chapter 10 Resources

AstroSeek. "Planetary Hours of the Day: Astrology Online Calculator." https://horoscopes.astro-seek.com/planetary-hours-today-astrology-calculator.

———. "Today's Current Planets." https://horoscopes.astro-seek.com/current-planets-astrology-transits-planetary-positions.

Global Monitoring Laboratory. "NOAA Solar Calculator." https://gml.noaa.gov/grad/solcalc.

Psychology Today. "7 Tips to Create Healthy Boundaries with Others." November 21, 2015. https://www.psychologytoday.com/us/blog/in-flux/201511/7-tips-create-healthy-boundaries-others.

University of Georgia. "Time Management: 10 Strategies for Better Time Management." Last modified February 19, 2024. https://extension.uga.edu/publications/detail.html?number=C1042&title=time-management-10-strategies-for-better-time-management.

University of Kentucky. "The Successful Person's Guide to Time Management." https://www2.ca.uky.edu/agcomm/pubs/fcs7/fcs7101/fcs7101.pdf.

CHAPTER 11
The Classical
Planets Together

We have now explored the classical planets, internalized them, and determined how they affect our lives. We have also interacted with them magically. In the Greco-Roman and Hermetic models, the classical planets personify basic human drives, affect our daily lives, and influence terrestrial events at large. Luminaries illuminate. Benefics give. Malefics take. Whether they yield positive or negative results depends on additional factors. In this chapter we will more scrupulously examine planetary interactions and how they may facilitate spiritual enrichment, life balance, and psychological well-being. At the end, you will learn about rites involving more than one planet revolving around these themes, which you are free to modify to your liking.

The Hexagram Revisited

The invoking and banishing planetary hexagrams follow a general formula. To invoke a planetary force, begin at its hexagram point and complete the first triangle by drawing clockwise. To draw the second triangle, begin at the point opposite the planet and again draw clockwise. To banish a planetary force, begin at its hexagram point and complete the first triangle by drawing counterclockwise. For the second triangle, begin at the point opposite the planet and again draw counterclockwise. The solar invoking and banishing hexagrams are a concatenation of the other planetary hexagrams drawn in Chaldean order. Traditional assignments of the planets to each hexagram point are shown in Figure 11.1.

Figure 11.1. The hexagram

As before, planets are denoted by their astronomical symbols and placed on their corresponding hexagram points, as given in Crowley's "777 Revised." Note their arrangement also reflects the relative positions of their respective Qabalistic spheres on the Tree of Life.

Thinking in Sevens

There are several sets of seven present in nature. There are seven metals of antiquity, commonly encountered colors, and more. There are also many sets of seven present in Western culture. Many of these sevens hold magical significance—each member of a set reflects the qualities of a specific planet, with all seven planets being ultimately represented. This is how magical correspondences are produced. Traditional Western magical correspondences for each classical planet we have explored thus far are summarized in Table 11.1.

Table 11.1. Traditional Western Magical Correspondences of the Classical Planets							
Attribute	☽	☿	♀	☉	♂	♃	♄
Day	Mon.	Wed.	Fri.	Sun.	Tue.	Thu.	Sat.
Metal	Silver	Mercury	Copper	Gold	Iron	Tin	Lead

Table 11.1. Traditional Western Magical Correspondences of the Classical Planets							
Attribute	☽	☿	♀	☉	♂	♃	♄
Number	9	8	7	6	5	4	3
Color	Purple or silver	Orange	Green	Yellow or gold	Red	Blue	Black

Correspondences such as these are commonly used to enhance magical work. You may incorporate as many or as few of them into your practice as you'd like. Note that alternate correspondence schemes with equally valid rationales exist. The ability to "think in sevens" will permit you to produce your own personally significant planetary correspondences. What other sevens in nature or Western culture can you think of? Which planet would you assign to each member of a set, and why? Example rationales justifying the correspondences in Table 11.1 are as follows:

Days
The traditional planetary days of the week are evident as early as the second century BCE, but relating the classical planets to deities goes back at least as far as Mesopotamia and ancient Egypt.[184] Each day of the week is named after the planet ruling the first hour of the day.

Metals
The traditional planetary metal correspondences originate from Byzantine scholar Stephanus of Alexandria, but relating the classical planets to metals goes back at least as far as the ancient Greek poet Pindar.[185]

Interestingly, early uses of the metals reflect key planetary characteristics. Like the Moon, silver (Ag) is an excellent reflector of visible light. It has long been prized in

---

184. Yannis Almirantis, "The Paradox of the Planetary Metals," 31–42.

185. Almirantis, "Planetary Metals," 31–42.

making mirrors.[186] Mercury moves quickly across the sky, and elemental mercury (Hg) is also very mobile—it is liquid at room temperature. Further, it easily forms alloys with other metals, and some ancient cultures may have used it for scrying.[187] Venus has long been associated with copper (Cu), the metal that brought mankind out of the Stone Age. In the Chalcolithic Age, copper was used to make decorative items, jewelry, and more.[188,189] Like the Sun, gold (Au) is bright and shiny. It has long been considered divine and was often used in idol-making or given as an offering to deities.[190] Mars has long been associated with warfare and engineering. Likewise, iron (Fe) has long been used to make weapons, armor, and more.[191] Like Jupiter, tin (Sn) may also exhibit a bright yellow-brown appearance. It has historically been a key ingredient in compounds used to make yellow paint.[192] Lead (Pb) is the heaviest and least conductive of the bunch, making Saturn an appropriate association. Lead has had many uses throughout history, including lining coffins.[193,194]

Numbers

The traditional planetary number correspondences reflect the order (*n*) of each planet's magic square. The sequence follows Chaldean order, with Saturn linked to the magic square of order 3 and the Moon linked to the magic square of order 9. These numbers also reflect the Qabalistic spheres associated with each planet.

186. "Silver," Periodic Table, Royal Society of Chemistry, accessed March 27, 2024, https://www.rsc.org/periodic-table/element/47/silver.

187. Paul F. Healey and Marc G. Blainey, "Ancient Maya Mosaic Mirrors: Function, Symbolism, and Meaning," *Ancient Mesoamerica* 22, no. 2 (2011): 229–44.

188. "Copper," Periodic Table, Royal Society of Chemistry, accessed March 27, 2024, https://www.rsc.org/periodic-table/element/29/copper.

189. Ralph S. Solecki, "A Copper Mineral Pendant from Northern Iraq," *Antiquity* 43, no. 172 (1969): 311–14.

190. George B. Kauffman, "The Role of Gold in Alchemy. Part I," *Gold Bulletin* 18, no. 1 (1985): 31–44.

191. "Iron," Periodic Table, Royal Society of Chemistry, accessed March 27, 2024, https://www.rsc.org/periodic-table/element/26/iron.

192. Nicholas Eastaugh, Valentine Walsh, Tracey Chapman, and Ruth Siddall, *The Pigment Compendium: A Dictionary of Historical Pigments*, (Elsevier, 2004), 231–33.

193. "Lead," Periodic Table, Royal Society of Chemistry, accessed March 27, 2024, https://www.rsc.org/periodic-table/element/82/lead.

194. A. Boddington, A. N. Garland, and R. C. Janaway, eds., *Death, Decay and Reconstruction: Approaches to Archaeology and Forensic Science* (Manchester University Press, 1987), 51, 76.

Colors

The traditional planetary color correspondences reflect the Queen Scale colors of their respective Qabalistic spheres. These colors are also frequently employed when visualizing planetary hexagrams. Regarding the luminaries, some practitioners assign the Moon and Sun the shiny colors of silver and gold, respectively. Further, some Hermetic magicians prefer to associate white with the Moon and purple with Saturn. Note that alternate correspondence schemes with equally valid rationales exist.[195,196]

Fundamentals: Planetary Dignities and Debilities

Examining the natal chart provides insight into how the planetary forces manifest in our lives and may also divulge potential knacks or challenges we may encounter when working with them magically. Planets with dignified (favorable) placements more easily express themselves, whereas planets with debilitated (unfavorable) placements find it more challenging.

Sign-Based Dignities and Debilities

Sign-based dignities and debilities refer to the innate expressive strength of a classical planet as determined by its sign and degree locale within that sign. Planets are dignified in their domicile, exaltation, triplicity, term, and decan. The latter three are important in traditional astrology but tend to be deemphasized in today's modern Western astrology. Planets are debilitated in their detriment or fall. Sign-based dignities and debilities are shown in Table 11.2. They later evolved into the *essential* dignities and debilities of Medieval and Renaissance astrology.[197,198] An explanation of each sign-based condition is given after the tables.

195. Greer and Warnock, *Picatrix*, 140–43.

196. Crowley, "777 Revised," 3, 7.

197. Greer and Warnock, *Picatrix*, 66–77.

198. Lilly, *Christian Astrology*, 101–05, 115.

Table 11.2. Traditional Western planetary rulerships

Sign	Domicile Ruler	Exal-tation	Triplicity Rulers			Terms					Decans			Detri-ment	Fall
			Day	Night	Co						1	2	3		
♈	♂	☉	☉	♃	♄	0° ≤ ♃ < 6°	6° ≤ ♀ < 12°	12° ≤ ☿ < 20°	20° ≤ ♂ < 25°	25° ≤ ♄ < 30°	♂	☉	♀	♀	♄
♉	♀	☽	♀	☽	♂	0° ≤ ♀ < 8°	8° ≤ ☿ < 14°	14° ≤ ♃ < 22°	22° ≤ ♄ < 27°	27° ≤ ♂ < 30°	☿	☽	♄	♂	–
♊	☿	–	♄	☿	♃	0° ≤ ☿ < 6°	6° ≤ ♃ < 12°	12° ≤ ♀ < 17°	17° ≤ ♂ < 24°	24° ≤ ♄ < 30°	♃	♂	☉	♃	–
♋	☽	♃	♀	♂	☽	0° ≤ ♂ < 7°	7° ≤ ♀ < 13°	13° ≤ ☿ < 19°	19° ≤ ♃ < 26°	26° ≤ ♄ < 30°	♀	☿	☽	♄	♂
♌	☉	–	☉	♃	♄	0° ≤ ♃ < 6°	6° ≤ ♀ < 11°	11° ≤ ♄ < 18°	18° ≤ ☿ < 24°	24° ≤ ♂ < 30°	♄	♃	♂	♄	–
♍	☿	☿	♀	☽	♂	0° ≤ ☿ < 7°	10° ≤ ♀ < 17°	17° ≤ ♃ < 21°	21° ≤ ♂ < 28°	28° ≤ ♄ < 30°	☉	♀	☿	♃	♀

Table 11.2. Traditional Western planetary rulerships

Sign	Domicile Ruler	Exal-tation	Triplicity Rulers			Terms					Decans			Detri-ment	Fall
			Day	Night	Co						1	2	3		
♎	♀	♄	♄	☿	♃	0° ≤ ♄ < 6°	6° ≤ ☿ < 14°	14° ≤ ♃ < 21°	21° ≤ ♀ < 28°	28° ≤ ♂ < 30°	☽	♄	♃	♂	☉
♏	♂	–	♀	♂	☽	0° ≤ ♂ < 7°	7° ≤ ♀ < 11°	11° ≤ ☿ < 19°	19° ≤ ♃ < 24°	24° ≤ ♄ < 30°	♂	☉	♀	♀	☽
♐	♃	–	☉	♃	♄	0° ≤ ♃ < 12°	12° ≤ ♀ < 17°	17° ≤ ☿ < 21°	21° ≤ ♄ < 26°	26° ≤ ♂ < 30°	☿	☽	♄	☿	–
♑	♄	♂	♀	☽	♂	0° ≤ ☿ < 7°	7° ≤ ♃ < 14°	14° ≤ ♀ < 22°	22° ≤ ♄ < 26°	26° ≤ ♂ < 30°	♃	♂	☉	☽	♃
♒	♄	–	♄	☿	♃	0° ≤ ☿ < 7°	7° ≤ ♃ < 13°	13° ≤ ♃ < 20°	20° ≤ ♂ < 25°	25° ≤ ♄ < 30°	♀	☿	☽	☉	–
♓	♃	♀	♀	♂	☽	0° ≤ ♀ < 12°	12° ≤ ♃ < 16°	16° ≤ ☿ < 19°	19° ≤ ♂ < 28°	28° ≤ ♄ < 30°	♄	♃	♂	☿	☿

The information in Table 11.2 is adapted from Dorotheus's *Carmen Astrologicum*, Maternus's *Matheseos*, and Ptolemy's *Tetrabiblos*. Triplicity rulers are Dorothean, terms are Egyptian, and decans are Chaldean. Detriment is a later concept, but is included here due to its importance in modern Western astrology.[199] Symbols of each zodiac sign in Table 11.2 are as follows: ♈, Aries; ♉, Taurus; ♊, Gemini; ♋, Cancer; ♌, Leo; ♍, Virgo; ♎, Libra; ♏, Scorpio; ♐, Sagittarius; ♑, Capricorn; ♒, Aquarius; and ♓, Pisces.

Domicile

When a planet is in a sign it rules, it is in its domicile. Here, the planet expresses itself easily and is autonomous and well-suited to the environment. A planet in its domicile at the time of birth is indicative of a strongly manifesting planetary force.[200]

When a planet is in another planet's domicile, it has to rely on its host planet for support. The condition of the host planet is a key factor in determining if it is capable of supporting its guest. For example, in a natal chart with the Moon in Leo, we would determine the condition of the Sun to gain insight into how well supported the Moon is as a guest in the Sun's domicile. If, for instance, the Sun is exalted in Aries, it facilitates providing support to the Moon. On the other hand, if the Sun is fallen in Libra, it may struggle to provide support to the Moon.

Exaltation

When a planet is exalted, it is an honored guest in another planet's domicile. Here, the planet is powerful but not autonomous, well-suited to the environment, and easily expresses itself. A planet that is exalted at the time of birth is indicative of a strongly manifesting planetary force.[201]

Triplicity

When a planet is in its triplicity (in older texts, *trigon*), it is in its element in another planet's domicile. Here, planets may also freely express themselves but not as much as when exalted or in their own domicile.

Each sign has a triplicity day, night, and co-ruler (Table 11.2 above). Day rulers are more influential in day charts, and night rulers are more influential in night charts.

---

199. Brennan, *Hellenistic Astrology,* 249–52.

200. Brennan, *Hellenistic Astrology*, 232–42.

201. Brennan, *Hellenistic Astrology*, 242–49.

Co-rulers are equally influential in both day and night charts. Signs of the same element share the same set of triplicity rulers.

Term

When a planet is in its term (in older texts, *bound*), it is a standard guest in another planet's domicile. Here, the planet is somewhat powerful, decently suited to the environment, and adequately expresses itself. Renaissance astrologer William Lilly states that a planet dignified only by term "… shows a man more of the corporature and temper of the Planet, then [than] any extraordinary abundance in fortune, or of eminency in the Commen-wealth [Commonwealth]."[202]

Decan

When a planet is in its decan (in older texts, *face*), it has minimal agency, ekes by in the environment, and struggles to express itself. Lilly states that a planet dignified only by decan is "… almost like a man ready to be turned out of doors, having much adoe [ado] to maintaine [maintain] himself in credit and reputation : and in *Genealogies* it represents a Family at the last gasp, even as good as quite decayed, barely able to support itself."[203]

Each sign is composed of three decans (Table 11.2 above) occupying a 10° segment of a sign. The first decan begins at 0°, the second decan begins at 10°, and the third decan begins at 20°.

Detriment

When a planet is in its detriment (in older texts, *adversity*), it is an uncomfortable guest in another planet's domicile. Here, the planet lacks agency, is not well-suited to the environment, and expresses itself in an unconventional or awkward manner. A planet in its detriment at the time of birth is indicative of a weak or negatively manifesting planetary force.[204]

---

202. Lilly, *Christian Astrology,* 102–03.

203. Lilly, *Christian Astrology*, 103.

204. Chris Brennan, "The Origins of the Concept of Detriment in Astrology," *The Astrology Podcast*, audio, 2:04:50, July 28, 2020, https://theastrologypodcast.com/2020/07/28/the-origins-of-the-concept-of -detriment-in-astrology.

Fall

When a planet is in its fall (in older texts, *depression*), it is an unwelcome guest in another planet's domicile. Here, the planet completely lacks agency, is ill suited to the environment, and severely struggles to express itself. A planet in its fall at the time of birth is indicative of a weakly manifesting planetary force.[205]

Other Dignities and Debilities

When planets lack sign-based dignities and debilities, other astrological conditions have a greater impact on their expressive strength. These conditions later evolved into the *accidental* dignities and debilities of Medieval and Renaissance astrology.[206,207] An explanation of each major condition follows. This is not an exhaustive list.

House

As discussed in chapter 7, planetary forces manifest strongest in angular houses and weakest in cadent houses. In Medieval and Renaissance astrology, planets in the first and tenth houses are the most dignified, whereas planets in the sixth, eighth, and twelfth houses are the most debilitated, with the twelfth house considered the most severe.[208,209] The other houses are considered more or less dignified.

Apparent Motion

Planets that appear prograde or are fast in motion are dignified, whereas planets that appear retrograde or are slow in motion are debilitated.[210] In antiquity, planetary speed was easy to deduce because astrologers used an ephemeris to find the daily positions of celestial objects, so they were familiar with their average speeds.

Solar Conjunctions

As previously covered, planets may conjunct the Sun in three different ways: under the beams, combust, or in the heart. Planets in the heart of the Sun are dignified, whereas

205. Brennan, *Hellenistic Astrology,* 242–46.

206. Greer and Warnock, *Picatrix*, 66–77.

207. Lilly, *Christian Astrology*, 115.

208. Ibn-Ezra, *The Beginning of Wisdom*, 137–38.

209. Lilly, *Christian Astrology*, 115.

210. Brennan, *Hellenistic Astrology*, 206–07.

planets under the beams or combust are debilitated. Combustion is considered more debilitating than being under the beams.[211,212]

When a planet is in chariot, this debilitation may be significantly mitigated.[213] A planet is in chariot when in domicile, exalted, or in term. Some also consider planets in their triplicity to be in chariot.

Orientation to the Sun

In Medieval and Renaissance astrology, planets may be dignified or debilitated by their rising and setting positions relative to the Sun.[214,215] Mercury and Venus are dignified as evening stars and debilitated as morning stars. Mars, Jupiter, and Saturn are dignified as morning stars and debilitated as evening stars. The Moon is dignified as an evening star but is not debilitated as a morning star.

Planets are morning stars (in older texts, *oriental*) when they rise and set before the Sun (i.e., are visible in the morning before sunrise) and evening stars (in older texts, *occidental*) when they rise and set after the Sun (i.e., are visible in the evening after sunset). You may think of planets conjunct the Sun as in the process of transitioning from one orientation to another.

Aspects

Generally, planets forming sextiles or trines are dignified, whereas planets forming squares or oppositions are debilitated.[216,217] In Renaissance astrology planets are dignified when they form a partile conjunction, trine, or sextile with Venus or Jupiter, and debilitated when they form a partile conjunction, square, or opposition with Mars or Saturn.[218] When planets form a partile aspect with each other, they are in the same degree of their respective signs. For example, the Moon at 10° Aries and the Sun at 10° Gemini form a partile sextile.

211. Ibn-Ezra, *The Beginning of Wisdom*, 129, 136–37.

212. Lilly, *Christian Astrology*, 113.

213. Brennan, *Hellenistic Astrology*, 203–04.

214. Abu'l-Rayhan Muhammad Ibn Ahmad Al-Biruni, *The Book of Instruction in the Elements of the Art of Astrology*, trans. R. Ramsay Wright (Astrology Classics, 2006), 75–78.

215. Lilly, *Christian Astrology*, 114–15.

216. Greer and Warnock, *Picatrix*, 71.

217. Dorotheus, *Carmen Astrologicum*, 221–21.

218. Lilly, *Christian Astrology*, 115.

One can easily spend a lifetime studying Western astrology—indeed, many people do. A detailed discussion of astrology is beyond the scope of this book but additional information and recommended reading are given in Appendix B should you wish to pursue it.

Fundamentals: Planetary Aspects

Since the planets are in continuous motion, they occasionally form aspects (angles) with each other (Figure 11.2). These aspects determine if the planets interact harmoniously or disharmoniously. You may think of them as social exchanges planets occasionally have with each other as they move through the sky. In the Greco-Roman model, five major aspects are recognized.[219]

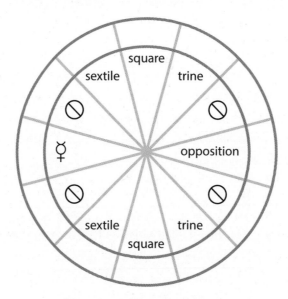

Figure 11.2. Planetary aspects

---

219. Ptolemy, *Tetrabiblos*, 72–73.

Conjunction

When two or more planets are conjunct, their forces mix. We have already seen this with the Sun, the most complex case of conjunction. Biblical commentator and philosopher Ibn-Ezra likens conjunctions in general to two companions travelling together.[220]

Sextile

When planets are sextile (60°), their interaction is harmonious. Ibn-Ezra likens sextiles to two people seeking each other's love.[221]

Square

When planets are square (90°), their interaction is disharmonious. Ibn-Ezra likens squares to two people competing for control.[222]

Trine

When planets are trine (120°), their interaction is harmonious. Ibn-Ezra likens trines to two people with a similar temperament.[223]

Opposition

When planets are in opposition (180°), their interaction is disharmonious. Ibn-Ezra likens oppositions to two people fighting each other.[224]

Planetary aspects are based on ancient Greek optical theory. In Figure 11.2, Mercury's locale is used as a reference point. The prohibition sign indicates locales where planets are averse to Mercury. When planets are averse, they cannot "see" each other in the sky.

Natal aspects reveal which planetary forces are inherently in harmony or in conflict within an individual. In the natal chart, aspects are typically shown as central lines connecting one planet to another. Some chart reports also convey aspect information in

220. Ibn-Ezra, *The Beginning of Wisdom*, 137.

221. Ibn-Ezra, *The Beginning of Wisdom*, 137.

222. Ibn-Ezra, *The Beginning of Wisdom*, 137.

223. Ibn-Ezra, *The Beginning of Wisdom*, 137.

224. Ibn-Ezra, *The Beginning of Wisdom*, 137.

grid format. To gain insight into the energetic tendencies underlying this harmony or conflict, examine the signs and houses of the planets involved.

All aspects have advantages and disadvantages; there is no "best" aspect configuration. Individuals whose natal charts have many squares or oppositions are not predisposed to a difficult life, though they may be required to put forth extra effort to reconcile disharmonious planetary forces. Likewise, individuals whose natal charts have many sextiles or trines are not predisposed to an easy life. They may be unable to deal with failure or unsure how to proceed during a crisis—these are learnable skills individuals with many squares and oppositions typically put into use more frequently. Unaspected planets are also not uncommon in natal charts. An unaspected planet does not interact with other planets. Left to their own devices, unaspected planets may manifest in powerful or unruly ways.

Active Work
Ritual: Orphic Adoration of the Luminaries

In traditional astrology, the Sun and Moon are the ruling lights of the day and night, respectively.[225] Here, you will perform an adoration of the luminaries incorporating elements of ancient Greek religious practice. In this paradigm, the deities Helios and Selene are personifications of the Sun and Moon, respectively. Helios is a titan who rides through the sky on a four-yoked chariot, providing the light of the day. Corinth and Rhodes were major centers of Helios worship.[226,227] Selene rides through the sky on a two-yoked chariot and provides the light of the night. In some genealogical accounts, she is the sister or daughter of Helios.[228,229,230] Statues of Selene (often co-present with Helios) were prominent in Thalamae and Elis, implying emphasis on her worship in those locales.[231,232]

Materials

- Matches
- Two tablets of incense charcoal

225. Valens, *Anthologies*, 25–26, 62.

226. Pausanias, *Description of Greece* 1, trans. W. H. S. Jones and H. A. Ormerod (William Heinemann, 1926), 247–51, 258–59.

227. Strabo, *Geography, Volume VI: Books 13–14*, trans. Horace Leonard Jones (Harvard University Presss, 1929), 269.

228. *Hesiod: The Homeric Hymns and Homerica*, trans. Hugh G. Evelyn-White (William Heinemann, 1914), 107, 458–59.

229. David Kovacs, trans., *Euripides: Helen, Phoenician Women, Orestes* (Harvard University Press, 2002), 228–31.

230. Nonnos, *Dionysiaca, Vol. III: Books 36–48*, trans. W. H. D. Rouse (Harvard University Press, 1940), 310–11.

231. Pausanias, *Description of Greece,* 2:163.

232. Pausanias, *Description of Greece,* 3:150–51.

- Tongs
- A fireproof container in which to burn your charcoal
- Frankincense
- A pleasant-smelling incense you associate with the Moon

Procedure: Sun Adoration

At sunrise, go outside and stand in the Sun's rays. If you live in an area where this is not practical, stand in the sunlight shining through a window instead. As you stand, center yourself using any preferred method. Feel the Sun's warm, radiant energy on your skin. Light your charcoal tablet in the fireproof container. You may use the tongs to move the charcoal tablet around if necessary. When it is sufficiently burning, add the frankincense. Say:

> *Hear golden Titan, whose eternal eye*
> *With broad survey, illumines all the sky:*
> *Self-born, unwearied in diffusing light,*
> *And to all eyes the mirror of delight:*
> *Lord of the seasons, with thy fiery car*
> *And leaping coursers, beaming light from far:*
> *With thy right hand the source of morning light,*
> *And with thy left the father of the night.*
> *Agile and vig'rous, venerable Sun,*
> *Fiery and bright around the heav'ns you run.*
> *Foe to the wicked, but the good man's guide,*
> *O'er all his steps propitious you preside:*
> *With various-founding, golden lyre, 'tis thine*
> *To fill the world with harmony divine.*
> *Father of ages, guide of prosp'rous deeds,*
> *The world's commander, borne by lucid steeds,*

Immortal Jove, all-searching, bearing light,
Source of existence, pure and fiery bright:
Bearer of fruit, almighty lord of years,
Agil [agile] and warm, whom ev'ry pow'r reveres.
Great eye of Nature and the starry skies,
Doom'd with immortal flames to set and rise:
Dispensing justice, lover of the stream,
The world's great despot, and o'er all supreme.
Faithful defender, and the eye of right,
Of steeds the ruler, and of life the light:
With founding whip four fiery steeds you guide,
When in the car of day you glorious ride.
Propitious on these mystic labours shine,
And bless thy suppliants with a life divine.[233]

As the incense continues to burn, spend a few moments in quiet gratitude, thanking the Sun for its life and light. Let the charcoal die out naturally. If you are in a hurry, you may smother it with sand, and *never* leave burning charcoal unattended. Make sure the ashes are completely extinguished and cool to the touch before disposal. Alternatively, they may be saved for use in future solar work. If you practice *Hellēnismos*, adding the ashes to your libation area is another option.

Procedure: Moon Adoration

That night, go outside and gaze up at the Moon. If you live in an area where this is not practical, look through a window instead. As you gaze, carry out rhythmic breathing using any preferred method. Carefully observe the Moon's silvery white color, as well as the quality of light it reflects. Feel the Moon's cool, reflective energy on your skin.

233. Taylor, *The Hymns of Orpheus*, 122–23.

Light your charcoal tablet in the fireproof container. You may use the tongs to move the charcoal tablet around if necessary. When it is sufficiently burning, add your lunar incense. Say:

Hear, Goddess queen, diffusing silver light,
Bull-horn'd and wand'ring thro' [through] the gloom of Night.
With stars surrounded, and with circuit wide
Night's torch extending, thro' the heav'ns you ride:
Female and Male with borrow'd rays you shine,
And now full-orb'd, now tending to decline.
Mother of ages, fruit-producing Moon,
Whose amber orb makes Night's reflected noon:
Lover of horses, splendid, queen of Night,
All-seeing pow'r bedeck'd with starry light.
Lover of vigilance, the foe of strife,
In peace rejoicing, and a prudent life:
Fair lamp of Night, its ornament and friend,
Who giv'st [gives] to Nature's works their destin'd end.
Queen of the stars, all-wife Diana hail!
Deck'd with a graceful robe and shining veil;
Come, blessed Goddess, prudent, starry, bright,
Come moony-lamp with chaste and splendid light,
Shine on these sacred rites with prosp'rous rays,
And pleas'd accept thy suppliant's mystic praise.[234]

As the incense continues to burn, spend a few moments in quiet gratitude, thanking the Moon for the tidal rhythms and nightly light. Let the charcoal die out naturally. If you are in a hurry, you may

234. Taylor, *The Hymns of Orpheus*, 124–26.

smother it with sand—and of course, *never* leave burning charcoal unattended. Make sure the ashes are completely extinguished and cool to the touch before disposal. Alternatively, they may be saved for use in future lunar work. If you practice *Hellēnismos*, adding the ashes to your libation area is another option.

> July 5, 2021. *Orphic Adoration of the Luminaries.* The Orphic Hymn to the Sun calls for a fumigation of frankincense and *mánna* (Gk. μάννα).[235] Since there is no consensus regarding what *mánna* actually is, it has been omitted. Some *Hellēnismos* practitioners use sap from the Flowering Ash—feel free to include it in addition to the frankincense if it is important in your tradition or if you feel it is necessary.
>
> The Orphic Hymn to the Moon calls for an incense offering of "aromatics," which are probably aromatic herbs and spices.[236] I typically use a mixture of storax, myrrh, sage, frankincense, and a fruit pit—*The Greek Magical Papyri* state this mixture is generally useful for benefic work with Selene.[237]

Ritual: Equilibrating Mercy and Severity

On the Tree of Life (see chapter 1), *Gebura* (associated with Mars) resides on the Pillar of Severity, while *Ḥesed* (associated with Jupiter) resides on the Pillar of Mercy. Although the Pillar of Severity and Pillar of Mercy occupy the left and right columns of the Tree of Life respectively, the Pillar of Severity is associated with the right side of the human body and the Pillar of Mercy with the left; when Primordial

---

235. Taylor, *The Hymns of Orpheus*, 122–23.

236. Taylor, *The Hymns of Orpheus*, 124–26.

237. Hans Dieter Betz, ed., *The Greek Magical Papyri in Translation, Including the Demotic Spells* (University of Chicago Press, 1986), 90–92.

Man (Heb. ʾAdam Qadmon) is superimposed on the Tree of Life, he faces the observer (Figure 11.3).[238]

Figure 11.3. ʾAdam Qadmon

When Primordial Man is superimposed on the Tree of Life, *Gebura* overlaps with his right arm and *Ḥesed* overlaps with his left arm. *Tifʿeret* (the central sphere residing on the Middle Pillar) is located in the center of his chest. The paths of *Lamed* and *Yod* connect *Gebura* and *Ḥesed* to *Tifʿeret* respectively.

The Pillar of Severity is generally associated with femininity (i.e., magnetic principle), whereas the Pillar of Mercy is generally associated with masculinity (i.e., electric principle). When these two forces are sufficiently balanced, we function more effectively in our daily lives. As Crowley said, "Remember that unbalanced force is evil; that unbalanced severity is but cruelty and oppression; but that also unbalanced mercy is but weakness that would allow and abet Evil. Act pas-

---

238. "Adam Ḳadmon," *The Jewish Encyclopedia*, 1:181–83.

sionately; think rationally; be Thyself."[239] Here, you will channel and then balance these two forces using solar energy.

Materials
- Your Sun, Mars, and Jupiter tools

Statement of Intent
It is my will to equilibrate mercy and severity.

Procedure
Place your Mars tool beside you in the north and Jupiter tool beside you in the south. Hold your Sun tool in front of you. Take six deep breaths and center yourself. When ready, use your Sun tool to perform an invoking solar GRH (chapter 8). Visualize a radiant golden light emanating down from the heavens, passing through your hexagrams and enveloping you.

Stand in the center of your circle and face west. Your Mars tool should be at your right (in the north) and Jupiter tool at your left (in the south). Place your Sun tool in front of you.

Pick up your Mars tool and draw an invoking earth Mars hexagram to your immediate right (in the north). Visualize it strongly in red. Set your Mars tool back down beside you.

Pick up your Jupiter tool and draw an invoking earth Jupiter hexagram to your immediate left (in the south). Visualize it strongly in blue. Set your Jupiter tool back down beside you.

Facing west, take six deep breaths and center yourself. Hold your Mars tool in your right hand and Jupiter tool in your left hand. Outstretch

---

239. Aleister Crowley, "Liber Libræ: Sub Figura XXX," *The Equinox* 1, no. 1 (1909): 17–21.

your arms in the shape of a cross, so your right arm extends through the center of your Mars hexagram and your left arm extends through the center of your Jupiter hexagram.

Visualize the letter *lamed* (ל) on your right collarbone and the letter *yod* (י) on your left collarbone. With arms still outstretched, allow the two planetary forces to flow through your tools, down your arms, past your shoulders, and into the center of your chest. When you are sufficiently filled with Martial and Jupiterian vibrations, set both tools back down beside you.

Pick up your Sun tool. Hold it with both hands in front of your chest. Take six more deep breaths while visualizing yourself emanating a radiant golden light. As you breathe, swirls of Martial (red) and Jupiterian (blue) light produce a marbling effect on the surface of the golden (solar) light. Say:

Strength and love,
death and life,
magnetic and electric,
darkness and light.
Between the pillars
of black and white,
I dwell in beauty,
combining mercy and might.

Still holding your Sun tool with both hands, visualize the Martian and Jupiterian light merging into the solar light. The red and blue marbling gradually fade as they are equilibrated by golden light. You may push any excess light down through your feet and into the ground beneath you. Set your Sun tool down in front of you and perform the Qabalistic Cross.

Banishing
To clear any remaining planetary vibrations, clap and banish with laughter.

> June 3, 2023. *Equilibrating Mercy and Severity.* I consistently feel more balanced and levelheaded afterward. I'm also convinced the aftereffects enhanced my ability to make impartial decisions when subsequent circumstances necessitated it. Others reported similar results.

Ritual: *Solve et Coagula*
The alchemical maxim *solve et coagula* (Lat. dissolve and coagulate) alludes to transforming matter (or the self) through separation and recombination. When a substance is dissolved, it is broken down into its component parts. Psychologically, this entails breaking down artificial and rejected constructs in the unconscious mind. When a substance is coagulated the component parts are reunited, possibly in a different form. Psychologically, this entails reuniting the refined components of the self. Together, these two processes form the basis of all alchemical operations.[240] Through repeated dissolving and coagulating of the self, we may undergo metamorphosis to reach our highest potential.

Here, you will harness these alchemical processes to balance the planetary forces in eight parts of your psyche. Each part corresponds to a classical planet (plus Uranus) and a ray of the chaos star (Figure 11.4).[241] The different aspects of your psyche that you will interact with are: the magical self (Uranus); war self (Mars); thinking self (Mercury); sexual self (the Moon); ego (the Sun); love self (Venus); wealth self (Jupiter); and death self (Saturn).

240. Mark Stavish, *The Path of Alchemy: Energetic Healing and the World of Natural Magic* (Llewellyn Publications, 2006), 214.

241. Carroll, *Liber Kaos*, 107–51.

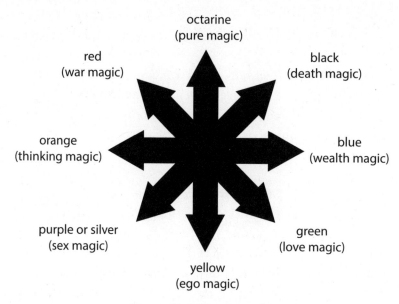

octarine
(pure magic)

red
(war magic)

black
(death magic)

orange
(thinking magic)

blue
(wealth magic)

purple or silver
(sex magic)

green
(love magic)

yellow
(ego magic)

Figure 11.4. The chaos star

In the chaos magic meta-paradigm magic is classified according to function, with each represented by a different color.[242] Octarine is the color of pure magic—everyone perceives it differently. Each ray corresponds to one of the selves you harbor, and together these selves comprise the totality of your being.

Materials

- No materials are required.

Statement of Intent

It is my will to achieve a state of internal planetary harmony.

---

242. Carroll, *Liber Kaos*, 107–51.

Procedure

Take a deep breath and center yourself. Visualize yourself standing on top of a two-dimensional chaos star. It is small enough for your feet to completely cover it. With each breath the star pulsates, gradually expanding until it is a few meters in diameter.

To undergo the process of psychological dissolution, visualize the chaos star slowly filling with water. As it overflows into the surrounding area, say:

> *I call forth the dissolving water*
> *which does not wet the hands.*
> *Hail the bath of the alchemical Queen!*
> *Hail its mother, the Moon!*
> *In this realm of slumbering dragons*
> *where hidden treasure lies in wait,*
> *I will to dissolve that which is below*
> *into that which is above!*

Visualize the dissolving water separating your eight selves from each other. They wade toward their respective points on the chaos star, each one connected to you by an umbilical cord. Each self glows its corresponding color.

Observe how your selves interact with each other. Which ones get along? Which ones conflict? Do any dominate the others? Do any look happy or sad? Talk to your selves one by one. Use the dissolving water to remove blockages, impurities, and anything else you deem necessary.

After you are finished interacting with them, begin the process of coagulation. Visualize the waters receding, leaving specks of golden light in their wake. Say:

I call forth the gold within me,
the Star in Man.
Hail the phoenix risen from the ashes!
Hail the child of the Sun and Moon!
United with the glory of the universe
and free from obscurity,
I will to integrate that which is above
into that which is below!

Again, talk to your eight selves one by one. Use the specks of golden light to mend connections, fill gaps, and anything else you deem necessary.

After you are finished interacting with your selves, visualize them walking toward the center of the chaos star. As they merge back into you, their different colored lights also merge, producing a brilliant white with golden flecks. The light slowly condenses in the center of your chest, and then disappears.

Open your eyes and become reacquainted with your surroundings.

Banishing

Banish with laughter.

June 10, 2023. *Solve et Coagula.* This rite was inspired by various alchemical texts and imagery. The interactions among various selves tended to reflect their relative planetary strengths and interactions in my natal chart. This was unexpected, but in retrospect not surprising. I also felt more integrated and had less internal conflict. Others reported similar results.

Chapter 11
Homework

After taking notes on the chapter, magical practice should be commenced for thirty minutes each day for a minimum of one month. Perform the assignments in the order presented. Remember to document your efforts in your magical diary.

- ☐ Meditate on the arrangement of planets in the hexagram. What new insights can you discover?

- ☐ Meditate on the planetary associations for each set of seven. Then, "think in sevens" to produce your own planetary correspondences. You may also rearrange any traditional associations to suit your personal practice if necessary.

- ☐ Examine your natal chart to determine sign-based (*essential*) and other (*accidental*) dignities and debilities of each classical planet. Overall, which of your natal planets is the most dignified? The most debilitated?

- ☐ Examine your natal chart to identify any aspects that are present. Which planetary forces are in harmony? Which are in conflict?

- ☐ Perform the multi-planet rites that facilitate spiritual enrichment, life balance, and psychological well-being before proceeding to the next chapter. Feel free to modify them to your liking or substitute your own.

Chapter 11 Resources

Carroll, Peter J. *Liber Null & Psychonaut: The Practice of Chaos Magic*. Weiser Books, 2022.

Enodian, River. "Banishing with Laughter: Not Sweating the Small Stuff." *Tea Addicted Witch*, February 28, 2018. https://www.patheos.com/blogs/teaaddictedwitch/2018/01/banishing-with-laughter.

Vayne, Julian. "Banish with Laughter." *The Blog of Baphomet*, February 17, 2014. https://theblogofbaphomet.com/2014/02/17/banish-with-laughter.

CHAPTER 12
Trans-Saturnian Planets

So far, we have explored the classical planets, internalized them, and determined how they impact our lives. We've also interacted with them magically and gained insight into how they interact with each other and work together. Here we will explore the trans-Saturnian planets, including the dwarf planet Pluto. In modern Western astrology, the trans-Saturnian planets are sometimes called the *generational* planets because they stay in a sign for years—roughly: Uranus, seven; Neptune, fourteen; and Pluto, twelve to thirty-one years. Common trans-Saturnian planetary symbols are shown in Figure 12.1. They are useful focal points in meditation and magical practice.

(a)   (b)   (c)

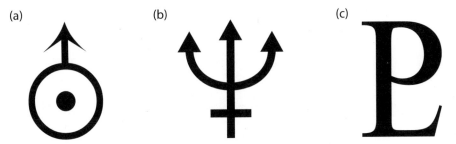

**Figure 12.1. Astronomical symbols
of (a) Uranus, (b) Neptune, and (c) Pluto**

The trans-Saturnian planets have no associated planetary seals, as they were discovered well after the publication of Agrippa's *Three Books of Occult Philosophy*.

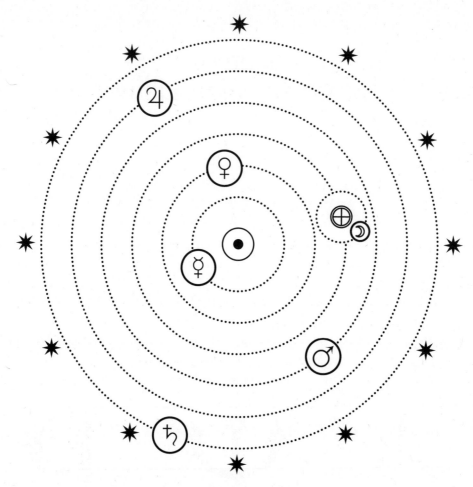

Figure 12.2. Renaissance model of the planets

Renaissance Model of The Planets

In ancient Greece, Aristarchus of Samos proposed a heliocentric model, but the idea did not gain popularity until the Renaissance, when it was revived by Nicolaus

Copernicus.[243,244] During the Renaissance, interest in observing astronomical phenomena was renewed in Europe—major advances in astronomy and astrology had already been made elsewhere during the Middle Ages.[245,246] In Copernican cosmology Mercury, Venus, Earth, Mars, Jupiter, and Saturn orbit the Sun, while the Moon orbits Earth (Figure 12.2). As subsequent discoveries catalyzed our understanding of the solar system and universe at large, the Copernican model underwent further revisions. Astronomy and astrology also separated, with the latter eventually deemed a pseudoscience.

In this model, the fixed stars appear to move through the sky due to Earth's rotation. The orbits of the wandering stars (including Earth) are circular, and celestial bodies move at a constant velocity. Information in this section is adapted from Copernicus's *On the Revolutions* (Lat. *De Revolutionibus Orbium Coelestium*).

We know today the planets orbit the Sun in an elliptical fashion. Their orbital velocity also varies. Further, the Sun is but one of many stars orbiting the center of our Milky Way. Some of the other stars in our galaxy have planets orbiting them and some do not. There are even rogue planets that do not orbit stars at all!

What Is a Planet?

In antiquity, the classical planets were *wandering stars* traveling through the heavens of a geocentric universe. In the heliocentric model introduced during the Renaissance, Earth was included among the wandering stars (Lat. *errantium siderum*). The Moon was considered a wandering star until the discovery of the Galilean moons, when they were deemed *satellites* (*satellites*; attendants) instead.[247] By the end of the seventeenth century, a *planet* was informally defined as a large celestial body that orbits the Sun. Evidence at the time was also mounting that the Sun is a star.[248]

---

243. T. L. Heath, ed., *The Works of Archimedes* (Cambridge University Press, 1897), 221–32.

244. Nicolaus Copernicus, *On the Revolutions*, trans. Edward Rosen (Johns Hopkins University Press, 1992), 385.

245. Marika Sardar, "Astronomy and Astrology in the Medieval Islamic World," in *Heilbrunn Timeline of Art History* (The Metropolitan Museum of Art, 2000).

246. Gad Freudenthal, ed., *Science in Medieval Jewish Cultures* (Cambridge University Press, 2011).

247. Johannes Kepler, *Narratio de Observatis a se Quatuor Iouis Satellitibus Erronibus* (Apud Cosmum Iunctam, 1611).

248. Miguel A. Granada, "New Visions of the Cosmos," in *The Cambridge Companion to Renaissance Philosophy*, ed. James Hankins (Cambridge University Press, 2007), 270–86.

Only six planets were known until the eighteenth century. Uranus (in older texts, *Herschel*) was discovered in 1781, followed by Neptune in 1846 and Pluto in 1930.[249,250,251,252] For a brief time, Ceres, the largest celestial object in the asteroid belt between Mars and Jupiter, was also considered a planet along with fellow asteroids Pallas, Juno, and Vesta. The discovery of additional trans-Neptunian objects (e.g., Haumea, Makemake …) soon made astronomers reevaluate what a *planet* actually is. In 2006, the International Astronomical Union issued a formal definition:

> *A planet is a celestial body that*
> *(a) is in orbit around the Sun,*
> *(b) has sufficient mass for its self-gravity to overcome rigid body forces so that*
> *   it assumes a hydrostatic equilibrium (nearly round) shape, and*
> *(c) has cleared the neighbourhood around its orbit.*[253]

Under this definition, Pluto was reclassified as a dwarf planet because it has not cleared its neighborhood enough to be considered the dominant celestial body. Ceres, Haumea, and Makemake are also considered dwarf planets.

Uranus

Uranus is the only planet that takes its English name from Greek mythology—its Roman counterpart is Caelus. It is one of the most unconventional planets: it was the first to be discovered via telescope, its axis of rotation lies nearly in the plane of its orbit (so it rolls like a ball instead of spins like a top), and its rings are composed of some of the darkest colored objects in our solar system.

249. William Herschel, "XXXII. Account of a Comet," *Philosophical Transactions of the Royal Society of London* 71 (1781): 492–501.

250. Papers of John Couch Adams, 1701–1996, St. John's College Library Special Collections, University of Cambridge, United Kingdom.

251. U. J. Le Verrier, "Recherches sur le mouvements d'Uranus," *Comptes Rendus Hebdomadaires des Séances de l'Académie des Sciences* 22, no. 22 (1846): 907–18.

252. Lowell Observatory, Lowell Observatory Observation Circular, May 1, 1930.

253. International Astronomical Union, "Resolution B5: Definition of a Planet in the Solar System," International Astronomical Union General Assembly, 2006.

Gk. *Ouranos* (Οὐρανός); Heb. *'Oron* (אורון);
Lat. *Uranus*; Ouranian Barbaric *UNGASCAB*

The Western View of Uranus

In the modern astronomical model, Uranus resides between Saturn and Neptune. Astrologically, Uranus represents a generation's uniqueness.[254,255] This includes their originality, innovative capabilities, and spontaneity. It is also generally associated with sudden change, technological advancement, and revolution. Uranus rules (or co-rules, depending on who you read) Aquarius. This is a suitable domicile because it is conducive to expressing the liberation and unpredictability underlying the Uranian force. Sign-based dignities and debilities of Uranus have long been debated—astrologers have not reached a consensus yet.

In the Hermetic model, Uranus affects the magical development on Earth.[256] It is also responsible for humanity's ability to recognize and practice magic. However, we cannot directly sense the Uranus sphere from Earth—its force is only detectable in the lunar sphere and beyond. According to Franz Bardon, a magician should be mentally saturated with a lilac light before visiting the Uranus zone.[257] This color of light emulates the Uranus zone's vibrations and is thus conducive to performing Uranian work.

The Uranus Archetype

Uranus is the disruptor. It represents your generation's unconventionality and manifests in your ability to change the status quo. It also has ties to one's sense of rebelliousness. Uranus oversees novelty and the unexpected, two important disruptors. Exoterically, it is the inventor who is ahead of the times. Esoterically, it is the Great Awakener overseeing revolution in the terrestrial and celestial realms. Deities typically associated with Uranus include Nut (Egyptian), Ouranos (Greek), and Caelus (Roman). Keywords relevant to Uranus are as follows:

---

254. Chris Brennan, "Uranus in Astrology: Meaning and Significations," *The Astrology Podcast*, audio, 3:23:56, September 23, 2021, https://theastrologypodcast.com/2021/09/23/uranus-in-astrology-meaning-and-significations.

255. Woolfolk, *The Only Astrology Book*, 210–15, 343.

256. Bardon, *Magical Evocation,* 293, 349.

257. Bardon, *Magical Evocation*, 357.

Disruption

Unconventionality is an important disruptor. Constructive disruption facilitates innovation, rapid advancement, and a healthy questioning of authority. Destructive disruption may instill a fear of change, hindering future progress. It may also lead to chronic feelings of unrest and rebellion for its own sake.

Uniqueness

You are unique, just like everyone else. The Uranian force may manifest through contrariety or be conveyed via eccentricity, such as marching to the beat of your own drummer.

Innovation

Originality confers no tangible benefit if a spark of genius receives no follow-through. Throughout history, innovation has powered numerous scientific, industrial, and cultural revolutions. This is also why Uranus is associated with electricity and technology.

Liberation

The Uranian force is heavily tied to freedom. Many astrologers view Uranus as free from Saturn's limitations. Further, in many paradigms Uranus is associated with celestial deities—the sky's the limit!

Western Uranus Magic

In many Western esoteric practices, Uranus is associated with astrological, technological, chaos, and pure magic. It is also generally associated with rebellious and spontaneous works. Uranus is not associated with a particular day of the week or metal—these were linked to the classical planets long before the discoveries of the trans-Saturnian planets.

In ceremonial traditions, Uranus is not associated with a sphere or path of the Qabala.[258] However, some magicians associate it with *Da'at* (Heb. Knowledge). This "sphere that is not a sphere" is typically depicted as an unnumbered circle crossing the Abyss (an imaginary horizontal line separating the upper three spheres from the lower spheres) on the Tree of Life. *Keter* (Crown) and *Da'at* are transpersonal and personal

---

258. Crowley, "777 Revised," 2–3, 5.

emanations of pure spirit, respectively.[259] Psychologically, *Da'at* allows us to integrate abstract concepts and relate to physical reality in novel ways.[260] Correspondences of *Da'at* often relate to knowledge and integration.

Some magicians also associate Uranus with *'Alef*, the path connecting *Keter* and *Ḥokma* (Wisdom). It connects the pure spirit of transpersonal self to transpersonal will and purpose. In ancient script the letter *'alef* resembles the head of an ox, the animal revered for its "sacred character."[261] Correspondences of *'Alef* often relate to elemental air. There is no magic square or Hebrew hierarchy traditionally associated with Uranus. However, I have seen some magicians attribute archangel *'Uri'el*. *'Uri'el* often appears with *Gabri'el*, *Mika'el*, and *Rafa'el*, and has been written about extensively.[262]

Neptune

Neptune's name pays homage to its deep blue color. It is one of the most mysterious planets: it was the first to be discovered via mathematics, its ring system exhibits arcs (clumps of dust that do not spread out), and the reason for its deep blue color remains unknown.

> Gk. *Poseidōn* (Ποσειδῶν); Heb. *Rahav* (רהב);
> Lat. *Neptunus*; Ouranian Barbaric *AKISEC*

The Western View of Neptune

In the modern astronomical model, Neptune resides between Uranus and the Kuiper belt. Astrologically, Neptune represents a generation's imagination.[263,264] This includes collective fantasies, dreams, and mystical qualities. It is also generally associated with myth, mystery, and illusion. Neptune rules (or co-rules, depending on who you read)

259. Yitzchak Ginsburgh, *The Hebrew Letters: Channels of Creative Consciousness* (Gal Einai Publications, 1990), 355.

260. Ginsburgh, *The Hebrew Letters*, 375.

261. "Ox or Bullock," *The Jewish Encyclopedia* 9:452.

262. "Uriel," *The Jewish Encyclopedia*, 12:383.

263. Woolfolk, *The Only Astrology Book*, 216–21, 343.

264. Chris Brennan, "How Did Pluto and the Outer Planets Get Their Meanings?" *The Astrology Podcast*, audio, 1:57:41, April 27, 2019, https://theastrologypodcast.com/transcripts/ep-202-transcript-how-did-pluto-and-the-outer-planets-get-their-meanings.

Pisces. This is a suitable domicile because it is conducive to expressing the nebulousness and fluidity underlying the Neptunian force. Sign-based dignities and debilities of Neptune have long been debated—astrologers have not reached a consensus yet.

In the Hermetic model, Neptune maintains the balance of macrocosmic forces on Earth.[265] It is also responsible for humanity's mystical knowledge. Bardon does not discuss what color of light a magician should be mentally saturated with before visiting the Neptune zone.[266] However, many magicians have successfully performed Neptunian work harnessing its deep blue.

The Neptune Archetype

Neptune is the transcender. It represents a generation's spiritual vision, which manifests in the ability to transition from the mundane to the magical. It also has ties to psychic sensitivity. Neptune oversees mystical insights and experiences, two important transcenders. Exoterically, it is the mystic who has a direct connection to the Divine. Esoterically, it is the Great Visionary overseeing faith in the terrestrial and celestial realms. Deities typically associated with Neptune include Nu and Hapi (Egyptian), Poseidon (Greek), and Neptune (Roman). Keywords relevant to Neptune are:

Transcendence

Imagination is an important means of transcendence. Constructive transcendence facilitates spiritual vision and a rich inner life. Destructive transcendence may leave people delusional, unable to distinguish fantasy from reality. It may also lead to escapist behavior, such as through maladaptive daydreaming or drug abuse.

Imagination

Imagination allows us to mentally construct counterfactual alternatives to consensus reality.[267] The Neptunian force may manifest through mystical experiences or be conveyed via faith, such as when you believe what you do not see.

---

265. Bardon, *Magical Evocation*, 293, 349–50.

266. Bardon, *Magical Evocation*, 356–57.

267. Ruth M. J. Byrne, *The Rational Imagination: How People Create Alternatives to Reality* (The MIT Press, 2005), 15–16.

Mysticism

If Uranus is the magician, Neptune is the mystic. Throughout history, mystical practices have facilitated spiritual vision and access to realms beyond physical reality. In modern times, mysticism aims to achieve union with the Divine.

Mystery

Neptune is not visible to the naked eye, a property that carries over esoterically: Neptune is associated with sacred knowledge and practices revealed only to initiates. The Eleusinian and Mithraic mystery cults of the ancient Greeks and Romans come to mind.

Western Neptune Magic

In many Western esoteric practices, Neptune is associated with enchantment, dream, illusory, and transcendental magic. It is also generally associated with mystical and hypnotic works.

In ceremonial traditions Neptune is not associated with a sphere or path of the Qabala.[268] However, some magicians associate it with *Ḥokma* (Heb. Wisdom), the second sphere. This wisdom is the divine imagination underlying physical reality. Psychologically, this sphere represents transpersonal will and purpose. Correspondences of *Ḥokma* often relate to wisdom and the divine masculine (i.e., electric principle).

Some magicians also associate Neptune with *Mem*, the path connecting *Gebura* (Strength or Might) and *Hod* (Splendor). It connects our personal will and power to our intellectual mind. In ancient script, the letter *mem* resembles waves of water, which may allude to the unknown washing upon the shore of the known. Correspondences of *Mem* often relate to elemental water. There is no magic square or Hebrew hierarchy traditionally associated with Neptune, though some magicians attribute it to "archangel Asariel." This could be *'Asri'el*, who is not present in *The Bible* but is identified as an angel in Aramaic incantations, "Azariel," an angel ruling one of the lunar mansions, or an entirely different entity.[269,270]

---

268. Crowley, "777 Revised," 2–3, 5.

269. Shaul Shaked, James Nathan Ford, and Siam Bhayro, *Aramaic Bowl Spells: Jewish Babylonian Aramaic Bowls 1* (Brill, 2013), 334.

270. Cornelius Agrippa, *Three Books*, 532–37.

Pluto

Pluto is one of the most beloved Kuiper belt objects. It did not receive a Hebrew name in 2009 due to its reclassification as a dwarf planet.[271] What it lacks in size it makes up for in intrigue: it was discovered by accident, its dynamic heart-shaped glacier powers its winds, and its orbit and rotation might be influenced by its weather.

Gk. *Hadēs* (Ἅδης) or *Ploutōn* (Πλούτων); Heb. Pluto (פלוטו);
Lat. *Pluto*; Ouranian Barbaric *CADEX-MENGO*

The Western View of Pluto

In the modern astronomical model, Pluto resides in the Kuiper Belt, along with other dwarf planets and trans-Neptunian objects. Astrologically, Pluto represents a generation's primordial power.[272,273] This includes their resilience, transformative capabilities, and the shadow self. It is also generally associated with life-altering events, catharsis, and the subterranean. Pluto rules (or co-rules, depending on who you read) Scorpio or Aries. These are suitable domiciles because they are conducive to expressing the tremendous pressure and duress capable of triggering the Plutonian force. Sign-based dignities and debilities of Pluto have long been debated—astrologers have not reached a consensus yet.

In the Hermetic model, Pluto does not currently have an influence on Earth but will after humanity enters a new epoch.[274] According to Bardon, a magician should be mentally saturated with a light gray light before visiting the Pluto zone.[275] This color of light emulates the Pluto zone's vibrations, making it conducive to performing Plutonian work.

The Pluto Archetype

Pluto is the transformer. It represents your generation's metamorphic process, which manifests in the ability to reinvent yourself. It also has ties to your sense of control.

---

271. Yair Ettinger, "Uranus and Neptune Get Hebrew Names at Last," *Haaretz,* (December 31, 2009), https://www.haaretz.com/2009-12-31/ty-article/uranus-and-neptune-get-hebrew-names-at-last/0000017f-ec5c-ddba-a37f-ee7ecaf10000.

272. Woolfolk, *The Only Astrology Book*, 222–27, 343.

273. Brennan, "Uranus in Astrology," *The Astrology Podcast*, 3:23:56.

274. Bardon, *Magical Evocation*, 349–50.

275. Bardon, *Magical Evocation*, 357.

Pluto oversees death and rebirth, two important transformers. Exoterically, it is the trauma survivor who finds a new normal. Esoterically, it is the Great Transformer who oversees evolution in the terrestrial and celestial realms. Deities typically associated with Pluto include Anubis and Osiris (Egyptian), Hades and Plouton (Greek), and Orcus and Dis Pater (Roman). Keywords relevant to Pluto are as follows:

Transformation

Primordial power is an important means of transformation. Constructive transformation facilitates personal growth, rebounding against the odds, and adapting to the times. Destructive transformation may result in an imbalance or abuse of power. It may also lead to chronic obsession and fanaticism.

Primordial Power

When a generation harnesses its primordial power, it is capable of irreversibly changing the course of humanity. The Plutonian force may manifest through regeneration or be conveyed via resilience—what doesn't kill you makes you stronger.

The Subterranean

Pluto reigns over all that lies beneath. The chthonic may be brought to the surface through force (such as a volcano erupting) or provocation (such as through shadow work). This is also why Pluto is associated with mineral wealth and buried treasure.

Evolution

The flow of life is unpredictable. Nature purges the old to make room for the new. As time passes, the new becomes old and is purged as well. The species that survive are not necessarily the strongest or the smartest—they are the ones who best adapt to change.

Western Pluto Magic

In many Western esoteric practices, Pluto is associated with death-rebirth, psychopomp, cathartic, and toxic magic.[276] It is also generally associated with metamorphic and apocalyptic works.

---

276. Joshua Wetzel, *Ill Thoughts, Ill Words, Ill Deeds: A Toxick Magick Primer, Vol. 1* (Megalithica Books, 2021).

In ceremonial traditions Pluto is not associated with a sphere or path of the Qabala.[277] However, some magicians associate it with *Keter* (Heb. Crown), the first sphere. This crown is the divine authority underlying physical reality. Psychologically, this sphere represents the pure spirit of transpersonal self. Correspondences of *Keter* often relate to divine union and illumination.

Some magicians also associate Pluto with *Sin/Shin*, the path connecting *Hod* (Splendor) and *Malkut* (Kingdom). It connects our intellectual mind to our physical body and the material world of the five senses. In ancient script the letter *sin/shin* resembles two front teeth, which may allude to the chewing required to break down the external so it may be transformed and used internally. Correspondences of *Sin/Shin* often relate to aether and elemental fire. There is no magic square or Hebrew hierarchy traditionally associated with Pluto. However, I have seen some magicians attribute archangel *ʿAzarʾel*. *ʿAzarʾel* is frequently identified as the Angel of Death in Arabic literature and has been written about extensively.[278]

Trans-Saturnian Planets in Chaos Magic

The trans-Saturnian planets may be integrated into magical practice in numerous ways. Various deities, egregores, or pop culture characters associated with them may be invoked or evoked. Divination may be practiced via astrological analysis. Magical items associated with the trans-Saturnian planets may be enchanted for purposes consistent with their nature. Illumination rites aimed at gaining insight into your generational cohort and others may also be performed.

The trans-Saturnian planets orbit the Sun more slowly than the classical planets, and reside billions of kilometers away. Thus, many magicians experience more slowly manifesting (but very powerful) results when utilizing them. There are no ceremonial planetary hexagrams traditionally associated with Uranus, Neptune, and Pluto.

For each trans-Saturnian planet, you'll find an attunement exercise and an additional ritual. As before, the attunements serve to familiarize you with the forces underlying each planet. The additional rituals serve to harness each trans-Saturnian planetary force in a manner consistent with its nature.

277. Crowley, "777 Revised," 2–3, 5.

278. "Angel of Death," *The Jewish Encyclopedia*, 4:480–82.

Active Work
Uranus Attunement

Here, you will attune with Uranus by imitating its movement in space. Find a clear area where you will not slip or bump into furniture. If you have limited mobility, feel free to modify the procedure to your liking, or you can perform the entire exercise mentally.

1. Begin orbiting counterclockwise around an imaginary Sun by walking in a nearly circular path. Uranus's orbit is slightly elliptical. Hold your arms out in front of your chest with rounded elbows in an oval shape to imitate Uranus's rings. Bend forward at your waist to imitate Uranus's unusual tilt. Since Uranus makes one revolution approximately every eighty-four years, walk slowly.

2. As you orbit the imaginary Sun, gyrate your arms clockwise as many times as possible per revolution. Uranus rotates one time approximately every seventeen hours.

3. As you orbit and gyrate, visualize yourself glowing blue-green or lilac. Uranus's blue-green color is caused by small quantities of methane in its atmosphere.

4. As you orbit, gyrate, and visualize, chant *XIQUAL UNGAS-CAB* (Ouranian Barbaric: Manifest Uranus).

5. As you orbit, gyrate, visualize, and chant, resonate with this unconventionality. Observe the unconventionality with all five senses as well as astrally. As time passes, the unconventionality grows stronger. Slowly adjust the rhythm of your body to match the vibrations underlying this unconventionality. Feel them awakening, individuating, and liberating you.

July 6, 2021. *Uranus Attunement.* A fun alternative method is to walk slowly in a counterclockwise direction while hula hooping (so the hoop rotates clockwise) as rapidly as possible. The chanting consistently becomes more erratic as time progresses, and it was not uncommon for it to transform into glossolalia.

Neptune Attunement

Fill a bowl or dish with cold water. Mix in a few drops of blue food coloring to mimic Neptune's deep blue. As the water stills, gaze into it in a well-lit area. Observe the reflections on the water's surface as well as the mutable patterns of light it refracts. Slowly stir the water. As it moves, observe the reflections warp and change. As you slowly become mesmerized by the reflections, take note of how they sometimes reflect reality obliquely and at other times not at all—this is the nature of Neptune.

July 13, 2021. *Neptune Attunement.* In addition to mimicking Neptune's deep blue, the food coloring helps reflections show up better on the water's surface. Stirring the water alludes to Neptune's intense winds, which surpass the speed of sound on Earth. The reflections and light patterns are not constant—they change with the winds. The overall exercise was inspired by data from NASA's *Voyager 2* mission.

Pluto Attunement

Take a bite of chewy food, such as a caramel or piece of beef jerky. (If you wear braces, substitute something softer and less chewy so the wires don't get damaged.) As you chew, feel your teeth mechanically breaking apart the food. Visualize the enzymes in your saliva beginning to digest any fats and starches present. Observe the chewing process with all five your senses, as well as astrally.

As you swallow, visualize the bite of food travelling down your esophagus into your stomach. Here, it mixes with gastric juice that kills microorganisms and further digests it. Visualize the macromolecules in your bite of food being broken down into their component parts. The barrage of enzymes in your gastric juice disassembles larger fats into fatty acids and glycerol, carbohydrates into simple sugars, and proteins into amino acids. Deconstructed by your gastric juices, they are no longer recognizable as your initial bite of food. In this state, these component parts can travel through your intestines, absorb into your body, and be transformed into something new.

Just as your digestive system breaks down and transforms your bite of food into something new, Plutonian energy breaks down and transforms *you* into something new. Spend a few moments contemplating the similarities of these processes.

July 20, 2021. *Pluto Attunement.* This attunement exercise was brought to you by the letter ש. Observing the chewing process and visualizing digestion is gross and unpleasant for many people. So is Plutonian transformation more often than not.

Ritual: "Sparking" Uranian Magical Innovation

A static charge occurs when electrons are transferred from one object to another. When these electrons are abruptly transferred, a brief flow of electricity occurs. For instance, when you shuffle across a carpet while wearing wool socks, the carpet gains electrons from your socks. If you touch a metal doorknob immediately after shuffling across the carpet, you might receive a brief shock and even see a small spark. Electrons abruptly transferred from the metal doorknob to your hand.

In this ritual, you will generate and discharge static to propel personal magical innovation. The static shock will be used to launch a sigil. A sigil is a symbolic glyph representing a specific intent.

Materials

- Pen and paper
- The means to generate a static charge (such as shuffling across a carpet in wool socks or rubbing an inflated balloon on dry hair)
- A nearby metal object (such as a doorknob)
- Optional: Playing sounds from Voyager 2's encounter with Uranus

Preparation

Ensure your means of generating a static shock is effective beforehand. Static shocks occur more frequently during winter due to the drier air—humidifiers may impede your ability to produce a static charge.

Statement of Intent

It is my will to magically innovate.

Procedure

Determine a suitable phrase (e.g., *I WILL MAGICALLY INNOVATE*) to create a sigil. Eliminate any repeating letters (e.g., *I ~~WILL MAGI-CALLY INNOVATE~~*). Construct a sigil from the remaining letters. Your sigil's appearance should not consciously remind you of its purpose. Take your time and do not rush.

When satisfied with your sigil, begin playing the (optional) recording if you are using it. As the recording plays, gaze at the sigil while you generate a static charge. Allow the sigil to embed itself in your mind.

When ready, launch your sigil. Touch the metal object to produce a static shock while still gazing at your sigil. As you are shocked, focus on the sigil as intensely as possible. Ideally, it should be the only thing occupying your conscious mind when you are shocked.

Banishing

Banish with laughter. To discharge any excess static, touch a small metal object (such as a coin or paper clip) to a larger one. You may keep your sigil in your magical diary or destroy it. Do your best to completely forget about the sigil—we will discuss why in chapter 13.

> March 20, 2023. *"Sparking" Uranian Magical Innovation.* A few weeks after I launched the sigil (and completely forgetting about it), two fellow magicians independently requested advice regarding how to go about performing Western planetary charity for…Uranus. I dug through my magical diary to see what worked (and didn't) during a past transit, and became super inspired! An initially short response grew into a longer, more comprehensive remediation document.
>
> June 18, 2023. *Update.* One magician reported the remediation was working! The other one has not responded back yet. The inspiration still continues—I am currently creating Western-style remediation suitable for Neptune and Pluto.

Ritual: Neptunian Bath for Mystical Awareness

Ritual bathing is a common magical practice. Though procedures vary among traditions, the overarching goal often involves purification or infusion with specific vibrations. Ritual bathing was a common practice in ancient Greece and Rome, where it served to cleanse, purify, prepare practitioners for entry into the spiritual realm, and more.[279,280]

---

279. Lionel Casson, *Everyday Life in Ancient Rome*, rev. ed. (Johns Hopkins University Press, 1999), 111.

280. Mirielle M. Lee, *Body, Dress, and Identity in Ancient Greece* (Cambridge University Press, 2015), 220.

Here, you will take a ritual bath to cultivate mystical awareness. After purifying your bath water, you will saturate it with Neptunian vibrations. You will then infuse yourself with Neptunian vibrations via the bath water.

Materials

- A bathtub
- Salt
- Myrrh incense
- An incense burner
- Matches
- Optional: additional bath items (such as a sachet containing ingredients to enhance mystical awareness or a bath bomb that turns the water Neptune's deep blue color)

   Note: If you are allergic to myrrh, incense or bath products that include marine constituents (such as seaweed or sea salt) also bear sympathetic correspondence with Neptune in many paradigms.

Preparation

Clean your bathroom and bathtub beforehand. Also, take a shower beforehand to ensure you are physically clean.

Statement of Intent

It is my will to cultivate mystical awareness.

Procedure

Take a deep breath and center yourself. Begin filling the bathtub with water as cool as you can stand it.

Once the water is a few inches deep, throw in a handful of salt and say, *Spirit of Salt, purify this water!* Visualize the salt removing any impurities present. You may also add any optional bath items at this time.

As the bathtub continues to fill, light your incense. Once it is sufficiently burning, waft the smoke over the water. Say:

> *Hear, Neptune, ruler of the sea profound*
> *Whose liquid grasp begirts the solid ground;*
> *Who, at the bottom of the stormy main,*
> *Dark and deep-bosom'd, hold'st thy wat'ry reign;*
> *Thy awful hand the brazen trident bears,*
> *And ocean's utmost bound, thy will reveres:*
> *Thee I invoke, whose steeds the foam divide,*
> *From whose dark locks the briny waters glide;*
> *Whose voice loud founding thro' the roaring deep,*
> *Drives all its billows, in a raging heap;*
> *When fiercely riding thro' [through] the boiling sea,*
> *Thy hoarse command the trembling waves obey.*
> *Earth shaking, dark-hair'd God, the liquid plains*
> *(The third division) Fate to thee ordains,*
> *'Tis thine, cærulian dæmon, to survey*
> *Well pleas'd the monsters of the ocean play,*
> *Confirm earth's basis, and with prosp'rous gales*
> *Waft ships along, and swell the spacious sails;*
> *Add gentle Peace, and fair-hair'd Health beside,*
> *And pour abundance in a blameless tide.*[281]

---

281. Taylor, *The Hymns of Orpheus*, 141–42.

As the incense continues to burn, visualize the water becoming infused with Neptunian vibrations. Stir the water with your hand while chanting *XIQUAL AHIKAYOWFA CHO AKISEC* (Ouranian Barbaric: Manifest Neptunian higher awareness) until the bathtub has sufficiently filled.

When the bathtub has sufficiently filled, turn off the water. Spend a few moments strongly visualizing the Neptunian vibrations infused in the bath water.

Step into the water. Sit down and close your eyes. Silently contemplate its nature for a few minutes.

Submerge yourself in the water. Visualize its mystical energy saturating every cell of your body. Take note of any transcendental impressions or mystical insights you receive.

Wash your entire body. Observe how the Neptunian water's vibrations affect your physical body, thoughts, and feelings.

Banishing

After you feel sufficiently inspired and refreshed, extinguish your incense if it has not burnt out already. Still standing in the water, chant *FACH SCHNAFFTASI AKISEC* (Ouranian Barbaric: I banish Neptune) as you drain the bathtub. Visualize your impurities draining along with the Neptunian water. After the water has completely drained, clean your bathtub again. Otherwise, undesirable side effects may occur during future use.

August 3, 2022. *Neptunian Bath for Mystical Awareness.* The Orphic Hymn to Neptune calls for a fumigation of myrrh.[282] I don't like burning incense indoors because it makes my cats

---

282. Taylor, *The Hymns of Orpheus*, 51.

sneeze. A viable alternative to burning incense is using a bath or spa product containing myrrh instead. I added it to the bathtub and then recited the Orphic Hymn.

Ritual: Plutonian Evolution of the Self

Butterfly metamorphosis is a Plutonian process. After consuming enough leaves, a caterpillar wanders in search of a place to pupate. Inside the pupa (chrysalis), the caterpillar's tissues are broken down and reorganized. Special cells in the caterpillar grow rapidly, while others are destroyed to provide energy. It may take weeks, months, or longer for these special cells to develop into adult structures. When transformation is complete, the chrysalis splits and a butterfly emerges. The butterfly spreads its wings and eventually flies off.

Here, you will magically undergo a similar metamorphic process. After eating leafy green food like a caterpillar, you will form a chrysalis around yourself and undergo an intense transformation process. You will ultimately be reborn as a more evolved version of yourself.

Materials

- A leafy green snack (such as collard greens or a bag of kale chips)
- A roll of cling film or a large blanket

Statement of Intent

It is my will to metamorphose into the most highly evolved version of myself.

Procedure

Crawl around on the floor for a few minutes, imitating the movement of a caterpillar. When you feel the time is right, binge on your leafy green snack with reckless abandon. Some caterpillars consume enough to double their body mass in a single day, but you don't need to go that far! As you eat, occasionally exclaim *FACH CHENCEB OBDAX-AZONGAGA* (Ouranian Barbaric: I consume higher chaos) while still visualizing yourself as a caterpillar.

When full, slink toward a secluded spot on the floor. Loosely wrap yourself in cling film or "burrito" yourself in the blanket from the neck down; you may leave your arms unwrapped if you feel it is necessary. This is your chrysalis. Inside the chrysalis, visualize yourself decaying and transforming while chanting *FACH COYANIOC CHO CADEX-MENGO ANGJABAGASS* (Ouranian Barbaric: I join together with the Plutonian magical current) for no less than ten minutes. As the old evolves into the new, embrace the discomfort and let go of what no longer serves you.

When fully transformed, spend a few moments silently contemplating the primordial power underlying this process. Begin breaking free of your chrysalis. After you emerge, stand up and stretch your arms toward the sky, akin to a butterfly spreading its wings. Spend a few moments silently contemplating your evolved form. Exclaim *SYCUZ!* (Ouranian Barbaric: It is done!).

Banishing

Banish with laughter.

> August 2, 2022. *Plutonian Evolution of the Self.* The entire rite took about 30 minutes to perform, primarily because I ate an obscene amount of kale chips. The metamorphic process was so disruptive that at times I stopped chanting entirely. A lot of unconscious rubbish was released! I feel more psychologically optimized and much lighter now.

August 15, 2022. *Addendum*. Over the last week or so, some relatives, friends, and coworkers have commented that I seem different, but not in a negative way. Nobody could pinpoint exactly why. Earlier today my cousin B. K. blatantly asked if I was doing magic to "wake up." I'm not sure if these are coincidences or not—I wouldn't have even thought back to this ritual if B. K. didn't ask me that today!

Chapter 12
Homework

After taking notes on the chapter, magical practice should be commenced for thirty minutes each day for a minimum of one month. Perform the assignments in the order presented. Remember to document your efforts in your magical diary.

☐ Meditate on the trans-Saturnian planets for a minimum of ten minutes each day. How do these planetary forces manifest in your life? How do you interact with them?

☐ Determine your natal Uranus, Neptune, and Pluto signs and houses using the tropical system and whole sign houses. Produce a broad delineation for each generational planet, using the examples in chapter 7 as a guide. Trans-Saturnian planetary forces are believed to be especially relevant when they form an aspect with a personal planet.

☐ Approximately every seven, fourteen, and twelve to thirty-one years, Uranus, Neptune, and Pluto enter a new sign, respectively. Visit a reputable website to determine the current Uranus, Neptune, and Pluto signs. In these signs, is their manifestation strong, weak, or somewhere in between? Are any of them retrograde or conjunct the Sun?

☐ Attune with the trans-Saturnian planets daily for a period of one week. You may either focus on one planet per week or attune with all of them at different times throughout the day over the same one-week span.

☐ Perform the rites for each trans-Saturnian planet before proceeding to the next chapter.

Chapter 12 Resources

AstroSeek. "Birth Chart Calculator." https://horoscopes.astro-seek.com /birth-chart-horoscope-online.

———. "Today's Current Planets." https://horoscopes.astro-seek.com /current-planets-astrology-transits-planetary-positions.

Chaos Matrix. "Sigils, Servitors, Egregores, and Godforms." http://www.chaosmatrix .org/library/sseg.php.

Space Audio. "Voyager 2 PWS Uranus Encounter." https://www.youtube.com /watch?v=JBFHG_Oraw0.

CHAPTER 13
Creating Your
Own Planetary Rites

Belief is a tool no different than any other. However, randomly throwing components together and haphazardly following through rarely achieves results. Effective magical rites require a solid foundation and the "nuts and bolts" of a working to be sound. As long as the key components that make magic work are intact, you can obtain quality results regardless of the paradigm you are using. Some crucial components to keep in mind are discussed point-by-point below. Following the discussion, an example planetary group rite is given. Feel free to modify it to your liking.

Statement of Intent

A statement of intent is your confident declaration of what you will to happen as a result of performing the rite, stated immediately beforehand. A basic format you may follow is "It is my will to _____." State the desired result as literally and as plainly as possible. Avoid use of idiomatic and colloquial language. Years ago, I declared it was my will to *run into* a long-lost friend. I did indeed meet my long-lost friend as I desired, but we almost crashed into each other on our bicycles!

Results will manifest through the path of least resistance. If you are not specific enough, the desired outcome might vaguely happen, and if you are too explicit, the universe may have difficulty manifesting a result within the confines of your specifications. Many magicians I know have stories of willing to obtain a large sum of money, performing their rite, and then obtaining that large sum of money via an inheritance when a beloved relative died shortly thereafter. Automobile and work accidents are other unfortunate variations.

Gnosis

Gnosis is an altered state of consciousness and key ingredient of magic. Achieving gnosis serves to bypass the conscious mind so your intent may be uploaded into the universe. The gnostic state is challenging to describe in words; it must be experienced directly. When you achieve this state, you will instinctively know it. Your internal dialogue freezes or disappears entirely. The surrounding environment becomes irrelevant. In that moment, a single point of focus is all that exists. Even if you do not achieve gnosis, the desired result may still manifest if the other components of your rite are technically sound.

Typically, the more frequently you achieve gnosis the easier it is to reach again. Some methods may yield an altered state of consciousness quickly and easily, while others require considerable effort. Though the most effective forms of gnosis may vary widely among individuals, don't become dependent on using only one method.

What will you do in your rite when you achieve gnosis? The answer varies widely and depends on the purpose of the rite, the planetary forces you are working with, and many other factors. For a lunar rite aimed at enhancing psychic abilities, you could evoke a lunar deity to bless your third eye and then visualize it opening. For a Mercury rite aimed at becoming a more effective speaker, you could invoke an eloquent deity and then anchor that state of eloquence to a word, gesture, laser pointer, or something else. For a Venus rite aimed at making new friends, you could enchant a piece of jewelry while focusing on positive inner feelings associated with friendship, and then wear the jewelry to a social event. For a solar rite aimed at maintaining good health, you could chant a Sun mantra while visualizing your cells radiating golden light. For a Mars rite aimed at winning a sports competition, you could create a "win the big game" sigil and launch it via physical exhaustion from practicing. For a Jupiter rite aimed at producing wealth, you could charge a lucky coin while visualizing your bank account balance increasing and then keep the coin in your pocket afterward. For a Saturn rite aimed at eliminating a specific target, you could hold a mock funeral for a symbolic representation of the target and then bury it. The possibilities are endless!

Method of Gnosis

Methods of gnosis may be broadly classified as inhibitory or excitatory.[283] Inhibitory gnosis involves gradually silencing the mind until a single point of focus remains, while excitatory gnosis involves exciting the mind until it overloads, paralyzing everything but a single point of focus. Chemognosis (gnosis reached by chemical means) is another option.[284,285] Though many magicians throughout time have used it effectively, it is risky because the mind may be difficult to control in this state. A short list of inhibitory and excitatory means to gnosis are as follows:

Inhibitory Gnosis

Methods of inhibitory gnosis include sleep deprivation, fasting, sensory deprivation (such as covering your eyes or ears), prolonged gazing or staring (such as into a mirror or crystal), repeating mantras, meditation, prolonged motionlessness, and focused visualization.

Excitatory Gnosis

Methods of excitatory gnosis include pain, exhaustion (such as through exercise or dancing), hyperventilation, strong emotion (such as confronting a fear), sensory overload (such as biting into a hot pepper while listening to loud music), holding your breath for as long as possible, spinning, and glossolalia.

The method of gnosis should be consistent with the paradigm and purpose of your rite. For example, if it is your will to evoke a lunar denizen, doing so via bright sunlight or a candle flame is not ideal. Gazing into moonlight or a dish of cool water would be more appropriate—it is more consistent with the nature of the Moon. On the other hand, if it is your will to evoke a Venusian denizen, marching around your triangle in militaristic fashion while boldly shouting is not ideal. Gracefully dancing around your triangle to pleasant music would be more appropriate—it is more consistent with the nature of Venus.

Although more than one method of gnosis may be incorporated into a rite, simpler is generally better, especially when you are first starting out. After you are comfortable

283. Carroll. *Liber Null*, 31–35.

284. Carroll, *Liber Null*, 147–50.

285. Wetzel, *The Paradigmal Pirate* (Megalithica Books), 14.

writing and performing simpler rites that achieve decent results, feel free to create more complex, layered rites. Regarding the latter, it is usually more efficient to perform an inhibitory method before an excitatory method.

Forget It

After performing your rite, document your efforts in your magical diary and then do your best to forget it. Detaching from your desire will prevent lust of result from short-circuiting its manifestation. The more you dwell on your desire, the more difficult it will be for the universe to shift probability in your favor and produce the requested outcome. An alternate way to look at it is that when you dwell on your rite, you are stealing energy from it that could otherwise be directed toward manifesting the result.

Magical Operations

Magical operations may be broadly classified into one of five categories: invocation, evocation, divination, enchantment, and illumination.[286] Some rites may use only one operation, while more complex ones may combine many.

Invocation

Invocation may be defined as bringing an external energy or vibration inside of you. Alternatively, some magicians perceive invocation as peeling away psychological layers to reveal hidden or dormant parts of the psyche. Generally, invocations vary according to what is being invoked, the nature of the paradigm, and the person performing the invocation. The experience of invocation varies heavily across paradigms. With some invocations it may feel as if you are performing a trust fall, while with others it may feel as if you are a marionette being controlled by a puppeteer.

Before invoking an entity of interest, determine as many sympathetic correspondences as you can. Research the entity's personality, talents, likes, dislikes, catch phrases, and anything else you feel is important. These crucial pieces of data will aid in the design of your invocation. With each entity, put in lots of thought beforehand and make sure your methods are consistent with its nature. If you lack experience with invocation, it is highly recommended you gain experience using conventional (as opposed to pop culture) paradigms first so you have some idea of what to expect.

---

286. Carroll, *Liber Null*, 27–56.

Evocation

In an evocation, you are bringing an energy or vibration outside, instead of inside as in invocation. Many of the aforementioned invocation concepts apply. If you are hesitant to invoke a deity, egregore, pop culture character, or something else, consider performing an evocation instead. This will allow you to become familiar with the energies involved. If you examine evocation methods across paradigms, many have the same core components. They often involve flattering the entity, offering it things it likes, and then flattering it some more. When the entity makes its presence known, a petition may be made. Often times, further flattering and offerings ensue before the entity is dismissed to complete its assigned task. After the task is complete, the entity is thanked and flattered again.

Divination

Divination allows you to extend your perception and acquire information that may not be accessible by conventional means. Divinatory systems may be broadly classified as active or passive. In active systems, you are shuffling cards, tossing coins, or otherwise manipulating objects that are a microcosmic representation of the universe. In passive systems such as astrology, you aren't actively manipulating objects—you are passively observing their natural behavior instead. Divination systems vary widely, but effective systems have clear components. A non-exhaustive list of things to consider when creating your own divination system is as follows:

- Will your system be active or passive?
- What archetypal forces or aspects of the universe will each card, stone, coin, or other item represent? How complete is this representation of the universe? Is it necessary to completely represent it?
- How will your system answer questions? In other words, will it produce a *yes* or *no* response, tell a story, give a time frame, or something else?
- What are the strengths and weaknesses of your system? What are its limitations?
- Will you say or do anything before, during, and after your divination? For example, will you recite a hymn, gaze at something, shuffle something, toss something, or perform some other action?
- Is your system completely novel, or is it comparable (archetypally or mechanistically) to other well-established systems (e.g., horary astrology, tarot, runes, reading tea leaves …)?

Enchantment

When you perform an enchantment, you are imposing your will on the universe to make stuff happen. As T. S. Eliot noted, "… Runes and charms are very practical formulae designed to produce definite results, such as getting a cow out of a bog."[287] The means to your desired end may involve the use of sigils, magic squares, talismans, metals, mantras, gestures, poppets, or other assorted magical items. The planetary tools you acquired in previous chapters may also play a role in your enchantments.

There are many ways enchantment may be accomplished. This topic will not be addressed in depth here, as it has been extensively discussed in the occult literature. A non-exhaustive list of things to consider when creating an enchantment is as follows:

- Is what you will to happen represented in the paradigm your enchantment will be performed in?
- What magical items are appropriate to use, and what are their roles in the paradigm the enchantment will be performed in?
- What forms of gnosis are suitable for your enchantment? Are they consistent with the purpose of your rite and the paradigm you are operating in?
- What will you do with your magical items after gnosis? After the rite is finished?

Illumination

Illumination involves objective contemplation void of delusion. It facilitates metamorphosis of the self so you may take your place in the universe and work in harmony with it. Much of your previous homework involved illumination via planetary meditations. You also analyzed your natal chart to determine how the planetary forces manifest in your life, and then took concrete steps to harness them for your benefit. Illumination may be achieved through meditation, invocation, evocation, divination, enchantment, and various amalgamations thereof.

---

287. T. S. Eliot, *On Poetry and Poets* (Farrar, Straus & Giroux, 2009), 22. Originally published in 1943 by Faber and Faber Ltd.

Active Work
Group Ritual: Eight Rays Empowerment

As previously discussed, each classical planet plus Uranus corresponds to a particular ray of the chaos star.[288] In this group ritual, participants will absorb the planetary essences underlying each ray so they may be harnessed in future magical endeavors. After participants individually absorb a particular planetary essence, they will gather on the rays of a large chaos star and collectively channel these essences into all group members, one by one, as they stand in the center of the chaos star. The planetary essences will then be directed toward individual and collective long-term well-being, magical success, and more. This rite requires at least eight participants.

Materials

- A large room (such as a living room or garage)
- Current locations of the classical planets, plus Uranus
- Sidewalk chalk (or duct tape and markers)

Preparation

Feel free to perform a divination beforehand to determine which particular planetary essence each participant should initially absorb in order to yield the most effective results.

Draw a large chaos star on the floor with the sidewalk chalk (or use duct tape and markers), as in Figure 13.1. It may be as simple or elaborate as you wish. It should be large enough for participants to stand on the rays, arm-width apart.

288. Carroll, *Liber Kaos*, 107–51.

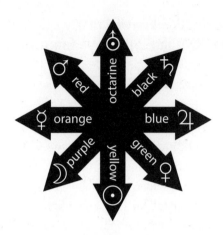

Figure 13.1. Chaos star setup

Statement of Intent

It is our will to empower ourselves with the eight rays.

Procedure

Participants should stand arm-width apart and face the general direction of their assigned planets. When ready, participants should begin absorbing their assigned planetary essence via the following Daoist-inspired techniques.

Close your eyes, take a few deep breaths, and center yourself. Place your tongue on the roof of your mouth. Stand with your feet hip-width apart and curve your arms slightly. If you are sitting, place your hands in your lap. Continue breathing deeply until you are calm and relaxed. Take your time and do not rush.

Transfer your focus to your assigned planet. Spend a few moments strongly visualizing and resonating with its appearance.

Continue breathing deeply while using your mind's eye to astrally see the assigned planet's light. Spend a few moments experiencing its innate nature.

Gently stretch your arms out toward the planet, as if to hold it in your hands.

As you inhale, bring the planet toward the space slightly above your eyebrows (your third eye). Visualize this area becoming filled with planetary light.

Transfer your focus to your third eye. Here, visualize the planetary light mixing with your personal energy and condensing to form a gently glowing colored drop. Feel free to hold your breath as you visualize.

As you exhale, visualize the colored drop descending down your throat and through the center of your body. Use your open palms to gently guide this drop. It eventually arrives in the area slightly below your navel, where a larger colored pool resides. As the drop falls into the pool, it ripples, radiating planetary qualities.

Continue inhaling and exhaling until the colored pool overflows, filling your entire body.

Fold your hands over the area slightly below your navel. In some practices males place the right hand on top, while females place the left hand on top. As you continue breathing deeply, visualize yourself filled with the colored liquid for as long as possible. Spend a few moments observing the physical and astral benefits conferred by this planetary essence.

After ten to fifteen minutes, all participants should be overflowing with their assigned planetary force.

Next, all participants should gather on the chaos star, standing on the ray corresponding to the absorbed planetary essence. Continue visualizing planetary light beaming into your third eye, continuously filling you with its essence.

One by one, take turns stepping into the center of the chaos star to become infused with all eight planetary essences. The individual in the star's center should close their eyes and command the planetary essences to *BATHUMS!* (Ouranian Barbaric: Congeal) while still visualizing planetary light beaming into their third eye. The other participants may then channel their planetary essences into the center individual using any method of their preference. After the center individual has sufficiently absorbed all eight planetary essences through their third eye, they should open their eyes and exclaim, *SYCUZ!* (It is done). The others should enthusiastically reply *CHOYOFAQUE!* (Do the Great Work) to the center individual.

The center may then return to their spot among the chaos star rays to continue channeling their assigned essence into the other participants. Going clockwise, repeat as necessary until everyone has stepped into the center to absorb all eight essences.

After all participants have absorbed the eight essences, collectively raise your open palms toward the sky. Say:

Uranus, Saturn, Jupiter, Venus,
Sol, Luna, Mercury, Mars,
planetary rays of the chaos star,
we hail you!
Instill in us
the innovation of Uranus,
the discipline of Saturn,
the abundance of Jupiter,
the cohesion of Venus,
the illumination of Sol,

the intuition of Luna,
the acuity of Mercury,
and the boldness of Mars!
Through these rays, we shall
do the Great Work!

To conclude, collectively cheer while enthusiastically exclaiming, *CHOYOFAQUE!*

Banishing

Banish with laughter.

> November 1, 2022. *Eight Rays Empowerment.* This iteration of the rite is slightly less clunky and still yielded decent results, but I'm still not happy with it...
>
> November 2, 2022. IDEA! *Can we absorb essences of fictional planets?* Ripped out the chaos star and rewrote using the founding members of the United Federation of Planets from *Star Trek.* The rewrite in the *Star Trek* paradigm flows more smoothly and is less energetically complicated. I see why this iteration so clunky now. [Ritual details follow.]
>
> November 27, 2022. *Star Trek Addendum.* Planetary light colors were determined via repeated meditation and absorbing planetary essences. The yellow-brown astral light of Earth is so consistent with the color of elemental earth.[289] Vulcan's astral light consistently appeared burnt orange—a subdued Martian red combined with a more fixed Mercurian orange comes to mind. Andoria's astral light typically appeared either light blue

---

289. Bardon, *Magical Evocation*, 41.

or light blue-gray. One participant described this essence as "…like *Mjölnir* [Thor's Hammer], if it was made of ice and transformed into a beam of light." Tellar's astral light typically appeared dark blue-green, with frequent hints of brown and purple. Another participant described this essence as "…like a rustic spa in the mountains that has the air conditioner cranked all the way up."

Chapter 13
Homework

After taking notes on the chapter, proceed with the following exercises. Magical practice should be commenced for thirty minutes each day for a minimum of one month. Perform the assignments in the order presented. Remember to document your efforts in your magical diary.

- ☐ Meditate on the types of magical operations (invocation, evocation, divination, enchantment, and illumination) for a minimum of ten minutes each day. What is each operation useful for? Are different operations better suited for particular planets?

- ☐ Create and perform a planetary invocation. For instance, you may invoke an entity embodying specific planetary qualities you would like to integrate into your personality.

- ☐ Create and perform a planetary evocation. For instance, you may evoke an entity bearing planetary significance and then charge it with a task complementary to its personality and the planet's nature.

- ☐ Perform a divination to determine the impact of the classical planets in your life, in ranked order. You may use an existing divination system or create your own.

- ☐ Create and perform a planetary enchantment. For instance, you may enchant a planetary metal to confer a beneficial characteristic congruent with that planet's nature and then carry it with you.

- ☐ Create and perform a planetary illumination rite. It may be something simple, such as a guided meditation to obtain insight from a planetary archangel, or something complex, such as a layered rite to promote harmony among planetary forces.

- ☐ Examine the overall structure of the example group ritual. Performing it is optional. What do you like and dislike about it? What would you change?

Chapter 13 Resources

AstroSeek. "Today's Current Planets." https://horoscopes.astro-seek.com
/current-planets-astrology-transits-planetary-positions.

Carroll, Peter J. *Liber Kaos: Chaos Magic for the Pandaemonaeon.* Rev. ed. Weiser
Books, 2023.

———. *Liber Null & Psychonaut: The Practice of Chaos Magic.* Weiser Books, 2022.

Hine, Phil. *Condensed Chaos: An Introduction to Chaos Magic.* The Original Falcon
Press, 2010.

Lee, David. *Chaotopia! Sorcery and Ecstasy in the Fifth Aeon.* Mandrake of Oxford,
2006.

Vitimus, Andrieh. *Hands-On Chaos Magic: Reality Manipulation Through the Ovayki
Current.* Llewellyn Publications, 2009.

Wetzel, Joshua. *The Paradigmal Pirate.* Megalithica Books, 2006.

Conclusion

You made it! You have successfully worked with each planet, gained insight into how they affect your life, and performed numerous planetary rites. You also have the tools to write your own. If you have been working at the suggested pace of no more than one chapter per month, this is your fourteenth month or more.

Where Do We Go from Here?

You can go anywhere you want. The planets are yours to use. Revisit them. Explore them in new paradigms of your choosing. Use them to facilitate spiritual enrichment, life balance, psychological well-being, and more. Use them in entirely novel ways that no one has imagined yet. Go nuts with dwarf, extrasolar, and fictional planets. Whatever you choose, keep in mind Lévi's words: "The seven planets are, in fact, the hiero-glyphic symbols of the keyboard of our affections."[290] Strive to maintain harmony among them to reach your highest potential.

The Moon Reflects

As the Moon reflects the light of the Sun, our unconscious mind reflects our "higher self." The Moon and Sun work together to sustain life on Earth. Our unconscious mind and personal self work together so we may manifest our True Will. Due to its synchro-nous rotation, we only see the near side of the Moon—the far side is not visible from

---

290. Lévi, *Transcendental Magic*, 82.

269

Earth. Likewise, we are only consciously aware of some of our drives, as much lies in the unconscious mind that has yet to be discovered. Further, lunar gravity produces tidal rhythms on Earth, so the Moon is frequently linked with water. Because the human menstrual cycle is roughly the same length as a lunar cycle, the Moon is also frequently linked with women's mysteries.

At its best, the lunar force provides a solid foundation and facilitates the manifestation of beauty (i.e., things of a divine nature). Our foundation is not rigid; it is malleable and changes as we do. We have the ability to create our own foundations, adapt to changing circumstances, and confront reality head on. At its worst, the corrupted lunar force rots a foundation and facilitates the manifestation of things that are not beautiful. Change is inevitable. The Moon changes phases as it travels on its monthly journey, and change occurs throughout our lives. The Moon has helped you build the foundation necessary to work with the classical planets. The fundamental concepts and principles of magic you practiced throughout this book will continue to serve you well in future endeavors. Be receptive and reflective, like the Moon at its best.

Mercury Inspects

As Mercury is never far removed from the Sun, our intellectual mind is never far removed from our personal self. Mercury's surface exhibits a dual nature—its daytime side (facing the Sun) is hot and bright, while its nighttime side (facing away from the Sun) is cold and dark. Our intellectual mind also exhibits a dual nature—our objective thinking is rational, logical, and analytical, while our subjective thinking is nonlinear, intuitive, and unsystematic. Like the Moon, Mercury lacks an atmosphere and is thus frequently linked with clear perception. Because Mercury orbits the Sun faster than the other planets, it is also frequently linked with speed and agility.

At its best, the Mercurian force provides a solid intellectual matrix and facilitates the unbiased transmission and reception of splendor. We must be brutally honest with ourselves to avoid self-deception. We must also keep in mind that the models we employ to explain the external world may be fallible, and not blindly accept them as absolute truths. At its worst, the corrupted Mercurian force poisons this splendor and facilitates the spread of faulty or dishonest information. Mercury has helped you inspect various planetary forces throughout this book. Be perceptive and inquisitive, like Mercury at its best.

Venus Connects

Venus's thick atmosphere reflects a large proportion of sunlight. Our inner feelings reflect a large proportion of our personal self. The surface of Venus is hot and pressurized due to its thick, heavy atmosphere and runaway greenhouse effect. Our inner feelings may also be hot and pressurized, brewing beneath a serene façade. Due to its retrograde rotation, the Sun would appear to rise in the west and set in the east on the Venusian surface. Likewise, our inner feelings may compel us to take unconventional action. Due to its stunning appearance in the sky, Venus is frequently linked with love, beauty, and attraction.

At its best, the Venusian force provides a solid emotional matrix and facilitates the triumph of beauty. As Virgil said, "Love conquers all."[291] Unselfishness allows us to join together in mutual integrity and respect, despite our differences. At its worst, the corrupted Venusian force scatters these efforts and prevents us from working together to achieve common goals. Venus has helped you connect with various planetary forces throughout this book. Be charming and unifying, like Venus at its best.

The Sun Projects

The Sun is the central star in our solar system. The personal self is the central point of our consciousness. Solar fusion produces immense energy released as heat, light, and other forms of radiation. This energy projects throughout the solar system, reaching the celestial bodies that orbit it. Likewise, through deliberate effort we may shine light on various aspects of our psyche. Since life as we know it would be impossible without the Sun, the Sun is frequently linked with health and vitality. Because the Sun and Moon are often viewed as complementary luminaries in the sky, the Sun is also frequently linked with men's mysteries.

At its best, the solar force provides an unalienable sense of self and facilitates devotion to the Great Work. The Great Work "… may mean the uniting of the soul with God, of the microcosm with the macrocosm, of the female with the male, of the ego with the non-ego—or what not."[292] It allows us to equilibrate with others and appreciate the unique beauty of everyone's "shine." At its worst, the corrupted solar force distorts our sense of self and may facilitate unwarranted self-importance. It may also divert us from

---

291. *Virgil's Eclogues*, trans. Len Krisak (University of Pennsylvania Press, 2010), 79.

292. Aleister Crowley, *Magick Without Tears*, ed. Israel Regardie (New Falcon Publications, 1991), 7. Originally published 1954 by Thelema Publishing Company.

pursuing the Great Work, or cause us to reject it entirely. The Sun has helped you project your higher self (i.e., divine consciousness) into the world. It has also equilibrated various parts of your psyche. Be radiant and illuminating, like the Sun at its best.

Mars Objects

Whereas Venus attracts our eyes in the sky, the vibrant red of Mars demands our attention. Intense dust storms are capable of saturating the planet's entire atmosphere with red particles, obscuring the Sun and other celestial bodies. Likewise, when we are consumed by anger, "seeing red" may obscure our personal self and other aspects of our psyche. Further, the Sun appears smaller when standing on the Martian surface. At times, our higher self may take a back seat to our passion, enthusiasm, or wrath. Due to its bold red appearance in the sky, Mars is frequently linked with war and bloodshed.

At its best, the Martian force provides a solid energetic matrix and facilitates the expression of raw energy and physical power (i.e., might). Having tangible goals and outlets to blow off steam will help you direct might constructively. At its worst, the corrupted Martian force overwhelms these channels and may divert might into unwarranted or misdirected aggression, cruelty, or wrath. Mars has helped you object to any timidity or fears you harbor regarding practicing magic throughout this book. It has also helped you develop strength of body and mind. Be bold and courageous, like Mars at its best.

Jupiter Protects

Jupiter is the largest planet in our solar system. At times, our focused aspiration may make us seem larger than life. Jupiter's far-reaching gravity field commands a complex arrangement of rings, satellites, asteroids, and more. Likewise, our obedience to principles aligned with the greater good commands the mercy necessary for us to protect people, places, and things we hold authority over. It has long been believed that Jupiter protects Earth from comets and asteroids. This carries over esoterically, as Jupiter is frequently linked with authority and protection. Due to its immense size, Jupiter is also frequently linked with expansion and abundance.

At its best, the Jupiterian force provides a solid philosophical matrix and amplifies our awareness of matters beyond our local community. This broader awareness allows us to rule our personal "kingdom" from a more merciful, magnanimous vantage point. As Seneca said, "The more tolerantly he rules the more easily he commands obedience."[293] At its worst, the corrupted Jupiterian force overinflates our sense of self and may create a control freak tyrant instead of a benevolent king. It may also tempt us to hoard surplus resources for ourselves instead of giving them where they are truly needed. Jupiter has helped you protect yourself, your assets, and those you love. Be jolly and generous, like Jupiter at its best.

Saturn Corrects

As Saturn resides at the boundary between the classical planets and rest of the geocentric universe, our restrictions and limitations reside at the boundary between our microcosmic self and the macrocosm. Saturn is bound by a set of stunning rings. Likewise, we are bound by numerous rules and regulations. Through silence, we may understand that constraint provides form and definition to physical reality. Further, Saturn is the most distant of the classical planets. This carries over esoterically, thus Saturn is frequently linked with solitude. Due to its slow orbital period, Saturn is also frequently linked with restriction and sacrifice.

At its best, the Saturnian force provides a solid structural matrix and provides the form necessary for boundaries to exist. Without this form, there would be no tangible structure to build our foundations or individuality upon. At its worst, the corrupted Saturnian force doubles down on this form, making boundaries overly rigid. It may also sever us from ourselves, others, and the macrocosm. Saturn has helped you correct your course, aligning you with the universe so you can work in harmony with it. It has also provided you with the discipline to make it this far. Be steady and enduring, like Saturn at its best.

Wander Often, Wonder Always!

As our knowledge of the cosmos grows, our model of the universe, astrology, and planetary magic will continue to evolve. Lévi states, "The planets […] are more truly the stars of the human mind than the orbs of heaven."[294] Likewise, as your magical practice grows, you will continue to evolve as well. With your feet on the ground and eyes toward the sky, wander often and wonder always!

---

293. Seneca, *De Clementia*, ed. Susanna Braund (Oxford University Press, 2009), 135.

294. Lévi, *Transcendental Magic*, 251.

Additional Resources

The planetary forces recur in many paradigms. If you would like to more deeply explore them in a particular tradition, a short list of recommended books follows below. Some focus entirely on the planets, while others have a specific section dedicated to them. They are available in most major bookstores or online. The list is by no means complete. There are many excellent books (and entire paradigms!) that are not included for brevity's sake.

Ceremonial Magic

Agrippa, Henry Cornelius. *Three Books of Occult Philosoph.* Edited by Donald Tyson. Llewellyn Publications, 2004.

Arbatel: Concerning the Magic of the Ancients. Translated by Joseph H. Peterson. Nicolas-Hays, 2009.

The Key of Solomon the King. Translated by S. L. MacGregor Mathers. Dover Publications, 2009.

Chaos Magic

Carroll, Peter J. *Liber Kaos: Chaos Magic for the Pandaemonaeon*, Rev. ed. Weiser Books, 2023.

Carroll, Peter J. "Planetary Rites." Chaos Matrix. http://www.chaosmatrix.org/library/magick/rites/planet9.txt.

Wetzel, Joshua. *The Paradigmal Pirate.* Megalithica Books, 2006.

Greek (*Hellēnismos*)

Betz, Hans Dieter, ed. *The Greek Magical Papyri in Translation, Including the Demotic Spells*. University of Chicago Press, 1986.

Athanassakis, Apostolos N., trans. *The Homeric Hymns*, 2nd ed. Johns Hopkins University Press, 2004.

Athanassakis, Apostolos N., and Benjamin M. Wolkow, trans. *The Orphic Hymns*. Johns Hopkins University Press, 2013.

Hermeticism

Bardon, Franz. *The Practice of Magical Evocation*. Merkur Publishing, 2001.

Clark, Rawn. *A Bardon Companion: A Practical Companion for the Student of Franz Bardon's System of Hermetic Initiation*, 2nd ed. CreateSpace, 2010.

Denning, Melita, and Osborne Phillips. *Planetary Magick: Invoking and Directing the Powers of the Planets*. Llewellyn Publications, 2011.

Islam

Warnock, Christpher, ed. *Astral High Magic:* De Imaginibus *of Thabit Ibn Qurra*. Translated by John Michael Greer. Renaissance Astrology, 2011.

Greer, John Michael, and Christopher Warnock, trans. *The Illustrated Picatrix: The Complete Occult Classic of Astrological Magic*. Renaissance Astrology, 2010–2015.

———. *Secrets of Planetary Ritual: Sabian Planetary Invocations from Picatrix*. Renaissance Astrology, 2009.

Judaism

Hayman, A. Peter. *Sefer Yeṣira*. Mohr Siebeck, 2004.

Isaccs, Ronald H. *Divination, Magic, and Healing: The Book of Jewish Folklore*. Jason Aronson, 1998.

Kude, Lorelai. *Astrolojew: The Big Book of Jewish Astrology*. Forthcoming.

Paganism and Neopaganism

Digitalis, Raven. *Planetary Spells & Rituals: Practicing Dark & Light Magick Aligned with the Cosmic Bodies*. Llewellyn Publications, 2010.

Shesso, Renna. *Planets for Pagans: Sacred Sites, Ancient Lore, and Magical Stargazing*. Weiser Books, 2014.

Barrabbas, Frater. *Talismanic Magic for Witches: Planetary Magic Simplified*. Llewellyn Publications, 2023.

Roman (*Cultus Deorum*)

Beard, Mary, John North, and Simon Price. *Religions of Rome: Volume 2, A Sourcebook*. Cambridge University Press, 1998.

Bernstein, Frances. *Classical Living: Reconnecting with the Rituals of Ancient Rome*. HarperCollins, 2010.

Cicero. *The Nature of the Gods*. Translated by P. G. Walsh. Oxford University Press, 2008.

Ovid. *Fasti*. Translated by Anne and Peter Wiseman. Oxford University Press, 2013.

APPENDIX A
The Hebrew *Alefbet,* Pronunciation, and Ceremonial Hierarchies

The Hebrew *alefbet* is put to use by a wide variety of magicians. Hebrew is read from right to left in horizontal lines. Biblical Hebrew lacks diacritics, so there is uncertainty as to how words were historically pronounced. The twenty-two consonants of the Biblical Hebrew *alefbet* are shown in Table A1. Some letters have a final form that occurs only at the end of a word. Going into further detail on this topic is beyond the scope of this book. However, if this subject interests you, there is an extensive body of scholarly literature on the evolution of Hebrew and its cognate languages.[295,296,297]

Try reading the two English phrases below by filling in the missing vowels where appropriate:

Y PT TH LM N TH CCNT
THS WH DNT BLV N MGC WLL NVR FND T

If you fill in the vowels, we obtain the phrases YOU PUT THE LIME IN THE COCONUT and THOSE WHO DON'T BELIEVE IN MAGIC WILL NEVER FIND IT.

---

295. Walter R. Bodine, ed., *Linguistics and Biblical Hebrew* (Eisenbrauns, 1992).

296. Joel M. Hoffman, *In the Beginning: A Short History of the Hebrew Language* (New York University Press, 2004).

297. Ian Young, ed., *Biblical Hebrew: Studies in Chronology and Typology* (T & T Clark International, 2003).

Although Hebrew lacks vowels, interpreting text in this manner is easy for native readers because they do it all the time.

Table A1. The Hebrew Alefbet			
Letter	**Letter Name**	**Romanization**	**IPA Pronunciation**
א	*'alef*	' or omitted	/ʔ/
ב	*bet*	*b* or *v*	/b/ or /v/
ג	*gimel*	*g*	/g/ or /ɣ/
ד	*dalet*	*d*	/d/ or /ð/
ה	*he*	*h*	/h/
ו	*waw*	*w*	/w/
ז	*zayin*	*z*	/z/
ח	*ḥet*	*ḥ*	/ħ/ or /χ/
ט	*ṭet*	*ṭ*	/t̪ʼ/
י	*yod*	*y*	/j/
כ (final: ך)	*kaf*	*k*	/k/ or /x/
ל	*lamed*	*l*	/l/
מ (final: ם)	*mem*	*m*	/m/
נ (final: ן)	*nun*	*n*	/n/
ס	*samek*	*s*	/s/
ע	*'ayin*	' or omitted	/ʕ/ or /ɣ/

Table A1. The Hebrew Alefbet			
Letter	**Letter Name**	**Romanization**	**IPA Pronunciation**
פ (final: ף)	*pe*	*p* or *f*	/p/ or /f/
צ (final: ץ)	*ṣade*	*ṣ*	/t͡s/
ק	*qof*	*q*	/q/
ר	*resh*	*r*	/r/
שׁ	*sin/shin*	*s* or *sh*	/s/ or /ʃ/
ת	*taw*	*t* or *th*	/t/ or /θ/

Planetary Hierarchy Names

Romanized Hebrew names (using conventions adapted from *The SBL Handbook of Style*), pronunciation (based on current understanding of Biblical Hebrew phonology), and etymology of planetary hierarchy denizens follow below.[298,299] Pronunciations, when known, are conveyed in IPA (International Phonetic Alphabet). If you want to use a different dialect instead, go for it. As long as you understand what you are saying, why you are saying it, and say it with conviction, it should not negatively impact your magical work.

---

298. *The SBL Handbook of Style*, 2nd ed. (SBL Press, 2014), 55–67.

299. *Encyclopedia of Hebrew Language and Linguistics*, ed. Geoffrey Khan, four vols. (Brill, 2013).

The Moon

Divine Names

Hod (Heb. הד)

According to *Sepher Sephiroth*, this is *hod* (Heb. הוד; n. splendor) without the ו. It is not present in *The Bible*. It is a Qabalistic divine name associated with the Moon.[300,301,302]

'Elim (Heb. אלים (/ʔeˈlɪim/); God)

This is the plural of *'el* (Heb. אל; n. god), which may be used to refer to any deity but is qualified with additional descriptors to distinguish *YHWH* from other deities. It is a Qabalistic divine name associated with the Moon.[303,304]

Archangel

Gabri'el (Heb. גבריאל (/ɡɑb.rɪiˈʔel/); Man of God)

The name is a combination of *geber* (Heb. גבר; n. man) and *'el* (אל; n. god). *Gabri'el* is identified as an angel in *The Bible* and an archangel in other texts (e.g., *The Books of Adam and Eve*, *Books of Enoch* …).[305] He frequently works with *Mika'el* to carry out the will of *YHWH*, and has been written about extensively.[306] *Gabri'el* is the archangel of *Yesod* and the Moon.[307,308]

Intelligence of Intelligences

Malka' Betarshishim We'ad Beruaḥ Shaharim
(Arc. + Heb. מלכא בתרשישים ועד ברוה שהרים)

The name as given by Agrippa and modified by Crowley does not appear in any known literature prior to the publication of Agrippa's *Three Books of Occult Philosophy*.[309,310,311]

300. Crowley, "Sepher Sephiroth," 1.

301. Agrippa, *Three Books*, 318–29.

302. Crowley, "777 Revised," 3.

303. Agrippa, *Three Books*, 318–29.

304. Crowley, "777 Revised," 3.

305. Luke 1:19 KJV 1611.

306. "Gabriel," *The Jewish Encyclopedia,* 5:540–43.

307. Agrippa, *Three Books*, 268–80, 287–91.

308. Crowley, "777 Revised," 21.

309. Agrippa, *Three Books*, 318–29.

310. Crowley, "777 Revised," 19.

311. Crowley, "Sepher Sephiroth," 69.

It is probably a mixture of Aramaic and Hebrew, and is generally regarded as untranslatable. Most magicians I know treat it as a proper name. It can be broken down into individual components, which are:

Malkà: This could be *malka'* (Arc. מלכא (/malˈkɔːʔ/); n. king).

Betarshishim: This is probably *betarshishim*, from the plural of *Tarshish* (Heb. תרשיש (/tarˈʃiʃ/)), an ancient port destination.[312] Jonah's unsuccessful attempt to flee *YHWH* by boarding a ship heading there resulted in his whale-swallowing fiasco.[313] Another possibility is a homophone for an unidentified type of gemstone incorporated into the priestly breastplate.[314] It may also refer to *Tarshishim* (/tar.ʃiˈʃim/), the angelic choirs associated with elemental water.[315]

We'Ad: This could be *we'ad*, from *'ad* (Arc. + Heb. עד (/ʕad̪/); prep. until/even to) or *'ad* (עד (/ʕad̪/); conj. until/while). Other possibilities include *wa'ed*, from *'ad* (Heb. עד (/ʕad̪/); n. forever), and *we'ed*, from *'ed* (עד (/ʕed̪/); n. witness).

Beruah: This is probably *beruah,* from *ruah* (Arc. + Heb. רוח (/ˈruː.aħ/); n. wind/spirit).

Shaharim: This could be a "mystic" spelling of *shaharim*, from the plural of *shahar* (Heb. שחר (/ʃaˈħar/); n. dawn).

Spirit of Spirits

Shed Barshehm'ot Shartathan (Heb. שד ברשהמעת שרתתן)

The name as given by Agrippa and Crowley does not appear in any known literature prior to the publication of Agrippa's *Three Books of Occult Philosophy*.[316,317,318] It could be a mixture of Aramaic and Hebrew; it is generally regarded as untranslatable. Most magicians I know treat it as a proper name. It can be broken down into individual components:

---

312. "Tarshish," *The Jewish Encyclopedia,* 12:65.

313. Jonah 1:3-17 KJV 1611.

314. "Tarshish," *The Jewish Encyclopedia,* 12:65.

315. Velchanes, *The Elemental Magic Workbook*, 237–38.

316. Agrippa, *Three Books*, 318–29.

317. Crowley, "777 Revised," 143.

318. Crowley, "Sepher Sephiroth," 69.

Shed: This is probably *shed* (Heb. שד (/ʃeḏ/); n. demon/devil) or *shad* (שד (/ʃaḏ/); n. breast).

Barshehmʿot: This could be a combination of *bar* (Arc. בר; n. son) and the proper name *Shimeʿath* (Heb. n. שמעת), the mother of one of King Jehoash of Judah's assassins, with an extra ת.[319] If the source language is Hebrew, its root could be *Sh-M-ʿ*, related to hearing or listening.

Shartathan: This could be *sheratten* (Heb. שרתתן; v. you f. pl. served/helped), from the root *sharat* (Heb. שרת (/ʃɔːˈraṯ/); serve/help).

Spirit

Ḥasmodaʾy (Heb. חשמודai)

The name as given by Agrippa does not appear in any known literature prior to the publication of his *Three Books of Occult Philosophy*.[320] It bears similarity to *ʾAshemeḋay* (Arc. אשמדאי), the "king of the demons" in *The Talmud* and *Hasmodaios* (Gk. Ἀσμοδαῖος), a malefic spirit in *The Bible*.[321,322] *Ḥasmodaʾy* is the spirit of the Moon.[323,324]

Mercury

Divine Name

ʾAzboga (Heb. אזבוגה)

The *eightfold name* contains three consecutive pairs of letters that sum to eight: *ʾalef* + *zayin* = 8, *bet* + *waw* = 8, and *gimel* + *he* = 8. It is not present in the Bible but is identified as a "secret name" in the *Lesser Hekalot* and a "great seal" (divine name) in the *Greater Hekalot*.[325] It is a Qabalistic divine name associated with Mercury.[326,327]

---

319. 2 Kings 12:21; 2 Chronicles 24:26 KJV 1611.

320. Agrippa, *Three Books*, 318–29.

321. Pesachim 110a:11, *The William Davidson Talmud*. https://www.sefaria.org/william-davidson-talmud.

322. Tobit 3:8, 3:17 KJV 1611.

323. Agrippa, *Three Books*, 318–29.

324. Crowley, "777 Revised," 19.

325. Gershom Scholem, *Jewish Gnosticism, Merkabah Mysticism, and Talmudic Tradition*, 2nd ed. (Maurice Jacobs, 1965), 65–74.

326. Agrippa, *Three Books*, 318–29.

327. Crowley, "777 Revised," 3.

Archangel

Mika'el (Heb. מיכאל /mɪ̯.kɔːˈʔel/); Who (is) like God?)

The name is a combination of *mi* (Heb. מִי; n. who?), *ki* (כִי; conj. is like), and *'el* (אל; n. god). *Mika'el* is identified as an archangel in the Bible and numerous other texts (e.g., *The Books of Adam and Eve, Books of Enoch* …).[328] He frequently works with *Gabri'el* to carry out the will of *YHWH*, and has been written about extensively.[329] *Mika'el* is the archangel of *Hod* and Mercury.[330,331]

Intelligence

Ṭiri'el (Heb. טיריאל)

The name as given by Agrippa does not appear in any known literature prior to the publication of his *Three Books of Occult Philosophy*.[332] It may bear connection to *Tīr*, the Zoroastrian *yazata* who is sometimes identified as Sirius or Mercury.[333] *Ṭiri'el* is the intelligence of Mercury.[334,335]

Spirit

Tafthartharath (Heb. תפתרתרת)

The name as given by Agrippa does not appear in any known literature prior to the publication of his *Three Books of Occult Philosophy*.[336] If the source language is Hebrew, its root could be *P-T-R*, related to solving or deciphering. *Tafthartharath* is the spirit of Mercury.[337,338]

---

328. Jude 1:9 KJV 1611.

329. "Michael," *The Jewish Encyclopedia,* 8:535–38.

330. Agrippa, *Three Books*, 268–80, 287–91.

331. Crowley, "777 Revised," 21.

332. Agrippa, *Three Books*, 318–29.

333. William W. Malandra, *An Introduction to Ancient Iranian Religion: Readings from the Avesta and Achaemenid Inscriptions* (University of Minnesota Press, 1983), 142.

334. Agrippa, *Three Books*, 318–29.

335. Crowley, "777 Revised," 19.

336. Agrippa, *Three Books*, 318–29.

337. Agrippa, *Three Books*, 318–29.

338. Crowley, "777 Revised," 19.

Venus

Divine Name

AHA (Heb. אהא)

According to *Sepher Sephiroth*, this is an acronym of *'Adonay Ha'areṣ* (Heb. (my) Lord of the Earth), a divine name associated with *Malkut*.[339] I have also seen it used as an acronym for *'Adonay Hu' 'Elohim* ((my) Lord is God) and *'Ish Ha'elohim* (Man of God). It is a Qabalistic divine name associated with Venus.[340,341]

Archangel

H'ani'el (Heb. האניאל)

The name as given by Agrippa does not appear in any known literature prior to the publication of his *Three Books of Occult Philosophy*.[342] It could be a combination of the interrogative form of *'ani* (אני; n. I) and *'el* (אל; n. god), which altogether may be interpreted as *Am I God?* Alternatively, it could be a "mystic" spelling of *Ḥani'el* (Heb. חניאל (/ħɑn̪ːi̯'ʔel/); Favored of God), who is not present in the Bible but is identified as an angel in other texts (e.g., *Zohar*, *Sefer Harazim* …). *H'ani'el* is the archangel of *Neṣaḥ* and Venus.[343,344]

Intelligence

Hagi'el (Heb. הגיאל)

The name as given by Agrippa does not appear in any known literature prior to the publication of his *Three Books of Occult Philosophy*.[345] If the source language is Hebrew, it could be a combination of a word derived from the root *H-G-H* (related to murmuring) and *'el* (אל; n. god), altogether implying divine pleasure. *Hagi'el* is the intelligence of Mercury.[346,347]

---

339. Crowley, "Sepher Sephiroth," 1.

340. Agrippa, *Three Books*, 318–29.

341. Crowley, "777 Revised," 3.

342. Agrippa, *Three Books*, 268–80.

343. Agrippa, *Three Books*, 268–80, 287–91.

344. Crowley, "777 Revised," 21.

345. Agrippa, *Three Books*, 318–29.

346. Agrippa, *Three Books*, 318–29.

347. Crowley, "777 Revised," 19.

Spirit

Qedem'el (Heb. קדמאל)

The name as given by Agrippa does not appear in any known literature prior to the publication of his *Three Books of Occult Philosophy*.[348] It bears similarity to *Qadmi'el* (Heb. קדמיאל (/k' aḏ.mii̯'ʔel/); God is Ancient), who is not present in the Bible but is identified as an angel in other texts (e.g., *Zohar Ḥadash, Sefer Harazim …*). *Qedem'el* is the spirit of Venus.[349,350]

The Sun

Divine Name

'Eloah (Heb. אלה (/ʔɛ̆'lo.ɑh/); God)

The name is probably an emphatic form of *'el* (Heb. אל; n. god) or a forced singular form of *'elohim* (אלהים; n. gods). It is present in the Bible and is a Qabalistic divine name associated with the Sun.[351,352,353]

Archangel

Rafa'el (Heb. רפאל (/rɔ.pɔː'ʔel/); God Healed)

The name is a combination of *rafa'* (Heb. רפא; v. he healed) and *'el* (אל; n. god). *Rafa'el* is identified as an angel in the Bible and an archangel in other texts (e.g., *The Books of Adam and Eve, Books of Enoch …*).[354] He frequently takes on the role of divine physician to carry out the will of *YHWH*, and has been written about extensively.[355] *Rafa'el* is the archangel of *Tif'eret* and the Sun.[356,357]

348. Agrippa, *Three Books*, 318–29.

349. Agrippa, *Three Books*, 318–29.

350. Crowley, "777 Revised,", 19.

351. Deuteronomy 32:17 KJV 1611.

352. Agrippa, *Three Books*, 318–29.

353. Crowley, "777 Revised,", 3.

354. Tobit 12:15 KJV 1611.

355. "Raphael," *The Jewish Encyclopedia,* 10:317–18.

356. Agrippa, *Three Books*, 268–80, 287–91.

357. Crowley, "777 Revised,", 21.

Intelligence

Naki'el (Heb. נכיאל)

The name as given by Agrippa does not appear in any known literature prior to the publication of his *Three Books of Occult Philosophy*.[358] If the source language is Hebrew, it could be a combination of a word derived from the root *N-K-H* (related to subtracting) and *'el* (אל; n. god), altogether implying divine individuality. *Naki'el* is the intelligence of the Sun.[359,360]

Spirit

Sorath (Heb. סורת)

The name as given by Agrippa does not appear in any known literature prior to the publication of his *Three Books of Occult Philosophy*.[361] If the source language is Hebrew, it could be derived from the root *S-R-T* (related to scratching). *Sorath* is the spirit of the Sun.[362,363]

Mars

Divine Name

'Adonay (Heb. אדני (/ʔɔ.doˈnɑiː/); (my) Lord)

This is an emphatic form of *'Adon* (Heb. אדון; n. lord).[364] In Jewish traditions, it is used as a proper name of *YHWH* and spoken in place of it. It is a Qabalistic divine name associated with Mars.[365,366]

Archangel

Kama'el (Heb. כמאל)

If the source language is Hebrew, the name could be a combination of a word derived from the root *K-M-H* (related to yearning) and *'el* (אל; n. god), altogether implying

---

358. Agrippa, *Three Books*, 318–29.

359. Agrippa, *Three Books*, 318–29.

360. Crowley, "777 Revised,", 19.

361. Agrippa, *Three Books*, 318–29.

362. Agrippa, *Three Books*, 318–29.

363. Crowley, "777 Revised,", 19.

364. "Adonai," *The Jewish Encyclopedia,* 1:201–03.

365. Agrippa, *Three Books*, 318–29.

366. Crowley, "777 Revised,", 3.

divine craving. *Kama'el* is not present in the Bible but is identified as an archangel in other texts (e.g., *The Key of Solomon the King, Three Books of Occult Philosophy* …). He has not been written about as extensively as other planetary archangels. *Kama'el* is the archangel of *Gebura* and Mars.[367,368]

Intelligence
Gra'fi'el (Heb. גראפיאל)
The name as given by Agrippa does not appear in any known literature prior to the publication of his *Three Books of Occult Philosophy*.[369] If the source language is Hebrew, it could be a combination of a word derived from the root *G-R-P* (related to sweeping clear) and *'el* (אל; n. god), altogether implying divine cleansing or banishing. *Gra'fi'el* is the intelligence of Mars.[370,371]

Spirit
Barṣab'el (Heb. ברצבאל)
The name as given by Agrippa does not appear in any known literature prior to the publication of his *Three Books of Occult Philosophy*.[372] It could be a combination of *bar* (Arc. בר; n. son), *ṣaba'* (Heb. צבא; n. host), and *'el* (אל; n. god), which altogether may be interpreted as "Son of God's Host" (i.e., "Soldier of God's Army"). *Barṣab'el* is the spirit of Mars.[373,374]

Jupiter

Divine Names
'Aba' (Arc. אבא; Father)
This is *'abà* (Arc. אבא; n. father) treated as a proper noun. It is not present in the Hebrew or Aramaic of the *Old Testament*, but is in the Greek of the New Testament as *Abba*

---

367. Agrippa, *Three Books*, 268–80, 287–91.

368. Crowley, "777 Revised,", 21.

369. Agrippa, *Three Books*, 318–29.

370. Agrippa, *Three Books*, 318–29.

371. Crowley, "777 Revised,", 19.

372. Agrippa, *Three Books*, 318–29.

373. Agrippa, *Three Books*, 318–29.

374. Crowley, "777 Revised,", 19.

(Gk. Ἀββᾶ (/αβˈβα/)).[375] In colloquial Hebrew, *'Abà* means *Daddy*. It is a Qabalistic divine name associated with Jupiter.[376,377]

'El 'Ab (Heb. אב אל (/ʔel ʔɔːb/); God (the) Father)

The name is a combination of *'el* (Heb. אל; n. god) and *'ab* (אב; n. father). It is not present in the Hebrew or Aramaic of the Old Testament, but is in the Greek of the New Testament as *Theou Patros* (Gk. θεοῦ Πατρὸς).[378] It is a Qabalistic divine name associated with Jupiter.[379,380]

Archangel
Ṣadqi'el (Heb. צדקיאל (/tsˤad.kiˈʔel/); Righteousness of God)

The name is a combination of *ṣedeq* (Heb. צדק; n. righteousness) and *'el* (אל; n. god). *Ṣadqi'el* is not present in the Bible but is identified as an angel in other texts (e.g., *Zohar*, *Sefer Harazim* …). He has not been written about as extensively as other planetary archangels. *Ṣadqi'el* is the archangel of *Ḥesed* and Jupiter.[381,382]

Intelligence
Yohfi'el (Heb. יהפיאל)

The name as given by Agrippa and Crowley does not appear in any known literature prior to the publication of Agrippa's *Three Books of Occult Philosophy*.[383,384,385] It could be a "mystic" spelling of *Yofi'el* (Heb. יופיאל (/yofːɪiˈʔel/); Beauty of God), which is the name of an angel who is not present in the Bible but is identified as an angel in other texts (e.g., *Zohar*, *Greater Hekalot* …). *Yohfi'el* is the intelligence of Jupiter.[386,387]

375. Mark 14:36; Romans 8:15; Galatians 4:6 KJV 1611.

376. Agrippa, *Three Books*, 318–29.

377. Crowley, "777 Revised,", 3.

378. Galatians 1:1; Ephesians 6:23; Philippians 2:11 KJV 1611.

379. Agrippa, *Three Books*, 318–29.

380. Crowley, "777 Revised,", 3.

381. Agrippa, *Three Books*, 268–80, 287–91.

382. Crowley, "777 Revised,", 21.

383. Agrippa, *Three Books*, 318–29.

384. Crowley, "777 Revised,", 19.

385. Crowley, "Sepher Sephiroth," 19.

386. Agrippa, *Three Books*, 318–29.

387. Crowley, "777 Revised,", 19.

Spirit

Hisma'el (Heb. הסמאל)

The name as given by Agrippa does not appear in any known literature prior to the publication of his *Three Books of Occult Philosophy*.[388] If the source language is Hebrew, it could be a combination of a word derived from the root *S-M-L* (related to symbolizing) and *'el* (אל; n. god), altogether implying divine representation. *Hisma'el* is the spirit of Jupiter.[389,390]

Saturn

Divine Names

'Ab (Heb. אב (/ʔɔːb/); Father)

This is *'ab* (Heb. אב; n. father) treated as a proper noun, in reference to *YHWH* as the father of his people. It is alluded to in the Hebrew of the Old Testament and more blatantly in the Greek of the New Testament.[391,392] It is a Qabalistic divine name associated with Saturn.[393,394]

Yah (Heb. יה (/jɔːh/); (the) Lord)

This is a shortened form of *YHWH* (Heb. יהוה; n. LORD). It is present in the Bible and is a Qabalistic divine name associated with Saturn.[395,396,397]

Archangel

Ṣafqi'el (Heb. צפקיאל)

If the source language is Hebrew, the name could be a combination of a word derived from the root *Ṣ-F-N* (related to hiding or concealing) and *'el* (אל; n. god), altogether

---

388. Agrippa, *Three Books*, 318–29.

389. Agrippa, *Three Books*, 318–29.

390. Crowley, "777 Revised,", 19.

391. Exodus 4:22–23; Isaiah 63:16; Jeremiah 31:9 KJV 1611.

392. Mark 14:36; Romans 8:15; Galatians 4:6.

393. Agrippa, *Three Books*, 318–29.

394. Crowley, "777 Revised,", 3.

395. Psalms 68:4 KJV 1611.

396. Agrippa, *Three Books*, 318–29.

397. Crowley, "777 Revised,", 3.

implying divine secrecy. Ṣafqi'el is not present in the Bible but is identified as an arch-angel in other texts (e.g., *The Key of Solomon the King*, *Three Books of Occult Philoso-phy* ...). He has not been written about as extensively as other planetary archangels. Ṣafqi'el is the archangel of *Bina* and Saturn.[398,399]

Intelligence

'Agi'el (Heb. אגיאל)

The name as given by Agrippa does not appear in any known literature prior to the pub-lication of his *Three Books of Occult Philosophy*.[400] If the source language is Hebrew, it could be a combination of a word derived from the root '-G-D (related to bundling or bunching) and *'el* (אל; n. god), altogether implying divine binding. *'Agi'el* is the intel-ligence of Saturn.[401,402]

Spirit

Zaz'el (Heb. זזאל)

The name as given by Agrippa and modified by Crowley does not appear in any known literature prior to the publication of Agrippa's *Three Books of Occult Philosophy*.[403,404] It bears similarity to *'Aza'zel* (Heb. עזאזל), the "scapegoat" in the Bible and *'Azaz'el* (עזזאל), a malefic angel in the Dead Sea Scrolls.[405,406] *Zaz'el* is the spirit of Saturn.[407,408]

398. Agrippa, *Three Books*, 268–80, 287–91.

399. Crowley, "777 Revised," 21.

400. Agrippa, *Three Books*, 318–29.

401. Agrippa, *Three Books*, 318–29.

402. Crowley, "777 Revised," 19.

403. Agrippa, *Three Books*, 318–29.

404. Crowley, "777 Revised," 19.

405. Leviticus 16:8, 10, 26 KJV 1611.

406. Andrei Orlov, "Eschatological Yom Kippur in the *Apocalypse of Abraham*: Part I. The Scapegoat Ritual," in *Symbola Caelestis: Le Symbolisme Liturgique et Paraliturgique Dans le Monde Chrétien, Scrinium* 5 (Gorgias Press, 2009), 79–111.

407. Agrippa, *Three Books*, 318–29.

408. Crowley, "777 Revised," 19.

APPENDIX B
Western Astrology

Astrology (Gk. ἀστρολογία) is a cornerstone of the Western esoteric tradition. It elucidates how the movements of celestial bodies impact our lives and terrestrial events at large, and will help you place your planetary work in a greater context. Astrology may be broadly classified into six modalities, which are as follows. They are not mutually exclusive.

Natal Astrology

Tells you about a person. The natal chart is based on the date, time, and city of birth. It elucidates the individual's personality, behavioral tendencies, strengths, weaknesses, overall life trajectory, and more. This is where we have focused much of our attention throughout this book.

Relationship Astrology

Tells you how compatible two people are. The natal charts of two individuals are compared through synastry (superimposing two natal charts) or via a composite chart (showing midpoints between natal planets). It is an offshoot of natal astrology.

Electional Astrology

Tells you auspicious times to hold future events. It is aimed at finding dates and times with astrological conditions favorable for talisman creation, starting a business, wedding ceremonies, and more. Throughout this book, we elected to perform magical work at times auspicious to a particular planet.

Horary Astrology

Tells you the answer to a defined question. The horary chart is based on the date, time, and city of the question's "birth." The answer is divined by examining the astrological conditions when the question was posed. Current evidence suggests horary astrology evolved from electional astrology.[409]

Medical Astrology

Tells you about a person's health. The natal chart and current astrological conditions are taken into account to prevent, diagnose, and treat disease. Different astrological phenomena correlate with particular parts of the human body, its processes, and treatment modalities. Although obsolete in modern evidence-based practice, astrology comprised a key part of medicine until the seventeenth century.

Mundane Astrology

Tells you about global affairs and events. The natal charts of countries and current astrological conditions are taken into account to predict occurrences of regional or worldwide impact. This includes but is not limited to political events, economic trends, natural disasters, and global health crises.

Further Reading

If you would like to learn more about astrology, a short list of recommended books follows. They are available in most major bookstores or online.

Hellenistic Astrology

Brennan, Chris. *Hellenistic Astrology: The Study of Fate and Fortune*. Amor Fati Publications, 2017.

Dorotheus. *Carmen Astrologicum*. Translated by David Pingree. Astrology Classics, 2005.

Ptolemy. *Tetrabiblos*. Translated by F. E. Robbins. Harvard University Press, 1940.

Valens, Vettius. *Anthologies*. Translated by Mark Riley. Amor Fati Publications, 2022. Accessed March 29, 2021. https://www.csus.edu/indiv/r/rileymt/Vettius%20Valens%20entire.pdf.

---

409. Brennan, "The Origins of Horary Astrology," *Astrology Podcast*, 1:57:52.

Medieval Astrology

Al-Biruni, Abu'l-Rayhan Muhammad Ibn Ahmad. *The Book of Instruction in the Elements of the Art of Astrology*. Translated by R. Ramsay Wright. Astrology Classics, 2006.

Ibn-Ezra, Avraham. *The Beginning of Wisdom*. Edited by Robert Hand. Translated by Meira B. Epstein. ARHAT, 1998.

Bonatti on Basic Astrology. Translated by Benjamin N. Dykes. The Cazimi Press, 2010.

Introductions to Traditional Astrology: Abu Ma'Shar and al-Qabisi. Translated by Benjamin N. Dykes. The Cazimi Press, 2010.

Renaissance Astrology

Culpeper, Nicholas. *Astrological Judgement of Diseases from the Decumbiture of the Sick (1655) and Urinalia (1658)*. Astrology Classics, 2003.

Ficino, Marsilio. *Three Books on Life*. Critical ed. Translated by Carol V. Kaske. ACMRS Press, 2019.

Houlding, Deborah, editor. *Lilly's Christian Astrology*. Independently published, 2022.

Ramesey, William. *Astrologia Munda, or, Astrology in its Purity*. London, 1653. https://archive.org/details/b30323149.

Modern Astrology

Hand, Robert. *Planets in Transit: Life Cycles for Living*. 2nd ed. Schiffer Publishing, 2002.

Hickey, Isabel M. *Astrology: A Cosmic Science*. CRCS Publications, 2011.

Tarnas, Richard. *Cosmos and Psyche: Intimations of a New World View*. Plume, 2007.

Woolfolk, Joanna Martine. *The Only Astrology Book You'll Ever Need*. 21st century ed. Taylor Trade Publishing, 2008.

Bibliography

Adams, John Couch. Papers of John Couch Adams, 1701–1996. St. John's College Library Special Collections, University of Cambridge.

Agrippa, Henry Cornelius. *Three Books of Occult Philosophy*. Edited by Donald Tyson. Llewellyn Publications, 2004. Originally published 1651 by R. W. for George Moule.

———. *The Fourth Book of Occult Philosophy*, edited by Donald Tyson. Llewellyn Publications, 2009. Originally published 1665 by J. C. for J. Harrison.

Al-Biruni, Abu'l-Rayhan Muhammad Ibn Ahmad. *The Book of Instruction in the Elements of the Art of Astrology*. Translated by R. Ramsay Wright. Astrology Classics, 2006.

Almirantis, Yannis. "The Paradox of the Planetary Metals." *Journal of Scientific Exploration* 19, no. 1 (2005): 31–42.

Aristotle. *De Caelo*. Translated by C. D. C. Reeve. Hackett Publishing Company, 2020.

———. *Metaphysics*. Translated by C. D. C. Reeve. Hackett Publishing Company, 2016.

———. *Nicomachean Ethics*. Translated by C. D. C. Reeve. Hackett Publishing Company, 2014.

———. *On Generation and Corruption*. Translated by H. H. Joachim, 467–531. In *The Basic Works of Aristotle*, edited by Richard McKeon. The Modern Library, 2001.

Aristotle. *Physics*. Translated by C. D. C. Reeve. Hackett Publishing Company, 2018.

Arlinghaus, Katherine R., and Craig A. Johnston. "The Importance of Creating Habits and Routine." *American Journal of Lifestyle Medicine* 13, no. 2 (2019): 142–44.

Ashcroft-Nowicki, Dolores, and J. H. Brennan. *Magical Use of Thought Forms: A Proven System of Mental & Spiritual Empowerment*. Llewellyn Publications, 2004.

Aurelius, Marcus. *Meditations*. Translated by George Long. Barnes & Noble Books, 2003.

Bardon, Franz. *Initiation Into Hermetics*. Merkur Publishing, 2001. Originally published in 1956 by Verlag Hermann Bauer.

———. *The Practice of Magical Evocation*. Merkur Publishing, 2001. Originally published in 1956 by Verlag Hermann Bauer.

Bargh, John A. "Our Unconscious Mind." *Scientific American* 310, no. 1 (January 2014): 30–37.

Betz, Hans Dieter, ed. *The Greek Magical Papyri in Translation, Including the Demotic Spells*. University of Chicago Press, 1986.

The Holy Bible, King James Version. Originally published in 1611.

Boddington, A., A. N. Garland, and R. C. Janaway, eds. *Death, Decay and Reconstruction: Approaches to Archaeology and Forensic Science*. Manchester University Press, 1987.

Bodine, Walter R., ed. *Linguistics and Biblical Hebrew*. Eisenbrauns, 1992.

Brennan, Chris. *The Astrology Podcast*. Audio. https://theastrologypodcast.com.

———. *Hellenistic Astrology: The Study of Fate and Fortune*. Amor Fati Publications, 2017.

Budge, E. A. Wallis. *An Account of the Roman Antiquities Preserved in the Museum at Chesters Northumberland*. Gilbert & Rivington, 1903.

Burton, Ernest DeWitt. *Spirit, Soul, and Flesh*. University of Chicago Press, 1918.

Byrne, Ruth M. J. *The Rational Imagination: How People Create Alternatives to Reality*. The MIT Press, 2005.

Campion, Nicholas. *Astrology and Cosmology in the World's Religions*. New York University Press, 2012.

Carroll, Peter J. *Liber Kaos*. Weiser Books, 1992.

Carroll, Peter J. *Liber Null & Psychonaut: An Introduction to Chaos Magic.* Weiser Books, 1987.

Casson, Lionel. *Everyday Life in Ancient Rome*, Rev. ed. Johns Hopkins University Press, 1999.

Copenhaver, Brian P. *Hermetica: The Greek* Corpus Hermeticum *and the Latin* Asclepius *in a new English translation, with notes and introduction.* Cambridge University Press, 1995.

Copernicus, Nicolaus. *On the Revolutions.* Translated by Edward Rosen. Johns Hopkins University Press, 1992.

Crowley, Aleister. *777 and Other Qabalistic Writings of Aleister Crowley*, edited by Israel Regardie. Samuel Weiser, 1999. Originally published in 1909 by Walter Scott Publishing Co.

———. *The Book of Lies.* Samuel Weiser, 1998. Originally published in 1913 by Wieland and Co.

———. "Liber Libræ: Sub Figura XXX." *The Equinox* 1, no. 1 (1909): 17–21.

———. *Magick: Liber ABA, Book 4*, 2nd ed. Edited by Hymanaeus Beta. Weiser Books, 1997. Originally published in 1913 by Wieland and Co.

———. *Magick Without Tears.* Edited by Israel Regardie. New Falcon Publications, 1991. Originally published 1954 by Thelema Publishing Company.

Daniels, Michael. "The Magic, Myth and Math of Magic Squares." Filmed November 2014 at TEDxDouglas, Douglas, Isle of Man. Video, 15:16. https://www.youtube.com/watch?v=-Tbd3dzlRnY

Dillon, Matthew. *Omens and Oracles: Divination in Ancient Greece.* Routledge, 2017.

Dorotheus. *Carmen Astrologicum.* Translated by David Pingree. Astrology Classics, 2005.

DuQuette, Lon Milo. *The Chicken Qabalah of Rabbi Lamed Ben Clifford.* Weiser Books, 2001.

Eastaugh, Nicholas, Valentine Walsh, Tracey Chapman, and Ruth Siddall. *The Pigment Compendium: A Dictionary of Historical Pigments.* Elsevier, 2004.

Eliot, T. S. *On Poetry and Poets.* Farrar, Straus & Giroux, 2009. Originally published in 1943 by Faber and Faber Ltd.

Ettinger, Yair. "Uranus and Neptune Get Hebrew Names at Last." *Haaretz,* December 31, 2009, https://www.haaretz.com/2009-12-31/ty-article/uranus-and-neptune-get-hebrew-names-at-last/0000017f-ec5c-ddba-a37f-ee7ecaf10000.

Evelyn-White, Hugh G., trans. *Hesiod: The Homeric Hymns and Homerica.* William Heinemann, 1914.

Ferrari, Joseph. "Why Clutter Stresses Us Out." Interview by Kim Mills. *Speaking of Psychology*, February 22, 2023. Audio, 35:35. https://www.apa.org/news/podcasts/speaking-of-psychology/clutter.

Fairclough, H. Rushton, trans. *Horace: Satires, Epistles, Ars Poetica.* William Heinemann, 1926.

Freudenthal, Gad, ed. *Science in Medieval Jewish Cultures.* Cambridge University Press, 2011.

Ginsburgh, Yitzchak. *The Hebrew Letters: Channels of Creative Consciousness.* Gal Einai Publications, 1990.

Gleadow, Rupert. *The Origin of the Zodiac.* Dover Publications, 2001.

Granada, Miguel A. "New Visions of the Cosmos." In *The Cambridge Companion to Renaissance Philosophy*, edited by James Hankins, 270–286. Cambridge University Press, 2007.

Grazier, Kevin R. "Jupiter: Cosmic Jekyll and Hyde." *Astrobiology* 16, no. 1 (2016): 23–38.

Greer, Johm Michael, and Christopher Warnock, trans. *The Picatrix: Liber Rubeus Edition.* Adocentyn Press, 2010–2011.

Grimassi, Raven. *Encyclopedia of Wicca & Witchcraft.* 2nd ed. Llewellyn Publications, 2003.

———. *Hereditary Witchcraft: Secrets of the Old Religion.* Llewellyn Publications, 2003.

Hand, Robert. *Whole Sign Houses: The Oldest House System.* ARHAT, 2000.

Healey, Paul F., and Marc G. Blainey. "Ancient Maya Mosaic Mirrors: Function, Symbolism, and Meaning." *Ancient Mesoamerica* 22, no. 2 (2011): 229–44.

Heath, T. L., ed. *The Works of Archimedes.* Cambridge University Press, 1897.

Herschel, William. "XXXII. Account of a Comet." *Philosophical Transactions of the Royal Society of London* 71 (1781): 492–501.

Hill, George. *A History of Cyprus, Volume 1: To the Conquest by Richard Lion Heart.* Cambridge University Press, 1940.

Hoffman, Joel M. *In the Beginning: A Short History of the Hebrew Language.* New York University Press, 2004.

Holford-Strevens, Leofranc. *The History of Time: A Very Short Introduction.* Oxford University Press, 2005.

Horowitz, Wayne. *Mesopotamian Cosmic Geography.* Eisenbrauns, 1998.

Ibn-Ezra, Avraham. *The Beginning of Wisdom.* Edited by Robert Hand. Translated by Meira B. Epstein. ARHAT, 1998.

International Astronomical Union, "Resolution B5: Definition of a Planet in the Solar System." International Astronomical Union General Assembly, 2006.

John Paul II. "Dies Domini–Apostolic Letter, John Paul II." Libreria Editrice Vaticana, 1998.

Jung, Carl. *Synchronicity: An Acausal Connecting Principle.* Translated by R. F. C. Hull. Princeton University Press, 2010. Originally published in 1952 by Princeton Univeristy Press.

Kaplan, Aryeh, ed. and trans. *Sefer Hapliy'ah* [Book of Wonder]. Zupnik, Knoller & Hammerschmidt, 1883.

———. *Sefer Yetzirah: The Book of Creation in Theory and Practice.* Rev. ed. Weiser Books, 1997.

Kauffman, George B. "The Role of Gold in Alchemy. Part I." *Gold Bulletin* 18, no. 1 (1985): 31–44.

Kepler, Johannes. *Narratio de Observatis a se Quatuor Iouis Satellitibus Erronibus.* Apud Cosmum Iunctam, 1611.

Khan, Geoffrey, ed. *Encyclopedia of Hebrew Language and Linguistics.* 4 vols. Brill, 2013.

Kim, Moonsil. "Food Distribution for the People: Welfare, Food, and Feasts in Qin/Han China and in Rome." In *Rulers and Ruled in Ancient Greece, Rome, and China,* edited by Hans Beck and Griet Vankeerberghen, 225–268. Cambridge University Press, 2021.

Kovacs, David, trans. *Euripides: Helen, Phoenician Women, Orestes.* Harvard University Press, 2002.

Krisak, Len, trans. *Virgil's Eclogues*. University of Pennsylvania Press, 2010.

Le Verrier, U. J. "Recherches sur le mouvements d'Uranus." *Comptes Rendus Hebdomadaires des Séances de l'Académie des Sciences* 22, no. 22 (1846): 907–18.

Lee, Mirielle M. *Body, Dress, and Identity in Ancient Greece*. Cambridge University Press, 2015.

Lenzen, Manuela. "Feeling Our Emotions." *Scientific American Mind* 16, no. 1 (2005): 14–15.

Lévi, Éliphas. *The History of Magic*. Translated by A. E. Waite. Cambridge University Press, 2013. Originally published in 1860 by Germer Baillière.

———. *Transcendental Magic: Its Doctrine and Ritual*. Translated by A. E. Waite. Weiser Books, 2001. Originally published in 1854–1856 by Germer Baillière.

Lilly, William. *Christian Astrology*. John Macock, 1659.

Lowell Observatory. Lowell Observatory Observation Circular. May 1, 1930.

Malandra, William W. *An Introduction to Ancient Iranian Religion: Readings from the Avesta and Achaemenid Inscriptions*. University of Minnesota Press, 1983).

Maternus, Firmicus. *Ancient Astrology Theory and Practice: Matheseos Libri VIII*. Translated by Jean Rhys Bram. Noyes Press, 1975.

Neulander, Judith. "Conjuring Crypto-Jews in New Mexico." In *Boundaries, Identity and Belonging in Modern Judaism*, edited by Maria Diemling and Larry Ray, 208–25. Routledge, 2016.

Nonnos. *Dionysiaca, Vol. III: Books 36–48*. Translated by W. H. D. Rouse. Harvard University Press, 1940.

Olivelle, Patrick, ed. *The Early Upaniṣads: Annotated Text and Translation*. Oxford University Press, 1998.

Orlov, Andrei. "Eschatological Yom Kippur in the *Apocalypse of Abraham*: Part I. The Scapegoat Ritual." In *Symbola Caelestis: Le Symbolisme Liturgique et Paraliturgique Dans le Monde Chrétien*. *Scrinium* 5: 79–111. Gorgias Press, 2009.

Ovid. *Metamorphoses*. Translated by Stanley Lombardo. Hackett Publishing Company, 2010.

Parker, R. A. "Ancient Egyptian Astronomy." *Philosophical Transactions of the Royal Society of London, Series A* 276, no. 1257 (1974): 51–65.

Pausanias. *Description of Greece*. Translated by W. H. S. Jones and H. A. Ormerod. 6 vols. London: William Heinemann, 1926.

Plato. *Epinomis*. Translated by W. R. M. Lamb, 423–87. In *Charmides, Alcibiades I and II, Hipparchus, The Lovers, Theages, Minos, Epinomis*. Harvard University Press, 1927.

———. *Protagoras*. Edited by Nicholas Denyer. Cambridge Univerity Press, 2008.

———. *Timaeus*. Translated by Donald J. Zeyl. Hackett Publishing Company, 2000.

Plotinus. *The Enneads*. Edited by Lloyd P. Gerson. Cambridge University Press, 2017.

Ptolemy. *Ptolemy's Almagest*. Translated by G. J. Toomer. Princeton University Press, 1998.

———. *Tetrabiblos*. Translated by F. E. Robbins. Harvard University Press, 1940.

Rogers, John H. "Origins of the Ancient Constellations: I. The Mesopotamian Traditions." *Journal of the British Astronomical Association* 108, no. 1 (1998): 9–28.

Rose, H. J., trans. *The Roman Questions of Plutarch*. The Clarendon Press, 1924.

Royal Society of Chemistry. "Periodic Table." Accessed March 27, 2024. https://www.rsc.org/periodic-table.

Sardar, Marika. "Astronomy and Astrology in the Medieval Islamic World." In *Heilbrunn Timeline of Art History*. The Metropolitan Museum of Art, 2000.

The SBL Handbook of Style. 2nd ed. Atlanta: SBL Press, 2014.

Scholem, Gershom. *Jewish Gnosticism, Merkabah Mysticism, and Talmudic Tradition*. 2nd ed. Maurice Jacobs, 1965.

Seneca. *De Clementia*. Edited by Susanna Braund. Oxford University Press, 2009.

Shaked, Shaul, James Nathan Ford, and Siam Bhayro. *Aramaic Bowl Spells: Jewish Babylonian Aramaic Bowls 1*. Brill, 2013.

Shaw, Frank. *The Earliest Non-Mystical Jewish Use of Ιαω*. Peeters, 2014.

Singer, Isidore, ed. *The Jewish Encyclopedia*. 12 vols. Funk & Wagnalls, 1906.

Smith, Pamela K., Daniël H. J. Wigboldus, and Ap Dijksterhuis. "Abstract Thinking Increases One's Sense of Power." *Journal of Experimental Social Psychology* 44, no. 2, (2008): 378–85.

Smith, William, ed. *A Dictionary of Greek and Roman Antiquities*. Taylor and Walton, 1842.

Solecki, Ralph S. "A Copper Mineral Pendant from Northern Iraq." *Antiquity* 43, no. 172 (1969): 311–14.

Spence, Lewis. *Ancient Egyptian Myths and Legends*. Dover Publications, 1990.

Starhawk. *The Spiral Dance: A Rebirth of the Ancient Religion of the Great Goddess*, 20th anniversary ed. HarperSanFrancisco, 1999.

Stavish, Mark. *The Path of Alchemy: Energetic Healing and the World of Natural Magic*. Llewellyn Publications, 2006.

Strabo. *Geography, Volume VI: Books 13–14*. Translated by Horace Leonard Jones. Harvard University Presss, 1929.

Taylor, Thomas, trans. *The Hymns of Orpheus*. 1792. Via Sacred Texts website. https://sacred-texts.com/cla/hoo/index.htm.

Three Initiates. *The Kybalion*. Yogi Publication Society, 1940. Originally published in 1908 by Yogi Publication Society.

Valens, Vettius. *Anthologies*. Translated by Mark Riley. Accessed March 29, 2021. https://www.csus.edu/indiv/r/rileymt/Vettius%20Valens%20entire.pdf.

Velchanes, Soror. *The Elemental Magic Workbook: An Experimental Guide to Understanding and Working with the Classical Elements*. 2nd ed. Megalithica Books, 2020.

Weinstock, Stefan. "Lunar Mansions and Early Calendars." *Journal of Hellenic Studies* 69 (1949): 48–69.

Weir, Kirsten. "Nurtured by Nature." *Monitor on Psychology* 51, no. 3 (2020): 50–56.

Wetzel, Joshua S. *Ill Thoughts, Ill Words, Ill Deeds: A Toxick Magick Primer, Vol. 1*. Megalithica Books, 2021.

———. *The Paradigmal Pirate*. 2001. Megalithica Books, 2006.

The William Davidson Talmud. https://www.sefaria.org/william-davidson-talmud.

Woolfolk, Joanna Martine. *The Only Astrology Book You'll Ever Need*. Scarborough House, 1990.

Yampolsky, Philip. "The Origin of the Twenty-Eight Lunar Mansions." *Osiris* 9 (1950): 62–83.

Young, Ian, ed. *Biblical Hebrew: Studies in Chronology and Typology*. T & T Clark International, 2003.

To Write to the Author

If you wish to contact the author or would like more information about this book, please write to the author in care of Llewellyn Worldwide Ltd. and we will forward your request. Both the author and publisher appreciate hearing from you and learning of your enjoyment of this book and how it has helped you. Llewellyn Worldwide Ltd. cannot guarantee that every letter written to the author can be answered, but all will be forwarded. Please write to:

Soror Velchanes
℅ Llewellyn Worldwide
2143 Wooddale Drive
Woodbury, MN 55125-2989
Please enclose a self-addressed stamped envelope for reply,
or $1.00 to cover costs. If outside the U.S.A., enclose
an international postal reply coupon.

Many of Llewellyn's authors have websites with additional information and resources. For more information, please visit our website at http://www.llewellyn.com.